Pamela Gerrish Nunn

Victorian Women Artists

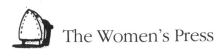 The Women's Press

Published by the Women's Press Limited 1987
A member of the Namara Group
34 Great Sutton Street, London EC1V 0DX

British Library Cataloguing in Publication Data

Nunn, Pamela Gerrish
    Victorian women artists.
    1. Women artists — Great Britain   2. Art,
    Victorian — Great Britain
    I. Title
    709'.2'2   N6796

    ISBN 0-7043-5015-7
    ISBN 0-7043-4034-8 Pbk

Designed by Suzanne Perkins and Stella Kane

Typeset by AKM Associates (UK) Limited
Ajmal House, Hayes Road, Southall, London
Printed and bound in Great Britain
by Nene Litho and Woolnough Bookbinding
both of Wellingborough, Northants.

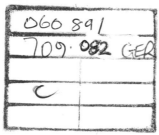

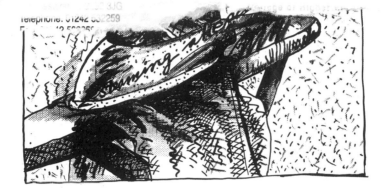

Pamela Gerrish Nunn studied the history of art at Leicester University and University College London and has taught the subject for the last ten years. She has played an active part in the feminist art movement both in Bristol and nationally, contributing to many conferences. Her published work, which includes articles in scholarly and feminist journals, several exhibition projects (The Women's Art Show, Nottingham, 1982; The Solomon Family of Painters, London, 1985; The Bristol Women and Art Group, Bristol, 1982 and 1983) and a collection of the writings of Victorian women artists (*Canvassing*, Camden Press, 1986), is indebted to the Women's Liberation Movement with which she has been actively involved since 1978.

Contents

Acknowledgements

I am grateful to Dr Will Vaughan, who supervised the thesis that gave rise to this book, and to the descendants of the artists without whose interest and co-operation neither thesis nor book would have come to fruition. They include Anne Christopherson, Beryl Sells, the late Helen Wightman, John and Jonathan Street, Dr Margaret Jackson, Julia Ford, Erika Charrington, David Pye, the late Peter Brett, Lord Michael Joicey, Bill Maddock and his daughters Sheila and Judy, Ione Brett, Commander Claude Sclater and his sister Susan Rose, the late Anne Wales, Michael Hickox, Phyllis Watson, Joan Mitchell, Katherine Scott and her daughter Susan. Numerous individuals and institutions have helped me in tracking down works and information, particularly Norma Watt at Norwich Castle Museum, Vivien Tubbs at the Fitzwilliam Museum Cambridge, Jill Knight at the Victoria Art Gallery Bath, the staff at the Victoria and Albert Museum Library and Print Room, the staff of the art library of Bristol Central Public Library, Dr Deborah Cherry and Andrea Garrihy.

I also wish to thank Ros de Lanerolle and Rachel Pyper at the Women's Press; Pauline Barrie of the Woman Artists' Slide Library; photographer Julie Phipps; other feminist art historians who are an encouragement just by being there; and the women who have supported and encouraged me over the years in a personal way: Joy Nunn, Clare Chapman, Rosemary van Arsdel, Mary Gormally and Ruth Hilary Bottrill.

List of Figures

List of Plates

1
Introduction

What were creative women doing while Edwin Landseer was immortalising dogs, stags and the British royal family? What experience did the female artist have of the natural environment while J.M.W. Turner was conducting a vaporous romance with sun, sea and mountains, and John Constable was recording his rustic idyll? What artistic sisterhood paralleled the Pre-Raphaelites' playing at secret societies? In short, what about Victorian women artists? We may think we know a lot about the nineteenth century – it is arguably the most investigated period of the whole of the western tradition – but feminism has in recent years exposed the claim of academic disciplines, including art history, to be offering a sound body of reliable knowledge as an oppressive myth, perpetrated by the white, male, middle and upper classes.

Simple answers are never adequate when it is a question of women and history, and the answers to the questions posed above are complex, although familiar from the current debates about women and art. For women to paint, sculpt or design professionally in Victorian Britain was to challenge western beliefs about the nature and status of art. At the same time, it was to challenge women's economic relationship to society and especially to men, and the relationship women had to culture. Since women begin from a position fundamentally different from men (whatever their class or race), it could be said that women are never engaged in precisely the same activity as men – a parallel one perhaps, but not a replica. Thus to study Victorian women artists is not to discover female Landseers or Turners, but to confront a moment when it seemed as if the world itself might be transformed. Which is not – despite the mutual self-aggrandisement by men of their activities – by and large what follows when men take up art. Certainly, in Victorian Britain, it was women's move into professional art practice which produced the greatest potential for change. As this book shows, ultimately that potential was only partially realised, and at the present moment we have a second chance to re-invent art, with the contemporary women artists' movement which feminism has brought into being in the last ten years. Though the nineteenth century was the era of the Great Exhibition and the invention of photography, of the Pre-Raphaelite movement and Impressionism, of Realism and the decline of the Academies' influence, if we ignore the question of women and art, which arose in Britain in the middle of the century and did not disappear from the agenda, so to speak, until the beginning of the twentieth century, we are guilty of tailoring and taming a picture of a very exciting, momentous and challenging period in the history of western art.

A self-serving history of art has largely suppressed the issue of women and art in the nineteenth century because it poses uncomfortable questions (or valuable questions, depending on your viewpoint) and diverts attention from traditional idols.[1] Art historians' corporate neglect of Victorian women artists cannot be explained as anything other than prejudice, when the number of female artists was increasing throughout the century, when the art press was teeming with articles and comment on women and art, and when a considerable number of female artists' names became familiar to the art-loving British public in the 1860s, 1870s and 1880s. Within the art worlds of Britain, France and other western countries the idea of the artist was under particular scrutiny in this period because of the changing circumstances under which fine art was practised. It has often been noted how numerous are the images of artists and their studios produced by painters and sculptors around the middle of the century.[2] The invention of

2

photography, for instance, caused many artists to look to their laurels – some said it would be the death of painting. The decline in academic traditions of the gentleman artist led to a new breed of painter and sculptor, more independent psychologically but more dependent economically on the market, which was a much more varied one in the mid-Victorian era than it had been, say, fifty years before.[3]

To take up the identity of 'artist' meant different things for different women, and it is this complexity which I hope will come through in my account of women artists in mid-Victorian Britain. The profession of artist would, by and large, only suggest itself to middle-class people, for reasons which will become clear. It was not a secure profession, economically speaking, but many women took it up in order to earn a living. It had (and has) a certain status which can be especially attractive as an opportunity for self-expression, and many women took it up as such, daring to believe that women had as much right to assert their creative vision as men. Other women, still, took it up almost accidentally, due to circumstances in their lives over which they had no control. Some saw themselves as gifted, some saw themselves as diligent, some saw themselves as lucky, some saw themselves as oppressed; although women are given a common character in patriarchal society, they do not necessarily have an identical experience.

In 1841, according to Census figures, 278 women in Britain identified themselves as artists (artist meaning here 'painter of pictures' but not, for instance, tile-painter: in the Census, artist denotes the traditional meaning of fine art worker). By 1871, this figure had risen to 1069. Correspondingly, it is during this period that the women's art movement became a central issue in British culture. It was an aspect of the larger women's movement, which can be dated from 1848, the 'year of revolutions'. Women's rights became an urgent issue in Britain, France, Germany and the USA from then on.[4]

If we look at the sort of things that were being said, written and pictured in British cultural circles at the mid-point of the century we can see clearly what a pivotal position the 'woman question' had. The Brontë sisters' first publications appeared in 1847, including notably Charlotte Brontë's novel *Jane Eyre*. In 1848, the first public women's college in Britain opened in Harley Street, London. In the next few years, female novelists came increasingly to the fore, some of whose female characters are themselves artistic (e.g. Anne Brontë's *The Tenant of Wildfell Hall* (1848), Dinah Craik's *Olive*

(1850)). In 1855, the French painter, Rosa Bonheur, became an overnight sensation in London when her huge picture 'The Horse Fair' [plate I] was exhibited by the art-dealer Ernest Gambart, and she was taken up by journalists as a model of the modern woman. In 1856, a Society of Female Artists was set up in London. (In the same year, a typical publication for middle-class women, *Elegant Arts for Ladies* (published by Ward Lock) would recommend that female creativity was best applied to such trivial pursuits as diaphanie, Persian painting, porcupine quill work, potichomanie and seaweed pictures.)

In 1857, the feminist and painter, Barbara Leigh Smith (later Bodichon), had published a booklet entitled *Women and Work*, in which she declared – amongst other things – that 'there is no reason at all why a woman should not build a cathedral if she has the instruction and the genius'. The same year, she and Bessie Parkes established a feminist newspaper, the *Englishwoman's Review* (EWR).[5] Finally, in 1858, it is not surprising to read a book review in the middle-class periodical the *Athenaeum* declaring that:

> Among the various classifications of the present day, there is one which is rising into importance, as well by the action of law as of opinion; we mean the division of the human race into men and women . . . [This] is not a joke: the distinction of man and woman, their separate as well as their joint rights, begins to occupy the attention of our whole community, and with no small effect.[6]

Truly, the very bases of Victorian society were being challenged. The dominant conviction that society comprised two spheres into which all people could be categorised according to gender, even though questions of class and race clearly cut across such a typology, combined itself with an individualistic, self-help ethic, to suggest that one's best efforts in life should be devoted to trying to attain the highest virtues attributed to one's gender. But the rationale on which the attribution of those virtues was based was being challenged and the patriarchal pattern for life was gradually exposed as the arrogation by men of the exciting, demanding, fulfilling and consequential activities in society and the complementary condemnation of women to the relative, supportive and dependent activities in society. Numerous publications instructed women – and, to a lesser extent, men – in their prescribed roles, and these forms of control did not necessarily blink at admitting what their intention and plan was, so unassailable did the established order seem to their complacent authors. Thus Mrs Strutt, in *The Feminine Soul* (1857):

> Man possessing superior physical strength, and having, through the agency of that strength, constituted himself master of the whole earth, can of course assign to woman whatever station in society may be most agreeable to himself.[7]

The position which it was most agreeable to men that women adopt might well be superficially different between social classes, but it revolved around the questions of marital status, of age, and of economic role, wherever in society a woman was placed. When it came to creativity, it was allowed that working-class women might work for a living, but it was not expected that they had any 'taste' or refinement of sensibility. A middle-class woman was expected to possess or cultivate sensitivity and an interest in 'culture', but as aids to her personal charm, not as work. While in the upper-class woman, artistic sensibility was presumed to be natural – some saw it as a defining characteristic. Of course she need not pursue artistic matters – or anything else – seriously, since her survival would never depend upon it; her survival had been otherwise assured. As long as a woman's artistic interests and performance were leisurely (not paid), she could call herself a lady, and 'ladies' were required in the upper and middle classes. If, as was the case for a working-class woman, her creativity was expressed in paid work (such as pattern-cutting), this was not 'ladylike', and certainly nothing to do with Art. Female creativity was the prerogative of the bourgeoisie and aristocracy and defined as amateur and unskilled, and desirably so. Since, thus, no class of women produced what could be called Art (or even art), no class of woman could be called artists; they were simply females, more or less sensitive in their creative endeavours, to be sub-divided by class as ladies or cheap labour.

'An English lady without her piano, or her pencil, or her fancy work, or her favourite French authors and German poets, is an object of wonder, and perhaps of pity', wrote the author of *The Habits of Good Society* (1859).[8] Those women who were not ladies did not even enter the picture for such an ideologue: creativity was only thought by such writers to exist in the receptive minds of the bourgeoisie and the superior hearts of the aristocracy. Who had ever heard, after all, of a working-class sculptor, or a proletarian composer?

The visualisation of this ideal relation of women to the artistic – the sensitive amateur, suitably modest in her ambition and flatteringly faithful to traditional (patriarchal) definitions of 'proper' art – is found in such paintings as Samuel Baldwin's 'Sketching from Nature' [fig. 1]. Far from being a threat to man's monopoly on the role of 'artist', this woman is herself the work of art: what she produces will very clearly be inconsequential, tentative, readily patronised and easily dismissed – in short, womanly.[9] The frontispiece to *Elegant Arts for Ladies* [fig. 2] endorses this image, and the promotion of it continued throughout the century, in men's paintings exhibited in galleries, in illustrations and stories in such organs as *The Girls' Own Paper* and *The Young Ladies' Journal*, and in less specialised branches of both the popular and the bourgeois press. At all costs patriarchy (and capitalism) wished to keep women's work categorised separately, as a phenomenon which could be given value and meaning as and when it suited the maintenance of the status quo. Images clearly defining women's relationship to art as decorative, trivial, sentimental, romantic and so on, stood out effectively against the numerous self-images produced by male artists in the period. They showed that the identity of artist was not one which a female person could seriously or effectively inhabit. Whatever an artist was in the modern age, he was a man. It is revealing that in a major review of Ellen Clayton's *English Female Artists* (1876), the writer opened anxiously with, 'The first effect produced by this book is to raise in our minds the question(s), – What constitutes an artist . . .?'[10] To my mind, this is still an essential question to pose in the face of the history of art, and it will be seen that, although I use the word artist here in its traditional sense of a person who paints or sculpts for a living, exhibiting, selling and expecting their products to be preserved for posterity, I also recognise it as a term which functions as a political formulation. It suggests, for instance, a seriousness, a degree of intellectual weight, a cultural status which are by no means unarguable.

How did the women who so named themselves 'artist' understand the term? Did they consider themselves artists purely because of their ambitions? Or once they had exhibited in public? Or only when they had sold a work? In society at large, of course, much effort went into assuring middle-class women of the meaninglessness of their own creative work over and above its contribution to their essential task of being a lady. In fact, the *only* meaning which their writing, their painting, their sewing, or their conversation

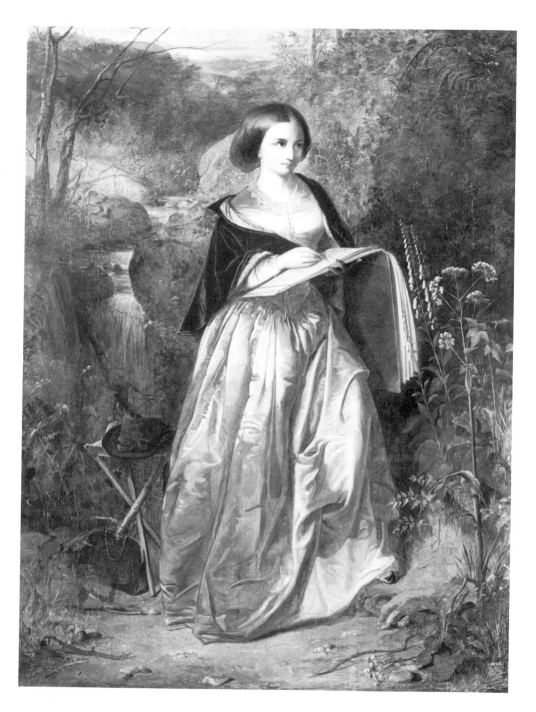

1. Samuel Baldwin, 'Sketching from Nature', 1857. Oil on canvas.
Private collection. (Photo: Maas Gallery, London)

could have was to identify their author as a true woman. So the writer of *The Habits of Good Society* goes on to tell his credulous readers that

> All accomplishments have the one great merit of giving a lady something to do; something to preserve her from ennui; to console her in seclusion; to arouse her in grief; to compose her to occupation in joy.[11]

The 'accomplishment' is well named, because its only true function is to accomplish woman's required goal of femininity. It is not to make her name, make her money or make herself heard; but to make her a good woman – that is, a lady. The activity is given no relation to music at large or art in general, say, with the result that women's creativity is maintained at the private, domestic and trivial level. Ultimately, also, this keeps women's *difference* absent from the culturally important fields of music, art, literature or philosophy.

The suppression of the contribution that women's experience and expression would make to culture was exposed by the upsurge of women into literature and art at the middle of the century. When exposed, it was boldly declared to be *friendly* to women, a form of gallantry which spared poor, inept and self-deluding woman from having her pathetic efforts at art, music, literature, thought exposed to 'real' culture, which is to say, men's work. By keeping women's creativity at an inconsequential level, by keeping women's art invisible (or, if that proved impossible, ghettoised as second-rate) men could claim their work to be true Art or Philosophy (or whatever). The fact that men's work is no more than the expression of one social group is thus concealed, and their point of view – their art – seems to be *the* point of view – Art. As Simone de Beauvoir has stated (with no particular reference to the nineteenth century): 'Representation of the world, like the world itself, is the work of men. They describe it from their point of view, which they confuse with absolute truth.'[12]

Articulation of this realisation in the mid-Victorian period was infrequent, and generally less than incisive; many women as well as men resisted the challenge that it presented. The spectre of 'de-sexing oneself' suppressed many women's tentative desires for personal fulfilment or greater social change. Most middle-class women – and in discussing female artists one is considering, for the most part, middle-class women – had an inadequate education, both in learning and in life, and were socially as well as economically dependent on their elders and especially on men. Becoming an artist did not necessarily mean that a woman could end her financial dependence – given the economic character of artworks as a market commodity, she was more likely to achieve that if she became an artisan – but it meant that she was trying to, in a way which also claimed cultural status and asserted its author as an individual psyche. In fact, you could say that the fundamental project on which the Victorian women's movement in Britain was engaged was the encouragement of the will to self-determination and the facilitating of the ability for self-determination. This project started in 1848 and culminated in the winning of the vote after the First World War, though we have been reminded in our own time that the reality is still a long way from completion.

A rare male voice of reason and insight on the question of women and art, which acknowledges that the whole issue is very broad, and must be seen to be so, is that of critic Philip G. Hamerton, writing in *Thoughts about Art* (1862). He vigorously entered the debate on women and art, which was then at its height:

> A feeble dilettantism in drawing seems to be considered essential to every young lady. But as Society requires that ladies should draw badly, so she carefully makes it impossible that they should ever have a chance of drawing well; the truth being, that respectable persons, for the most part, have no interest in art sufficiently powerful to overcome their intense horror of whatever they are pleased to consider 'unfeminine'.[13]

Despite his revealing indentification of the society that is to blame as itself female, Hamerton has hit the nail on the head. Femininity is the enemy of woman's ambition and fulfilment: it is femininity which Baldwin's sketcher of nature personifies, and it was femininity which Victorian society required of women of all classes. The definition of femininity, though regrettably widely accepted and promulgated by women, was not the invention of women: it was the 'station in society . . . most agreeable to himself' which Mrs Strutt steadfastly told her deluded readers men would consign woman to. Barbara Leigh Smith might rail, in *Women and Work*, that 'To think a woman more feminine because she is frivolous, ignorant, weak, and sickly, is absurd,'[14] but *The Leisure Hour* – which, as 'a family journal of instruction and recreation' was assured of many more readers than Leigh Smith – could comfortably declare in the same period (1856/57) that 'What a Woman should be Alphabetically' was 'Amiable, Benevolent, Charitable, Domestic, Economical, Forgiving, Generous, Honest, Industrious, Judicious, Kind, Loving, Modest, Neat, Obedient, Pleasant, Quiet, Reflecting, Sober, Tender, Urbane, Virtuous, 'Xemplary, Zealous.'[15] In short, feminine.

The insistence on femininity was most strident and implacable in the middle-class press and in bourgeois literature, drama and art, because the middle-class woman had nothing other to do than fulfil this requirement. To be a lady, and reap the rewards thereof, (while paying the price therefor), was her only legitimate task. But because at the middle of the century marriage was no longer assured for middle-class women (women outnumbered men, and, anyway, their ideas were changing) a demand arose for work that women might do, in order to be self-supporting and autonomous. No longer could it be assumed that a woman passed from being her father's social and economic possession to playing the same role in her husband's repertoire. However, society saw these women as 'redundant': there was no provision for them. In her art, as in her person, woman was subjected to the demands of femininity. It is not hard to see that this was bound to fashion a certain sort of art, as it fashioned a certain sort of woman. Baldwin's sketcher might be counted on to provide it, but other women, like Barbara Leigh Smith, had something very different in mind. As a middle-class woman who refused and refuted dominant prescriptions of womanhood, Leigh Smith and her work irritated the aware critic and discomfited the unaware.[16]

It is this disruption of established ideas about society and about art that the Victorian women artists' movement achieved, and this is why they, their work and the debate they generated have been excised from conventional accounts of the period. The feminist art historian recognises this disruption for what it is, and far from suppressing it as irrelevant or dismissing it as a side issue, she welcomes it. As the American art historian, Linda Nochlin, writes:

> A feminist critique . . . can pierce cultural–ideological limitations, to reveal biases and inadequacies not merely in regard to the question of women artists, but in the formulation of the crucial questions of the discipline as a whole. Thus the so-called woman question, far from being a peripheral sub-issue, can become a catalyst, a potent intellectual instrument, probing the most basic and 'natural' assumptions.[17]

This account of women artists in the nineteenth century is

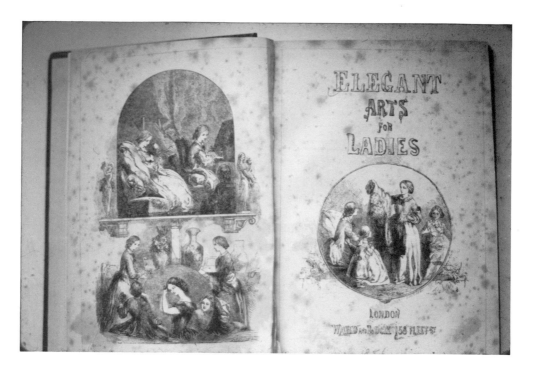

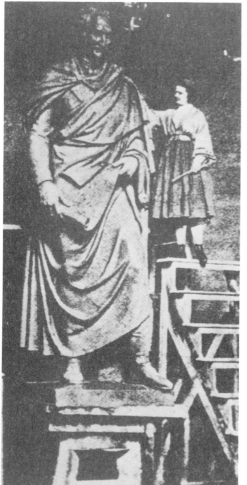

2. Anonymous engraving,
Ward Lock's *Elegant Arts for Ladies*, 1856.
(Photo: author)

3. Anonymous photograph,
Harriet Hosmer at work on her statue
of Thomas Hart Benton, *c.* 1860.

limited to the British scene, but where artists from other countries figured in the British debate on women and art, they have been included. Rosa Bonheur has already been mentioned: her popularity became, in fact, greater and more enduring in Britain than in her native France. Other French women to attract notice in Britain were Henriette Browne and Sophie Anderson, both figure painters.[18] Americans were thought of as generally more progressive than any other nation, and though this generalisation was often meant as an insult rather than as a compliment by British writers, it brought the sculptor Harriet Hosmer to the notice of women in Britain as an inspiring example of the possibility of women becoming established fine artists. Those few women who took up sculpture as their medium had difficulties to face which women specialising in painting or drawing did not, and Hosmer's case highlights this fact: she was even accused of not being the author of her own work, because it seemed to some inconceivable that a mere woman could or should successfully practise that most monumental of arts [fig. 3].[19]

In fact, the arguments that swirled around this new tide of women painting, sculpting, drawing and exhibiting from the middle of the century on, were often crude, usually muddled and frequently contradictory. The chief concern of critics was the question of 'female art': Was there a woman's art? Many patriarchs hoped there was not, many assumed that there must be. After all, women were required to be so different from men that of course their art would be different too. The difficulty was, could it possibly be Art? Though ideologically women's work would never be admitted into the same camp as men's by some commentators, a number of women artists of the time gave even hardened misogynists pause for thought: Joanna Boyce's and Elizabeth Thompson's paintings, and Mary Thornycroft's sculptures, seemed, for a moment at least, to be Art, yet they were by women. How could this be explained?![20] The twists and turns of thought and discussion which the women artists' movement provoked must now be discussed, and if the critics' and the artists' lines of argument seem confused, this will be a reflection of the overlapping and contradictory paths which the debate took throughout the period.

There were two main strands to the discussion. One concerned genius: Could a woman be a great artist? The other concerned diligence or education: If a woman would only work hard, she could get somewhere. These two strands interwove according to the prejudice of the writer and according to the developments of the situation. By and large, the 'genius' argument was used to stonewall any further discussion, and was considered the ultimate and irrefutable answer, being employed by people who would not conceive of any breach of male monopoly in cultural authority. The 'diligence' argument was deployed by people who imagined themselves sympathetic to women's cause, and was considered a very reasonable position to take. It also had a built-in escape clause for its proponents, because if women did not appear to improve after training and opportunity, they could be blamed for having let themselves down and need no longer be supported. The contradictions that these discussions exposed between assumptions based on gender and assumptions based on class, were largely avoided at the time, though we cannot help but acknowledge them now, and I have exposed them where it seems useful to do so.

Notes

1.   Widely available accounts of the Victorian period or of the nineteenth century in general include Quentin Bell, *Victorian Artists* (1967) (eight women artists indexed); Jeremy Maas, *Victorian Painters* (1978) (thirteen women artists indexed); Benedict Read, *Victorian Sculpture* (1983) (ten women artists indexed); Fritz Novotny, *Painting and Sculpture in Europe* (1970) (seven women artists indexed). In all these cases, the women are merely mentioned.
2.   See, amongst others, Michael Levey, *The Painter Depicted: painters as a subject in painting* (1981); and *In the Studio* (Sterling and Francine Clark Institute of Art, Williamstown, Massachusetts, 1981).
3.   For some art historians, the only major shifts in artists' own consciousness of what it meant to be an artist occurred in the French avant-garde, and consist of the so-called alienation evidenced by the life and work of Edouard Manet and some others. This interpretation of what was significant about being an artist in the mid-nineteenth century fails to consider gender as a relevant issue at all, and tends to confirm traditional negligence of female artists by its assumption of the intellectual outsider as the most meaningful of artists alongside a tacit assumption that only men have an intellectual engagement with the dilemmas of their own time.
4.   For a useful account of the women's movement in Britain from the beginning of the nineteenth century to the 1920s, see Ray Strachey, *The Cause* (1928).
5.   The *EWR* ran till 1859, and was then emulated by the *Englishwoman's Journal*, which ran from 1858 to 1864. For information on Barbara Leigh Smith see Hester Burton, *Barbara Bodichon* (1949).
6.   'Man and Woman', *Athenaeum*, 31 July 1858, p. 139.
7.   Mrs Strutt, *The Feminine Soul* (1857), quoted in the *EWR*, 21 March

1857, p. 2. For a selection and critique of writings on women at this time, see Bauer and Ritt, *Free and Ennobled* (1979).

8.   *The Habits of Good Society* by Man in a Club Window (1859), p. 230.

9.   For discussion of the workings and influence of men's images of women in the visual arts, see John Berger's seminal *Ways of Seeing* (1972), and Rozsika Parker and Griselda Pollock, *Old Mistresses* (1981). This discussion can be found related specifically to the Victorian period in Susan P. Casteras (ed.), *The Substance or the Shadow: Images of Victorian Womanhood* (Yale, 1982).

10.   *Spectator*, 29 July 1876, p. 956. For further comment on this important book, see Appendix.

11.   *op. cit.*, p. 230.

12.   Simone de Beauvoir, *The Second Sex* (1949), quoted in Shulamith Firestone, *The Dialectic of Sex* (New York, 1970), p. 176.

13.   P.G. Hamerton, *Thoughts About Art* (1862) p. 349. Being unfeminine might be anything from going out alone (ie. without a chaperone) to using oil paints (dirty and smelly).

14.   Barbara Leigh Smith, *Women and Work* (1857) p. 18. See also Harriet Martineau, 'Female Industry', *Edinburgh Review*, vol. 222 (1859), p. 297.

15.   *The Leisure Hour*, December 1856, no. 260, p. 816. A man should be: 'Affectionate, Bold, Candid, Daring, Enterprising, Faithful, Grateful, Honourable, Indefatigable, Just, Kind, Loving, Moral, Noble, Obliging, Polite, Quick, Religious, Social, Truthful, Upright, Valiant, Watchful, 'Xemplary, Zealous.'

16.   For an elementary account of her art, see John Crabbe, 'An Artist Divided', *Apollo*, May 1981, vol. 113, p. 311. Bodichon's paintings can be seen at Girton College, Cambridge and Hastings Art Gallery.

17.   Linda Nochlin, 'Why have there been no great women artists?', *Art and Sexual Politics*, Hess and Baker (eds.) (New York, 1973) p. 2.

18.   See Dore Ashton and Denise B. Hare, *Rosa Bonheur* (1981). There is nothing published on Browne as yet, and Anderson appears only as one entry among many in Christopher Forbes, *The Royal Academy Revisited* (privately published 1975); and Ellen C. Clayton, *English Female Artists* (1876).

19.   See Cornelia Crow Carr, *Harriet Hosmer* (New York, 1912).

20.   Mary Thornycroft's career is described in Elfrida Manning, *Bronze and Steel* (1932) (the author is the sculptor's grand-daughter); Thompson (later Butler) wrote her own life story, *An Autobiography* (1923) and had two volumes of memoirs published, *Letters from the Holy Land* (1903) and *: Recollections by Six Victorian Women Artists*, (1986).

2
Issues and Ideas

There was undoubtedly a widespread belief that a woman could
not be an artist, that the two were mutually exclusive. Ruskin wrote
in the late 1850s to a female acquaintance who aspired to become a
painter: 'You *must* resolve to be quite a great *paintress*; the
feminine termination does not exist, there never having been such
a being as yet as a lady who could paint. Try and be the first . . .'[1]

The claim that the past provided no evidence either of the
existence or the probability of female artists was often put forward
in the 1850s, 1860s and 1870s by those people who were impatient
even of discussing the 'woman (and art) question' (see below,
Chapter 3, for some instances). However, opponents of this
argument could be relied on to recall for doubting, sceptical and
prejudiced minds the names of the European painters Margaret van
Eyck, Elisabetta Sirani, Angelika Kauffmann and Elisabeth Vigee-
Lebrun, and sculptor Anne Damer. That such an argument, based
on an appeal to historical precedent, was very simplistic is obvious
to us now, but it was at the time often utilised to explain away the
absence or proscription of women from other fields, both cultural

and socio-political. Many, if not most, of the arguments put forward in the 1850s to represent the oppression of women as natural, rational, morally good or inevitable were based chiefly on the arguing party's convenience, and became clearly invalid when the line of argument collapsed once applied to more than one class of women. The arguments thus show themselves to be founded, not on truths concerning the female half of the race or population, but on political interest contingent on other systems of inequality, such as social class and ethnic origin.

That Ruskin tacitly believed the great 'paintress' to be an impossible creature came to light when the success of Elizabeth Thompson (later Butler) in the 1870s seemed to many to demand a reassessment of established prejudices. He wrote in *Academy Notes* in 1875:

> I never approached a picture with more iniquitous prejudice against it than I did Miss Thompson's: partly because I have always said that no woman could paint: and secondly, because I thought, what the public made such a fuss about *must* be good for nothing . . .[2]

The painting he was considering was the young artist's 'The Roll Call' [fig. 4], a subject from the Crimean war, and the first of several large-scale war or battle scenes with which she gained public and critical popularity. Obviously, a woman who painted war, in a manner acceptable to the Academy, went a long way towards contradicting many established ideas about Woman, femininity, and women's creativity.

Less than a decade later, he was over-compensating for his previous bias sufficiently to declare, in 'The Art of England' lectures, with reference to Francesca Alexander and Lilian Trotter:

> For a long time I used to say, in all my elementary books, that, except in a graceful and minor way, women could not paint or draw. I am beginning, lately, to bow myself to the much more delightful conviction that nobody else can.[3]

Ruskin is not a typical case, in that he was constantly contradicting himself throughout his career, but his importance in the second half of the nineteenth century cannot be denied, and he *is* typical in his adaptation to the developments of the women artists issue. He is also representative of those who took part in the debate in that his

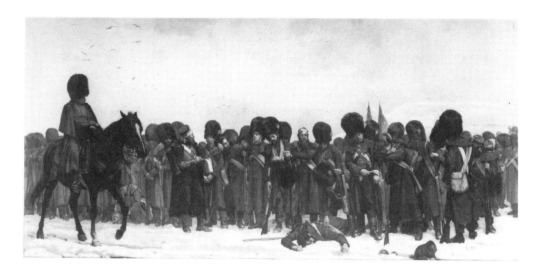

4. Elizabeth Thompson Butler, 'Calling the Roll after an Engagement, Crimea'
('The Roll Call'), 1874. Oil on canvas. Reproduced by gracious permission of
Her Majesty the Queen.

ideas of what constituted great art were tortuously entangled with notions of genius and standards of technical ability, in a complex and largely unresolved way. Thus, Ruskin was endlessly urging the women whom he 'taught' to improve their technical skills – to learn to draw properly, to copy the best models, to take their talent seriously, to apply themselves – yet he saw the artist as having a special innate quality (whether or not it be called genius) which he neither envisaged women as possessing nor encouraged women to cultivate. Passages from the now notorious 'Sesame and Lilies' lectures (1864), and from his correspondence with protegées, are ample illustration of this.[4] The mutual incompatibility of the concepts 'woman' and 'artist' was seen to devolve more perhaps upon this point than on any other. Genius seemed to many minds emphatically not an inhabitant of the female psyche. Discussing 'the natural mode of exercising female influence', the *Spectator* in 1856 allowed that women might operate in many fields, including art, but with crucial limitations:

> Women have appeared in the arts, in literature, in public business, as the handmaids of the greatest human influences. They can give expression to music where music becomes the voice of woman. They contribute a very important and useful portion of literature. They can appear as the ruling governors of the world. But into none of these cases enters that process which we may call the working out of reason, which is essentially a masculine function.[5]

It was popularly believed that women's brains were smaller than men's,[6] and that smaller meant lesser, as well as that women's physiology was inherently weak and vulnerable: so women's inability to create great art need be seen as no discredit to them but simply as a fact of life. Equally (went this line of reasoning) if it was not women's failure neither was it society's fault. As a fact of life, it was needless to rail against it, and not only fruitless but impious to question it. This allowed mockery, pity and indignation to be levelled at women who tried to make art. On the other hand, female creativity was seen to be suited to craft, or design, and the Victorian era was one in which an endless variety of pastimes (more or less creative) was invented for girls and women to spend their energies on. The invidious division of creative activities into art and craft or fine art and applied art has been exposed and discussed in feminist writings and research, and it can now be seen that such categorisations are a product of a competitive attitude which prioritises certain values over others for purely ideological ends. Oil painting (a fine art) was often said to be too smelly and dirty for women to practise, yet sand pictures, feather pictures and shell-box-making (hobbies) were praised to the skies for their suitability for girls, women and ladies, the messiness of such contrived pastimes being just as emphatically glossed over. Though the women described in these pages might have recognised the politics of these distinctions, their aspirations towards the so-called fine arts testify to a determination to succeed on these terms: only in some cases was the intention to thereby overturn them.

The critical reception given to different sorts of art-work produced by women was greatly affected by such hierarchical attitudes. Some critics embraced the idea that women's art could never be the product of genius, nor even show the trace of intellectual invention. Some, on the other hand, protested it. In some quarters, women's work was evidently judged from the premise that it was bound to be uninspired, yet such misogynists might also enjoy criticising the artists for such a lack. Amongst those who imagined themselves supportive of women artists, the same criticism could be found, though ostensibly because the critic hoped to spur the artists on to the higher position which he claimed to believe they could attain. The *Athenaeum's* reviewer wrote in 1866:

> It is strange to find so few who display intellectual grasp, not merely of any method of treating a given subject in Art, but of the subject itself. Nine tenths of the work in question must have been made by those who have no insight beyond that of their eyes.

This comment was given in a review of the Society of Female Artists exhibition. The same context prompted a similar remark by the critic of the *Spectator*, usually more perspicacious on the subject than other reviewers, in 1861: 'There are many [works] which are very clever handiwork, in the manner of certain painters of the day, with all the trick of colour and touch; but thought and originality are seldom felt to have had much concern in the production.' Other critics avowed, at the outset, that they did not even expect such things from women: 'Strength of will and power of creation belonging rather to the other sex, we do not of course look for the more daring efforts in an exhibition of female artists.'[7]. In this presumed absence of insight, industry was recurrently recommended to women whose work appeared not to meet the male-defined standard of excellence:

> If a lady will labour with a portion of the earnestness and in-dustry a man must employ she might succeed as well . . . We know that if the same concentration of mind had been applied to these pictures which is so often devoted with perfect taste and charming success to the disposition of a walking costume or the tint of a bonnet the result would have been far other . . .
>
>   . . . ladies, if they would compete in fine art with men, whether in an exhibition open to both sexes, or in one like this, should *work* like men. There is nothing for it at last but work: no cleverness, no compliments, avail to supply its place.[8]

Some 25 years later, the analogy with women's traditional sphere of creative effort – the domestic and consumerist – would be used by critics who were still unsympathetic to women's fine art aspirations to suggest that, after all, the home and the person were the only sites congenial to women's creativity.

In the 1850s criticism at least allowed that there was a way in which artistic success *might* prove attainable by women, and, indeed, some writers pointed out to their readers a living example of this possibility being achieved. This specific example, which this latter critic (writing in the *Spectator*) would hold up to women for their emulation, was the French artist Rosa Bonheur, who was used throughout the period as a paradigm of all sorts of excellence for women to note. Her industry was recommended to *Spectator* readers in the following terms:

> Rosa Bonheur is the first woman who has taken up art without one vestige of dilettantism, that fatalest of cankers in any serious pursuit. What men study, she can and does; what men can endure, she can and does; what men can work, she can and does . . .[9]

The fundamental contradiction between this demand for earnest study and the desire for a feeble 'dilettantism' of which Hamerton was so vigorously critical, is seldom tackled head-on by critics promoting either position: in this, Hamerton shows rarely expressed insight. But women themselves could also express a wish for greater diligence from women artists: the *Victoria Magazine* commented in 1866:

> It is a great pity that so few women ever work up to the point where their paintings cease to be studies and become pictures. Of course we do not mean to infer that every man or woman who can produce a clever correct study, can produce original inventive work, but we regret to see such a number of aimless sketches on the walls of the Royal Academy . . .

Few women, however, in the 1860s – which seemed such a boom time for women artists – would go so far as Mrs Sutherland Orr in her article on the subject of 'The Future of Englishwomen' in 1878, who gave no hope even to the diligent:

> Women are intelligent; they are not creative. Whether in their home or beyond it, their successes can only be achieved through the contact with other minds; the impulse to mental action must always come to them from without, or at least the form in which the impulse will be clothed. That men possess the productiveness which is called genius, and women do not, is the one immutable distinction that is bound up with the intellectual idea of sex . . . [10]

That such a view, though perceptibly reactionary, was still feasible in 1878 indicates how deeply ingrained was the idea that women could not, by their very nature, be 'special' enough to be artists of any note, that they lacked the capacity for genius. Thus, the constant emphasis by critics, commentators and many women alike, on the fact of a woman artist's gender in the 1850s and 1860s, indicated a fundamental acceptance of the idea that anything done by women in this field was necessarily different, and negatively so, and must be signalled as such. For women's art to be different – or Other, in de Beauvoir's terms [11] – there had to be a norm, from which it was different and which it was other than, and this norm is thus revealed to be male artists' work. Just as Ruskin, in introducing the term 'paintress' to describe women painters, had revealed the ostensibly neuter term 'painter' as signifying a male artist, most critics distinguished female practitioners as different from the norm by describing them as 'the fair artist', 'the gentle painter', 'this accomplished lady', and so on. Inescapably, such terms read as indications that this artist and this work were not to be considered as one would consider other (i.e. male) artists and art. They were to be viewed from a position which did not expect to find genius present, did not expect to see that quality which identifies the 'proper' artist and 'real' art. Henrietta Ward, for instance, one of the most successful of the artists who will be discussed here, hardly ever escaped the identification as woman first and artist second: 'The lady artists are getting now a powerful body. First comes Mrs Ward . . .'; 'Among the ladies, Mrs Ward makes a distinguished figure . . .'; '[This is a picture] placing Mrs Ward decidedly at the head of the lady contributors'; 'Mrs E.M. Ward takes precedence of the female contributors . . .'[12]

This approach effectively set women apart from men in the reader's mind, presenting for consideration a number of works of art and a number of works by women. This did not, as far as I can tell, reflect the way in which works were hung, but simply the way in which works were approached and assessed. Emphatically implied is the supposition that the women's art will be 'women's work' first, and art second. The question of what female art was supposed to be, and to what extent it was so, can best be considered through individual cases, but suffice it to say here that, unless a commentator was very progressive or very acute, it mattered not whether an artist's work in fact confirmed or contradicted the prevalent stereotype of the woman's picture. The work was considered as stereotype, or as if it should have been such.

A selection of critical comments on the work of particular artists will serve to make this point clear, as well as to hint at the gradual embarrassment felt by a few critics at this implicit and predetermined categorisation. Emily Mary Osborn was a woman conspicuous amongst the new wave of female artists: in 1861 her Academy exhibit, 'The Escape of Lord Nithsdale' [fig. 5] produced the following review in the *Illustrated London News*:

> . . . a capacity for historical painting to an extent quite extraordinary in a female, and which places her in an elevated rank in comparison with the most celebrated of her male compeers.

The same paper greeted her 1870 'Lost' [fig. 6] as 'creditable to its author both as woman and painter'. This same work, however, was greeted by the more alert *Art Journal* as 'worthy, we will not say, of a "female artist", now a term of contempt – it holds its place strongly by its genuine pictorial merits'.

Emily Mary Osborn, born in 1834, had one of the most enduring

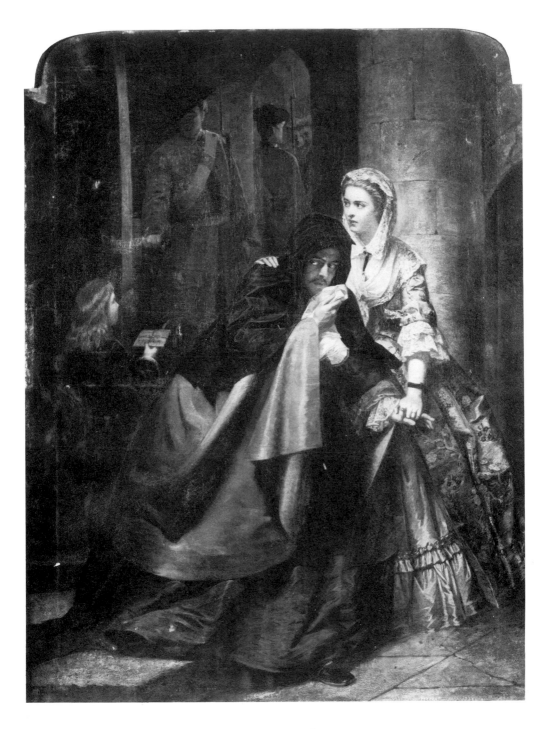

5. Emily Mary Osborn, 'The Escape of Lord Nithsdale', 1861. Oil on canvas.
Private collection. (Photo: Christie's)

careers of her generation; though no one has yet established the date of her death, she was still exhibiting in 1905, and had moved on from her earlier work, embracing altogether in her career a wide variety of genres. The lack of ladylike modesty which the critics noted in 'Lord Nithsdale', seems to be characteristic of this artist, whose paintings have begun to come to light in recent years though she has had up till now no reputation to speak of. She evidently led a very independent life – she remained single, and travelled to Munich and parts of France for her subjects, eventually producing landscapes of Algeria in the 1880s. Her work fitted in to a middle-of-the-road notion of Realism, picturing modern life in the style popularised by William Frith in the 1850s, though clearly from a point of view which could discomfit the male critic. Her subjects, mostly predicated on female protagonists, included such topical motifs of contemporary life as women workers and the governess, as well as standard mid-Victorian literary subjects from sources such as Oliver Goldsmith and Tennyson.

Joanna Mary Boyce (later Wells) also presented critics with work that defied definition as 'woman's work' as they understood it: 'Mrs H.T. Wells vindicates her claim to be considered one of our best female painters by her striking "Veneziana" [fig. 7] . . . there is unusual force in the execution', commented the *Saturday Review* at the Academy in 1861, with *The Times* echoing: 'There are few more workmanlike pieces of painting in the Exhibition than this.' '. . . Without sinning on the side of the masculine, Miss Boyce paints with a manliness which there are few men to emulate,' the *Spectator* had said in 1855.[13] The *Athenaeum*'s obituary notice excused her lack of feminity: 'As a young and consequently incompletely practised artist, Mrs Wells' work erred rather in excess of strength than the common fault of feminine tameness.'[14]

As feminist opinion became more evident in the art world, the singling out of women as women could be done in a positive way, in the spirit of what would nowadays be called positive discrimination,[15] but at the start of the mid-century, and continuingly so for some quarters of opinion, this ghettoising of women artists was motivated by a real conviction that their work was, because performed by women, less interesting and less meritorious than 'proper' (male) art. This was widely accepted to be the true state of affairs, but commentators sympathetic to women explained this circumstance by pointing out women's lack of art education and poverty of encouragement from the right quarters (specifically the Academy); and gradually, in fact, the education argument came to

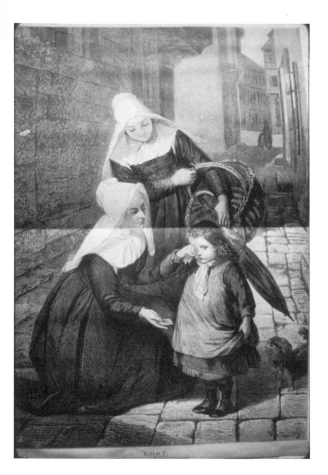

6. Anonymous engraving after
Emily Mary Osborn, 'Lost', 1870.
Anderdon album, Royal Academy of Arts.
(Photo: author)

7. Joanna Boyce Wells, 'La Veneziana', 1860.
Oil on canvas. Destroyed.
(Photo: courtesy Julia Ford)

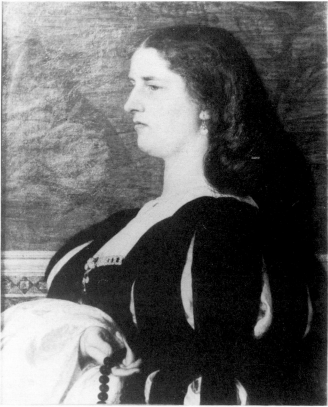

eclipse the discussion of genius. Before appraising women's art education, however, further examination of the social fabric which militated against the acceptance of women as artists is necessary.

There were great structures of reasons why female artists were what they were, built upon various factors in mid-Victorian society, as well as upon the aims and practices of mid-Victorian art, but few critics took these up for analysis. Elizabeth Ellet, a woman interested in art and in women, in her book *Women Artists in all Ages and Countries* (see Appendix), attempted to point out to the undiscerning but increasingly concerned critic and public, some of the reasons *why* women and art appeared to relate in such an unsatisfactory way:

> Such occupations [as copper engraving and miniature painting] might be pursued in the strict seclusion of home, to which custom and public sentiment consigned the fair student. Nor were they inharmonious with the ties of friendship and love, to which her tender nature clung. In most instances women have been led to the cultivation of art through the choice of parents or brothers. While nothing has been more common than to see young men embrace the profession against the wishes of their families and in the face of difficulties, the example of a woman thus deciding for herself is extremely rare.[16]

The selection of the art world as a career was, of course, almost exclusively a choice which offered itself to the middle class and it is the particular lack of freedom of the middle-class female that Ellet conjures up here: the working-class woman was a worker outside the home and a worker within it, while the aristocratic female could quite acceptably find some enthusiasm with which she could earnestly occupy some of her yawning leisure time. However, the bourgeois woman was supposed to appear idle within her home (if not, she was not handling her servants properly or she was in the embarrassing position of having too few of them) and to be inactive outside it (for her husband or father was supposed to be able to afford almost total leisure for her). Such women were relative creatures, to borrow Françoise Basch's term:[17] they had practically no autonomy, and their choices were largely determined by their place in the social system of mid-Victorian society. They were identified as women, and to seek an identity as artists also was to come into conflict with that fundamental, socially imposed identity.

26

Home and the family were the essential context for women, the domestic scene their natural habitat, marriage and motherhood their destiny.[18] These factors conspired to rule out any other possibilities for the bourgeois woman who wished for respectability and social acceptance. The assumptions that went particularly with the married state – that one would confine one's interests and energies to the home, that one would be economically dependent, that one would have neither time nor interest for anything but the fulfilment of one's prescribed duties – were indeed forbidding to women's ambitions and fatal, in most cases, to women's imagination. For women aspiring to be fine artists, the particular issues raised here are twofold: first, the family connection had a great influence on a woman's ability to become an artist, and secondly the assumption that a middle-class woman need not earn her living seemed to doom her to eternal amateurism. These two points need close examination, especially since it was recognised at the time that most successful women artists seemed to come from artistic families and since the preponderance of women over men in British society (notably from the 1850s) rendered the theory of dependent womanhood impractical. Questions about art, then, can be seen to be equally about the maintenance of the Victorian status quo. The danger of women's ambitions 'de-sexing' them was created as a deterrent and much bruited about by defenders of femininity, womanliness and the institutions of patriarchal capitalism. Thus the *Saturday Review*, again discussing 'Womanliness' in 1870:

> Women are swarming out at all doors, running hither and thither among the men, clamouring for arms that they may enter into the fray with them, anxious to lay aside their tenderness, their modesty, their womanliness, that they may become hard and fierce and self-asserting like them, thinking it a far higher thing to leave the home and the family to take care of themselves, or under the care of some incompetent hireling, while they take up the manly professions and make themselves the rivals in trade of their husbands and brothers.

A few months later, the *Review* returned to this theme in 'Young Ladies as they are':

> We have lately heard so much discussion of what is called 'the movement on behalf of women', that it is a relief to find that there

27

are still women in the world whose thoughts are occupied with love, dress, and cookery, and who seem to have neither grand aims nor lofty aspirations, nor any desire for what is called the 'intellectual development' of their sex . . . Let women enter trades and professions freely, but let them not expect, after they have done so, that they can compete for men's affection with our Rosebud.

Clearly, the challenge which the idea of professions for middle-class women presented was a challenge to femininity, marriage, the family and the home.[19] Some women saw that challenge as dangerous and undesirable, because they thought women would not gain more than they had to lose, and women who became artists were not necessarily progressive or radical people, never mind feminists. Even so, it was of course mainly men who were to be heard resisting the idea of women taking up seriously any non-domestic activity. Men's own interests were fundamentally involved, though they usually guilefully presented the threat of emancipation as a threat to women. The *Athenaeum* carried a review of the American Virginia Penny's *The Employment of Women* in 1863, which uses this strategy blatantly:

It is some consolation, too, that woman will not necessarily lose 'that softness and gentleness that render her so lovely'. Our charming author seems to forget that in her ideal state of society there would be less opportunity of cultivating those graces, and fewer admirers to be ensnared . . .

Within the art world, there was just as much antagonism but less sophistry: the following is from the memoirs of the painter Sir Martin Archer Shee, on women entering the medical profession:

If women are found anxious to indulge such questionable tastes, let them by all means do so. I would, if it rested with me, keep the sex *pure* and *undefiled*; and confine them to their own recognised sphere of usefulness, and I believe that a majority of the fathers, sons, and brothers of England would agree with me, if they were polled.[20]

And Ruskin, in 1873:

I cannot find expression strong enough for the hatred and

contempt I feel for the modern idea that a woman should cease to be mother, daughter, or woman so that she may become a shop assistant or an engineer . . . The duty of a man is to support his wife and children, that of a woman to make him happy in his home, and to bring up his children wisely. No woman is capable of more than that. No man should do less.[21]

This brings us back to the two aspects of the question of woman's social identity and role which particularly affect the woman aspiring to the arts – domestic location and relationship, or relativity, to men. Clearly, though the mid-Victorian woman might move from the home of her father to that of her husband, for her to seek to escape from home was not in order at all, and this belief is often reflected in discussion of women and art. The following comments come from an article that appeared in the *Art Journal* in 1872 entitled 'Art-work for Women':

Designing seems to offer peculiarly suitable work for women. To whom should we so confidently apply for all that concerns the beautifying of home life as to the presiding spirit of the home? . . . Engraving again is an art little practised by, but quite possible for, women; and attractive from the fact that it may be done at home . . . There is perhaps no branch of art-work more perfectly womanly and in every way desirable than painting on china.

Since woman's place was assumed to be in the home, activities which could take place within that environment and which accorded with its routine and ambience were viewed favourably, in a way that a pastime – never mind a career – which took her out of the house was not.[22] At the same time, of course, it must be noted that domestic creativity such as handwork and sewing, collecting, and compiling albums, command no artistic status at all, generally speaking. Keeping clean and tidy and retaining the outward signs of femininity were considered a more desirable achievement for her to aspire to.

Although the writers of the article quoted above state firmly early in the piece that 'No reason can possibly be urged why talent in women, if as much cultivated as by men, should not produce the same results', they go on to assume that her talent will in fact be cultivated within the domestic sphere. (This crucial difference between might and will is typical of the spurious liberality of some writers on this subject.) Only if art were already practised within the family (say, by a parent), and thus did not violate the domestic hearth, might a woman enter into it reasonably readily. Thus the family connection was such an important factor in the fate of aspiring women artists.

As has already been indicated, this was recognised in the period; Sarah Tytler's *Modern Painters and their Paintings* commented:

> I may observe, in proof of the difficulty which the technicalities of art must present to women, that of all the women painters whom I have chronicled, I am not aware of one . . . who did not overcome the difficulty, by the advantage of an early familiarity with art, from having been the daughter of a painter, or, at least, of an engraver.[23]

Such daughters in the period under discussion were legion: Agnes Bouvier, Catherine and Lucy Madox Brown, Adelaide and Florence Claxton, Isabel Constable, Emily Desvignes, Mary Rosenberg, Constance Fripp, Maria Gastineau, Emma Kendrick, Eliza Lance, Jessie and Emma Landseer, Hannah Linnell, Matilda Lowry, Mary Chalon, Elizabeth Heaphy, Maud Naftel, Anne, Barbara, Charlotte, Elizabeth, Jane and Margaret Nasmyth, Julia Pocock, Frances, Louise, Margaret, Nancy and Rose Rayner, Frances Redgrave, Mary Severn, Charlotte Vawser, Henrietta Ward and Emily and Julia Weigall. As well as being the daughter of a painter, the mid-Victorian woman artist was often the wife of an artist – Henrietta Ward, Hannah Palmer, Mary Thornycroft, Louise Jopling, Anne Bartholomew, Mary Duffield and Joanna Mary Wells; or the sister of one – Rosa Brett, Emma and Jessie Landseer, Joanna Mary Boyce, Emma Sandys and Rebecca Solomon. (Such a list shows that the fathers, husbands and brothers, as well as the daughters, wives and sisters, achieved very varied degrees of fame.) Thus expressions like the following abound in exhibition reviews:

> Naturally, with a father, sister, and brothers all painting, it would have been almost strange had she not taken up the pencil . . . the house in London, people laughingly said, was '*all* studio'.
>
> . . . there was hereditary tendency enough to account for Miss Mary Forster's taking to the brush, and continuing the succession . . .[24]

It was, noticeably the case that on the mid-Victorian art scene, the family connection played a large part generally, and the dynasties of such as the Nasmyths, the Rayners, the Landseers and the Hayllars – to say nothing of fathers and sons or families of brothers like the Stones or the Goodalls – characterise the nineteenth-century British art world. (It is interesting to note, however, that the most successful artists of the period, with the exception of Landseer, were unique in their families.) The Nasmyth sisters were of a pre-Victorian generation, born between 1790 and 1804. Anne, Barbara, Charlotte, Elizabeth, Jane and Margaret were daughters of a father who established a fashionable art-training practice in Scotland. The family gradually migrated south to set up an equally successful 'family business', so to speak, in London, the daughters in fact taking on much of the teaching as well as the production of Nasmyth landscapes. These were very successful until the middle of the century, when they became old-fashioned (especially in the light of the new Pre-Raphaelite movement). Needless to say, however, it is their father Alexander and their brother Patrick who are usually the best-remembered artists of the family.

The Rayners, similarly, are to be found described in relation to their father Samuel: 'His five daughters, Louise, Frances, Margaret, Nancy and Rose were all painters', says Christopher Wood's *Dictionary of Victorian Painters* (1978); 'Five of his daughters became painters of repute', says M. H. Grant in his *Chronological History of Old English Landscape Painters* (1957). Unlike the Nasmyths, whose staple product was the oil painting, the Rayner family (including the sisters' mother Anne and a brother) special-ised in watercolours. Of the five sisters, born in the late 1820s and early 1830s, Louise became the most well-known and became the supporter of the family after Samuel's death. She lived until 1924.

The women of the Landseer dynasty were little known, though their father John and their brothers Thomas and Edwin were amongst the most familiar characters of the mid-Victorian art world. The Landseers did not have a family product, and so the women of the family were not automatically drafted in to be cogs in the wheel. With the Landseers, it was rather that every member of the family took an interest in art, and it seems that, in the absence of a defined practice into which they could easily and must easily slot, the two daughters of the family, Emma and Jessie, got caught in a much more typical familial role of lesser lights reflecting the greater glory of their brothers' talent. Emma exhibited animal paintings in the shadow of her fabulously famous brother Edwin, while Jessie painted landscape, still life and pets, and left her money to animal charities. Biographers of Edwin like to suggest that both sisters thought the sun shone out of his eyes.

The Hayllar sisters, born in the middle of the century and achieving success in the 1880s, were a product of their father's devotion to painting. Although he and his wife had nine children, it was Jessica, Edith, Mary and Kate who continued the Hayllar name in the Academy after their father's career had passed its peak. Christopher Wood suggests that James Hayllar's sons were less malleable than these four daughters, whom he moulded to the production of a streamlined and unified product, oil scenes of middle-class idylls, usually domestic.[25]

The family connection had a particular effect on women artists, very different and more important in its meaning than for the male artist. It was both positive and negative, for, while the artistic family gave a woman opportunity and encouragement, her relatives' support was very much of a mixed blessing, for while giving with the one hand, it took away with the other: it took her individuality away, contributing to the invisibility that she has suffered from. The shadow in which the mid-Victorian woman artist has stood has often been cast by her male relatives, especially if they worked in the same medium. Thus Henrietta Ward was usually known as Mrs E. M. Ward, Rebecca Solomon was known as the sister of Abraham and Simeon, Charlotte Nasmyth as Alexander's daughter and Patrick's sister, and so on. The woman did, of course, bear the man's name, and the contemporary custom of the woman taking, on marriage, not only her husband's surname but his first name too, effectively reduced her to an appendage of his fame or position: thus Anne Fayermann was known as Mrs Valentine Bartholomew, Emma Eburne as Mrs William Oliver, Mary Rosenberg as Mrs William Duffield and Joanna Mary Boyce as Mrs H. T. Wells.

Some women kept their maiden name if they had established a reputation for themselves before they married, conscious no doubt that a reputation can easily be lost when the name by which they are known to the public is lost from view. When Emma Brownlow married the singer Donald King in 1867, after she had been exhibiting for almost two decades, she subsequently exhibited as Emma Brownlow King rather than as Emma King or Mrs Donald King. Jane Benham, painter and illustrator, exhibited as Benham Hay after her marriage in 1859. Henrietta Ward was in the peculiar position of having married a man who bore the same name as herself, so that her single and married names had a continuity which was only marred by critics' tendency to neglect her own first name, and call her Mrs E. M. Ward. Much-married artists, changing their names and titles more than once in their careers, were a confusion to the public and remain so for the historian.[26]

The shadow cast by the family connection is very apparent in press write-ups of women artists. It seems that if there were so much as a hint of an artistic father, brother or husband in the woman's pedigree, he was brought forth by critics to stand as a witness for her – more often than not, to stand in front of her – and was used as a yardstick by which to measure her failings. To adopt the negative sense here is nothing more than typical of the critical tendency to think in terms of her failings rather than her merits: the comparison was usually to the woman's disadvantage. Thus, discussion of a woman's work often ran like this:

> . . . executed with somewhat of the feeling of the gifted father of the artist, but yet of course far below his standard. The work wants the harmonious colour and cohesion of those of Patrick Nasmyth . . . (Charlotte Nasmyth's 'Burnham Beeches', 1861)

> Mrs McIan follows her husband as closely as possible, in subject and in manner (Fanny McIan's 'Captivity and Liberty', 1850).[27]

The point here is not so much whether or not husband and wife or father and daughter were indeed producing the same genre, a family style or a shared view of a similar subject, but that the male artist would never be appraised by the same critic through his wife's or his daughter's work. Alexander Nasmyth did not have to put up with a comparison with any of his daughters' work, neither were Patrick Nasmyth's pictures judged by his sisters'. Robert McIan was not praised or blamed according to his wife's work.

A conspicuous victim of such comparative criticism was Henrietta Ward, and a range of the critical comments she typically received will show to what lengths this approach was sometimes taken, depending on the condescension of the critic:

> 'The Young May Queen' by Mrs E. M. Ward shows a decisive advance, and hints that the lady, if this is entirely her own handi-work, may at no distant day rival her lord in the laying on of colour.

> We should have pointed to the 'Scene from the camp at Chobham' as a specimen of the manner by which he [E. M. Ward] is best known, did not the catalogue inform us that *Mrs* E. M. Ward was the painter of the work in question.

The children in Mrs E. M. Ward's 'Henrietta Maria' are the most praiseworthy features of that elaborate, skilful, but somewhat theatrical picture, in which the lady has imitated with marvellous accuracy the style and manner of her husband.

['Mary Queen of Scots'] is vigorously painted, with good, quiet expression, excellent feeling and colour, and an easy command of the technical resources of composition, drawing and effect, which shames much man's work round about it. If Mrs Ward indicates her master in her method, this is only natural [fig. 8].

Some traces of this artist's [E. M. Ward] manner are naturally seen in Mrs Ward's picture, 'Mary of Scotland giving her infant to the charge of Lord Mar'.

['Joan of Arc'] if too faithfully reproducing the manner of her distinguished husband, has excellent points both of conception and execution.[28]

In some cases, a surrogate father/husband was found by critics in the male mentor or master, with similarly negative results for the artist: 'the pupil imitates the master, the daughter the parent', commented the *Spectator*'s reviewer of the Society of Female Artists show in 1862.[29]

This brings the discussion here on to the other major effect of the fact that women's place was socially conceived as being properly in the bosom of the family (even in the case of working-class women, whose absence from the home was seen as a necessary evil), for it bears on the deeply felt conviction that women's art was inevitably not serious – that the female artist was irresistibly an amateur, and dependent on the originality which only men possessed.

Since it was taken for granted that woman's primary interest should be in marriage and a family, and only secondarily might she be drawn to some additional complementary activity (probably philanthropic), that other activity would necessarily be subject to the demands of breeding, nurturing and servicing which was the wife and mother's lot in the Victorian middle classes. If she were thus drawn, traditional opinion assumed it would be for Christian, altruistic purposes (doing good for others, showing a womanly compassion and charity for those less fortunate than herself), not for personal gain: to complement or amplify the character she was already assumed to have, not to challenge it. Hence *Elegant Arts for Ladies*, Baldwin's sketcher and Hamerton's frustrated artist. Not

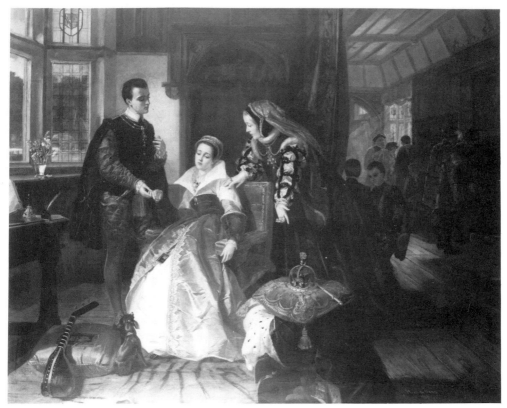

8. Anonymous engraving after Henrietta Ward, 'Queen Mary quitting
Stirling Castle', 1863. *Art Journal*. (Photo: Julie Phipps)

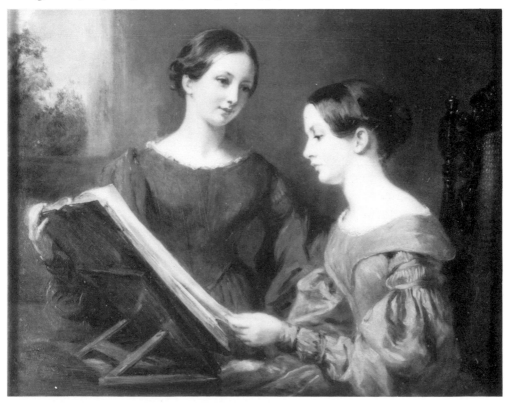

9. Margaret Carpenter, 'The Sisters', 1839. Oil on canvas. Reproduced by
courtesy of the Board of Trustees of the Victoria and Albert Museum.

only was the woman assumed to be almost exclusively a wife, mother and lady, but she was assumed to *desire* to be this – her entire upbringing had been devoted to inculcating this sole desire in her – and therefore to have no ambition to rise higher than the dilettante, the amateur, the dabbler, the modest and well-meaning Sunday painter. One of the major reasons why the question of women artists became *such* a question during the later nineteenth century is that it became obvious that more and more women were practising art with the intention and ambition of being 'proper', or professional, artists, and that they meant their work for sale and serious attention.[30]

One of the factors which has militated against Victorian women's art being paid any serious attention in later periods is that it rarely featured in public collections, apparently was not bought by major collectors and was therefore rarely bequeathed under conspicuous circumstances to the nation, or to a prominent institution commanding public attention. I say apparently, because even where women's pictures or sculptures were among prominent collectors' legacies or gifts, they were overlooked: Margaret Carpenter's work [fig. 9] is to be found in the Sheepshanks collection which now forms the Victoria and Albert Museum's painting exhibit, for instance, and the Burdett-Coutts collection included work by Rebecca Solomon [fig. 10], but in both cases other (male) artists' work has always been picked out as forming the chief interest of such a sale or collection. It is ironic that the British public collection with the highest proportion of women's art work is the National Portrait Gallery, which selects works on the basis of the subject/ sitter, not the artist.

For most artists, it is selling work that confirms one's identity, whether the era is one of stable and monolithic patronage by church and state or one of a wide and free-ranging market open to many social groups. Yet to earn money was anathema to many women's sensibilities, even when it might have been the obviously sensible way to proceed. The society around them was only unwillingly persuaded that for them to earn money was tolerable, and the confusion of both women artists and their public at the contradictions presented here was very evident in the press. Reviewers vacillated in their criticism between guffaws and gallantry, between scholarship and small talk: was women's art really to be judged as if it were Art? Was a critic who liked his reputation seriously to recommend these paintings to the picture-buying public? Despite their own ambivalent feelings in many

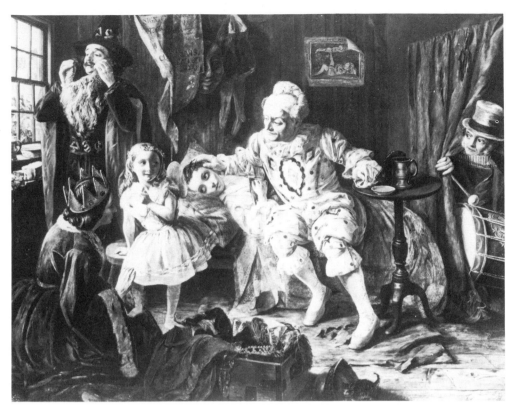

10. Rebecca Solomon, 'Behind the Curtain', 1858. Oil on canvas.
Private collection. (Photo: the owner)

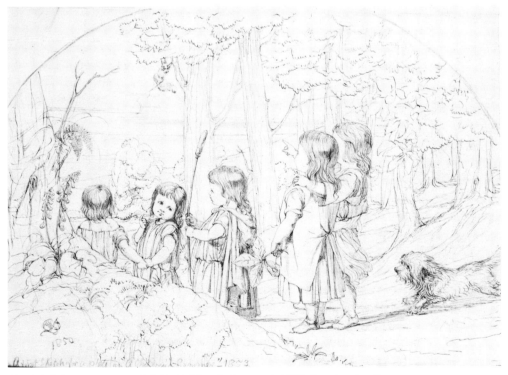

11. EVB (Eleanor Vere Boyle), 'A Children's Summer', 1853. Pen drawing for
etching (one of eleven plates). Private collection. (Photo: Sotheby's)

cases, increasing numbers of women (as the Census figures show) saw art-making as their profession, approaching painting, say, as an activity which they enjoyed but which primarily was meant to earn them a living. They actively sought commissions, and hoped for buyers, while pursuing other commercial opportunities such as illustration. Such concerns, a simple fact of life to the male artist, constituted a major transgression of social habits and norms if the artist was a woman. Yet she had to prove to herself and to her potential patron that she was not an amateur pursuing a hobby: she wanted serious, financially backed attention from the gallery-goer.

It is obviously important to examine the definition of amateur. A comment on the work of Eleanor Vere Boyle (EVB) [fig. 11] made in the *Spectator* in 1853, indicates the distinction between an amateur and a professional:

> Art is a pleasure to her as well as a study; and this alone would separate her widely and for ever from the crowd of artists for whom designing is a profession, and from amateurs who rate it as an accomplishment.[31]

The point is expanded by this observation on the work of Ruskin, exhibited at a charity exhibition in 1863, amidst professional and amateur work:

> Mr Ruskin stands on the debatable ground between artist and amateur. As not following the art for money, he belongs to the latter category; as following it with the entire devotion of an earnest mind, he is, above most men of his time, an artist.[32]

These statements immediately encourage the reader to expect from the amateur something which is equivalent to an art for art's sake, and yet also less accomplished than the work presented by someone producing for remuneration. Writings on art in both books and press throughout the period reflected not only an acceptance of this distinction, but a conviction that it was a very important one to maintain.

To take the latter point first, this is the opening passage of the *Spectator* critic's reaction to Clayton's *English Female Artists*:

> The first effect produced by this book is to raise in our minds the questions, – What constitutes an artist, and where are we to draw the line, especially in the case of women, between an artist and

an amateur? The rough-and-ready money test, though the most obvious, is, after all, the least reliable, for the veriest dauber may sell his or her paintings, when a true artist may never gain a penny from the discerning public. But if all the fine ladies who have ever dabbled in oil painting, in conjunction with fancy work and paper flowers, are to go down to posterity as Female Artists, we shall be more puzzled than ever to discover the right application of the word![33]

The amateur exhibitions provoked comment which shows what the label connoted, and indicates women's expected position in such a company:

The collection on the whole is a creditable one; not offering, as was not to be expected, any great daring in choice of subject or originality in method, but showing in many cases a cultivated sense of beauty, and adequate power in its expression. There are not many works of a decidedly inferior character. The ladies are generally among the best contributors, as, indeed, they will be found to be in most collections of the kind – copies of pictures, flower-painting, etc. – in all the minor branches and amid the minor votaries of art.[34]

Amateur exhibitions invariably held more female work than male – there was an assumption that amateurism was fundamentally more in keeping with being female than with being male. Martin Hardie has described this notion in *Watercolour Painting in Britain* (1968):

After 1850, people changed and conditions altered. Women had just as much leisure, and watercolour painting before marriage and between confinements became recognised as one of their especial occupations. Men, however, turned aside from such trivialities. More manly pursuits were encouraged at the public schools. Grown men found dabbling with colours on a piece of paper incompatible with a sense of their own dignity. Leisure could be better spent on sport or courtship, on the reading of newspapers and scientific journals, on experimental science itself, on travel, billiards, literary compositions, and, most important of all, in serious converse away from the ladies.[35]

Here we see very clearly that art as a hobby was appropriate for women, but unsuitable for men; this led to the assumption that art produced by women was *necessarily* amateur, that it was of the character that Eliot describes so caustically in *Middlemarch*:

> Dorothea, whose slight regard for domestic music and feminine fine art must be forgiven her, considering the small tinkling and smearing in which they chiefly consisted at that dark period . . .

> Rosamund, though she would never do anything that was disagreeable to her, was industrious; and now more than ever she was active in sketching her landscapes and market-carts and portraits of friends, in practising her music, and in being from morning till night her own standard of a perfect lady.[36]

However, I have already mentioned that many women in this period either chose or were obliged to use their art as a source of income, despite the conventions, and found their polite accomplishment having to come into its own as their livelihood, practising, not so much like Eliot's Rosamund, but rather like Brontë's Mrs Huntingdon, the tenant of Wildfell Hall, who supports her son and herself by her landscape painting.[37]

When economic necessity – the result of a deceased or truanting husband, continued spinsterhood, dependant parents or offspring – demanded earning activity from a middle-class woman (women in the lower classes had, of course, always worked for the family's livelihood), it was often to an occupation that she had legitimately enjoyed in the home as a genteel and decorous pastime that she looked, rather than turning to work of a nature 'unbecoming' to a 'lady'.[38] Thus, it was often with a 'make do and mend' attitude that a woman became a professional. There were also feminist artists who, on the tide of public opinion and in the face of the 'redundancy' of women in the 1850s, claimed professional status on principle, as a statement about the substantiality and consequence which their art had for them, and which they wanted others to acknowledge.

Cases in point include Anna Blunden, described by Virginia Surtees as 'a young, ambitious woman, impecunious', 'with apparently little choice other than that of earning a precarious living as a governess'.[39] She sought the assistance of Ruskin. Her paintings, initially of modern life, and subsequently more often of landscape, apparently adhered to the Pre-Raphaelite ethic of close and meticulous study of natural detail, giving a highly focused and often vividly coloured image. I say 'apparently' because little of her work is now known, though she received much critical comment during the 1850s and 1860s, which picked on her miniature and painstaking finish, and almost 'photographic' exactitude. The *Art Journal* critic commented in 1867 that 'At one time it was feared that this artist was going the way of all Pre-Raphaelites. Mannerism, however, has been corrected in time.'

Numerous other examples of female artists who earned their living by their work can be discovered, but they were by no means necessarily well known. Blunden had to support herself, and even after her marriage she continued her output, exhibiting as Mrs Martino from 1874 till 1915. Other women had to support themselves and their relatives, or themselves as single women with no family. Harriet Ludlow Clarke was another: she was a stained glass artist and wood engraver, and the *Dictionary of National Biography* says that 'having a turn for art, and wishing to earn an independent living, she adopted about 1837 the practice, unusual for a woman, of engraving on wood'.[40] Ellen Clayton gives another example, of an artist who was in fact very well known in the middle of the century:

> Very early in life, Fanny [Corbaux] displayed a marked love for drawing. When she was but fifteen, the childish fancy was suddenly turned into a matter of stern necessity. Her father lost a considerable competence, and became enfeebled both in body and mind. The young girl bravely faced the difficulties of an arduous profession, and set to work in right earnest.[41]

Another of Corbaux's biographers makes the important point that is often missing from the romanticised picture of the artist as free agent which tends to be given: 'Thenceforward her success as a portrait painter has been rapid and steady, and to this branch of art she has chiefly devoted herself, more, perhaps, from necessity than choice; for she has a vigorous and lively fancy, and, as many of her paintings shew, possesses all the requisites for excelling in imaginative subjects.'[42]

Margaret Gillies' situation was the same: reverses in family fortunes led to her taking up art professionally, and she was obliged to specialise in portrait-painting, often miniature. The DNB notes with a flourish that 'she determined to earn for herself an honourable livelihood, and . . . took the somewhat bold step of becoming a professional artist'.[43] Yet again, Mary Harrison, the flower painter from Liverpool, was obliged to be a professional artist, having 'a large family of children for whom, through the invalided condition of their father, she was compelled to provide'.[44] One of the later generation of women active in the mid-century, who, benefiting from the change in opinion on the 'woman question', could see the impositions that were placed on women artists by convention, exclaimed in her autobiography: 'How my relations in England would have stared, and thought me little less than mad, to entertain the idea of becoming a professional – I, a married woman!'[45] (The speaker, Louise Jopling, had removed to France at this point in her life.) She too was obliged to practise portraiture because it was in that genre which she was most likely to get patronage, although she also exhibited fancy pictures of women – always a marketable commodity. To paint for the market is obviously to paint within established prejudices, and when female artists especially violated those prejudices, they would simply not find patrons.

Little consistent information on the sales achieved by such artists as Jopling is available, and the picture that can be built up of the commercial success of female artists in this period is therefore patchy. To evaluate the significance of the price of a painting, it is necessary to know the size and the venue at which it was presented, the running for that sort of subject, as well as the standard of prices the artist was striving to reach. That women artists' work seems to have sold much more easily within the Art Unions than on the open market, is an indication that much women's work was priced relatively low and appealed to the small buyer rather than the more pretentious and self-conscious patron. (Art Unions were subscription organisations based on a German model whereby 'ordinary' people could become purchasers of exhibits from the annual London shows by winning lotteries run by these societies. The most successful one in Britain was run by the *Art Journal*, which awarded prizes ranging from £10 to £100: see Table pp. 114–8) How often a work changes hands, and how the price declines, is also an indication of the artist's hold o the market: one of Henrietta Ward's history paintings, exhibited at the Academy during the height of her popularity, 'Princes in the Tower' (1864) was sold for 200 guineas, but was on sale again the next year and changed hands at only £141. Then, in 1871, after changing hands more than once in between, it could command only 120 guineas when sold from the Wallis collection (in all three of the cases cited, the seller and the buyer were private individuals from the business class, established as collectors of modern paintings).

It is clear that for many female artists, how to conduct yourself in a business-like way was a mystery: Rosa Brett, for instance, clearly left all to her artist brother – placing work in exhibitions, interesting potential buyers, setting viable prices. She would know, however, that by producing only small-scale paintings (whatever the subject) she was restricting herself to a particular price-range. Equally, an artist who worked in watercolour knew that her prices would always be proportionately lower than the same sort of work in oil.

Clearly, then, in the face of the changing facts of the situation, it could no longer be assumed that women's art *was* amateur (though some quarters of opinion would always believe it to be so and more believed that it *should* be so) and feminist writing proclaimed this: Caroline Dall, an American author of a book called *Woman's Right to Labour*, published in 1859, was quoted in the *Athenaeum* the following year:

> The *amateur* element has hitherto pervaded women's attempts to labour. They have not been *thoroughly* taught and trained to any trade or business; and, until they *are* so trained and taught, their work will not be worth wages adequate to the labour it has cost them. Good work, of whatever kind, will always command good pay. The present generation of women are beginning to feel this, and *to desire to learn thoroughly* whatever form of industry they adopt.

Indeed, as discussion about women artists increased and developed in complexity and subtlety, the question of their education came more and more to the fore. Women, critics and commentators, all came to see education as the key factor in the matter (whether they wanted to provide or withhold it).[46]

The idea that drawing and painting were skills that could be 'picked up', combined with the notion that women's attitudes were by definition unskilled (that is to say, that even if it was allowed that some tasks undertaken by women were difficult, it was considered that there was no science to such tasks, nor any great body of knowledge of which one had to be mistress in order to practise them), conspired to allow women for a long time to go on thinking that for them to demand serious art training was both unnecessary and unfeminine; and to allow men – many of whom were artists themselves who should have known better – to go on supporting this idea. (Male artists can be seen as having a vested interest in perpetuating this belief among women.) The image of the born artist – whose natural gifts seemed a wonderful substitute for training – was a dear and popularly held belief, and despite the fact that the born artist's distinguishing characteristic of innate genius was not easy for the popular mind to couple readily with the name of woman, the persuasive influence of this image introduced itself time and time again in attempts to represent women as serious artists.

Clayton reflects this clearly in her accounts in which the eventual painter (or writer) was to be seen emerging in the nascent woman's scribblings (or jottings). Although Clayton's evident susceptibility to the sentimental may well have encouraged her to interpret her subjects in this way, it can reasonably be conjectured that the artist in question also shared this image of the artist being born rather than made, since Clayton apparently took her material from the subject's mouth, if she was alive. Thus Emma Walter 'was a mere child, only five years old, when she made her first attempt with a pencil . . . From that time, she found her chief delight in drawing everything she could see, not only from the flat, but, by her father's desire, from real objects.'[47] And thus Elizabeth Ellet, in 1859, on Fanny Corbaux (born 1812), tries to glorify what was patently a deprived situation:

> When she was only fifteen years of age, her father suddenly lost his property, and became indigent. The daughter had received only superficial instruction in drawing, but determined to use her small skill to support her father and herself. With the ardent spirit of youth she threw herself into the undertaking, sparing herself no severe labour; and so well directed were her efforts that, before the end of the year, she obtained a silver medal for her watercolour drawings.[48]

What then did women's art education consist of in 1850? In the middle of the century, women could receive an art education at a government school of design, especially the Female School (out of London, these schools were called branch or regional schools); at Cary's or Leigh's if one lived in or near London; by means of the old-fashioned drawing-master; and by various forms of self-help.[49] It was with the establishment in 1857 of the Society of Female Artists (see below, Chapter 3) that the inadequacies of these opportunities became all at once resoundingly obvious, because of the type and standard of the work displayed at the Society's exhibitions. Critical response to these first shows demonstrated this, but only the more perspicacious of reviewers, like the *Art Journal* critic, immediately linked the limitations of women's work with their lack of education:

> . . . that which we see at the Egyptian Hall is the result of assiduous self-tuition, for we have no school for the instruction of ladies in painting from the living model. Labouring under such disadvantages as the female student does, we are not disappointed to see here so many drawings of flowers, fruit, and still-life objects – we are only surprised into exultation to see so much excellence in the higher departments of Art . . .[50]

A woman who was more adventurous, moneyed or lucky in family and circumstances, might go abroad to study. Such a move, if not occasioned by family business, marriage or death, must have indicated in the 1850s an already strong conviction in her art, for it was not until the 1870s and 1880s that it became less than unusual for a young woman to go abroad to study,[51] although individual women did take this step more often than was publicly realised.

Women making such a bold move before the middle of the century included Mary (Francis) Thornycroft, who went to Rome to study under the sculptor, John Gibson; Elizabeth Murray (née Heaphy), who had studied in Rome also; and Susan Durant, who learned sculpture in Paris under Baron Triqueti. More women followed their example in the 1850s: Gillies was in Ary Scheffer's studio in 1851; Mary Severn was taught by the same artist in the early 1850s; Boyce spent six months in the studio of Thomas Couture in 1855; Eliza Turck studied in Antwerp in the latter part of the decade. There was another wave in the early 1860s, despite the amelioration of art education in Britain, which included Benham Hay going to Italy (having already been to Munich with A.M. Howitt), Jopling and Maud Naftel both going to Paris, Henrietta Montalba to Venice, Clara Montalba to Paris, and Elizabeth Thompson to Italy. The tutors under whom these women worked varied enormously in prestige and skill: some artists were known, as in England, for specialising in female pupils (Chaplin and Cogniet, for instance), some artists might be particularly admired by their would-be pupils: Howitt is an example of this latter process, while Boyce intended to ask Bonheur to take her as a pupil.[52] It should be borne in mind that, although the intention in going abroad to study was to obtain training which could not be had in Britain, there was an element of spurious prestige attached to taking a period of study abroad. As a result a young woman might find herself training under a mediocre French painter in the provinces so that it could be said she had studied abroad.[53]

But it was a prestigious education at home that was wanted, and in 1861 women effected a *coup* to force open the doors of the Royal Academy Schools. Before that, women had orchestrated a vigorous campaign to force the reluctant Academy's hand. In April 1859, a letter appeared in the columns of the *Athenaeum* which was simultaneously sent to every Academician:

> Sir – we appeal to you to use your influence, as an artist and a member of the Royal Academy, in favour of a proposal to open the Schools of that institution to women. We request your attentive consideration of the reasons which have originated this proposal. When the Academy was established in 1769, women artists were rare; no provision was therefore required for their Art-education. Since that time, however, the general advance of education and liberal opinions has produced a great change in this particular; no less than one hundred and twenty ladies have exhibited their works in the Royal Academy alone, during the last three years, and the profession must be considered as fairly open to women.[54] It thus becomes of the greatest importance that they should have the best means of study placed within their reach; especially that they should be enabled to gain a thorough knowledge of *Drawing* in all its branches, for it is in this quality that their works are invariably found deficient. It is generally acknowledged that study from the Antique and from Nature, under the direction of qualified masters, forms the best education for the artist; this education is given in the Royal Academy to young men, and it is given gratuitously. The difficulty and expense of obtaining good instruction oblige many women artists to enter upon their profession without adequate preparatory study, and thus prevent their attaining the position for which their talents might qualify them. It is in order to remove this great disadvantage, that we ask the members of the Royal Academy to provide accommodation in their Schools for properly qualified Female Students, and we feel assured that the gentlemen composing that body will not grudge the expenditure required to afford to women artists the same opportunities as far as practicable by which they themselves so greatly profited.[55]

There were 38 signatories to this memorial, forming an array of the female art talent of the time, drawn from several generations. The issue was forced the year after the women's petition by one of its signatories, Laura Herford, gaining entry to the Schools by submitting work anonymously to the usual entrance examination. The *Englishwoman's Review*'s obituary notice of the artist recalled:

> ... what was needed was that a lady should send in a drawing as a candidate, and thus get the question fairly brought before the Council for decision. This Miss Herford did, and the question was discussed and ultimately decided in her favour, and she duly entered upon her seven years' studentship.[56]

A rather less sympathetic account of the business was given retrospectively by G.D. Leslie in his recollections, *The Inner Life of the Royal Academy* (1914); he referred to the 'invasion of the school by the ladies', writing:

> The invasion was artfully planned. In 1860 one female was passed into the establishment by an entirely unsuspecting Council; she had sent in her drawings with her Christian names in initials only. It was a good enough drawing. The laws were searched, nothing was found in them prohibitory to the admission of females, and so she took her place amongst the boys. The drawing she made as a probationer was quite good, and in due course she received her ivory ticket with a copy of the laws and took her seat in the School as a Royal Academy student. Two or three more soon followed, and the number of female students kept increasing.[57]

Academic resistance to equal opportunity for women remained influential, however, and a few years later, the door which had been thrown open by Herford's admission – and which apologists for the Academy maintained had never been locked – was effectively shut, for in the minutes of the Academy's Council meeting of 14 May 1863 one reads: 'It was moved by Mr Webster, seconded by Mr Pickersgill and resolved unanimously, that no more Female Students are to be admitted to the Academy at present.'[58] Thus, the records of female Academy students for the first decade after Herford's trail-blazing, read as follows: 1860, 1; 1861, 4; 1862, 5; 1863, 3; 1864, 0; 1865, 0; 1866, 0; 1867, 0; 1868, 3; 1869, 6; 1870, 13.[59]

Although this intemperate ban on women students was lifted in

March 1867 to allow the number of women present in the Schools to remain constant, and was revoked completely two months after that, the itch for entry into the Academy itself had started, and would be scratched until it was alleviated. In 1866 the *Times* critic returned to the fray, in his Academy review:

> With Mrs Ward, Miss Edwards, Miss Osborn, Miss Swift, the Misses Mutrie, Mme Jerichau, Miss Wells, Miss Martineau, Miss Blunden, Mrs Robinson and Miss Dundas among the painters here – to say nothing of such exhibitors in the French Gallery at Pall Mall as Rosa Bonheur and Henriette Browne – and Miss Durant, Mrs Thornycroft, Mrs D.O. Hill, Mme Ney and the Duchess of Castiglione Colonna among the sculptors, it is time that the Royal Academy should be reminded that its original list included Mary Moser and Angelika Kauffmann. It is much to be hoped that in the proposed extension of the Associate class the ladies will not be forgotten.

But forgotten they were, ultimately, though membership for women was proposed during the course of the Government Commission of 1863. (The proposer was Roberton Blaine, whose wife was one of the mainstays of the Society of Female Artists.)[60] Between 1868 and 1881 rebel Academicians proposed female candidates (Henrietta Ward, Martha Mutrie and Elizabeth Thompson) despite their ineligibility.

Art education provided by the state was of a very different order from the training which the Academy offered its students. Female students were admitted, under varying circumstances, in the regional schools, and in 1842/43 a special Female School of Design (sometimes called the Female School of Art, sometimes more prudently the Female School) was set up [fig. 12]. Like the branch schools, the Female School was posited on a notion of art applied to manufacture, rather than art as an end in itself. A paper issued by the School's Committee of Management, quoted by F.D. Maurice in 1860 in *Macmillan's Magazine*, stated the objects of the establishment to be: 'I. Partly to enable Young Women of the Middle Class to obtain an honourable and profitable employment; II. Partly to improve Ornamental Design in Manufactures by cultivating the taste of the Designer.'[61] It takes little imagination to see that women were admitted to schools of the applied arts – design or industrial design – while they were not to a school of fine art, because the former, having a less prestigious character, were acceptable ground for women to work, while the truly creative and inspirational area of the latter was seen to be out of bounds for women. But it was fine art to which the middle-class woman aspired.

The Female School followed a peripatetic course, from Somerset House to the 'wrong' side of the Strand (in 1848), partially transferring to South Kensington in 1852 when Henry Cole came in to reorganise the government schools, to Gower Street, and finally to Queen Square, Bloomsbury from 1861 (although it continued to be called the Gower Street School by some).[62] Before this, the School's funding from the Council was withdrawn, obliging it to adopt the status of a charitable institution, holding bazaars and *soirées* to raise money for its continuation. The *Builder* reported in April 1860: 'The public should be made acquainted with the fact that in July next the school will be finally closed, unless sufficient funds be raised before that time.'[63]

It is unclear why it had been thought a separate school for women was necessary, for none of the government schools was professedly male only, and in many of the branch schools women and men were taught in segregation (if it was separation of the sexes that was desired). Although female attendance at branch schools was widespread in the 1840s, 50s and 60s, the proportions of male to female students in the different schools were very varied.[64] It can be deduced from the schools' reports that this may well have been due to widely differing facilities and attitudes vis-à-vis women students. In many schools, it is quite clear, the staff and the male students did their best to deter women from enrolling, or continuing their studies. Classes were held both in the daytime and in the evening, and came under the heading 'public' or 'special': it looks as if the 'special' class was instituted as a device for keeping undesirable students (e.g. middle-class women) out of the principal ('public') classes. In fact the demand from women up and down the country for entry into the government schools in an effort to get *some* art training, was quite an embarrassment to the architects of the idea of government-sponsored design education, who felt they were being dragged into an issue (art education for women) which was none of their concern. Some of the school reports display a veiled anxiety which the powers that be had to dispel somehow or another: 'The attendance of the female class has been doubled during the year, and the course of instruction carried out has induced many young persons of a higher grade of society to join it' (York, 1849).[65]

The problem was that the use of state education serving industry by middle-class women (whom it was assumed did not want to become breadwinners) contradicted the cosy – and self-interested – aim of improving the taste and skill of the working classes, which was at the back of the government's initiative. Such women as those ladies who joined up in York were condemned as muscling in on a facility which was aimed at those who were more *properly* needy and therefore more deserving of places on the courses. However, once the question of 'redundant women' became an issue, the authorities claimed to be doing their bit by allowing such females to enter their classes.[66] It was even asserted that this had been their aim all along.

Unlike the Female School (as originally intended or as it was obliged to become), the Slade was declaredly a training-ground for fine artists. The place which it could take among other art institutions was outlined by the first principal, Edward Poynter, in his inaugural address of 2 October 1871:

> Except at the Royal Academy there is no school of any importance in London for the study of high art. In the various branches of the Government Schools, the primary object is confessedly the study of ornamental design, as applied to the industrial arts, and attention is only paid to high art in so far as the study of the figure is necessary for some particular branch of ornamental manufacture. There are no doubt in London private schools where the study of the figure, from nature or the antique, is made the principal object, but these are chiefly used by students as preparatory for admission to the Royal Academy, where, as the schools are open to the public without payment, it is necessary to impose a certain test of proficiency before admission. There are also in London various clubs or societies, where artists subscribe and meet together for study from the living model . . . Considering therefore the large number of students of art to be found in London, and the fact that there are no schools of importance for the study of the figure, except those of the Royal Academy, where the space is necessarily limited, it is to be presumed that there is room for a School of Fine Art, where the study of high art may be encouraged to the extent of its being the only object of the institution.[67]

From the start, the Slade was of particular benefit to female students. Despite its bias towards high art and, therefore, the nude – a difficult ground for women to exploit successfully – women

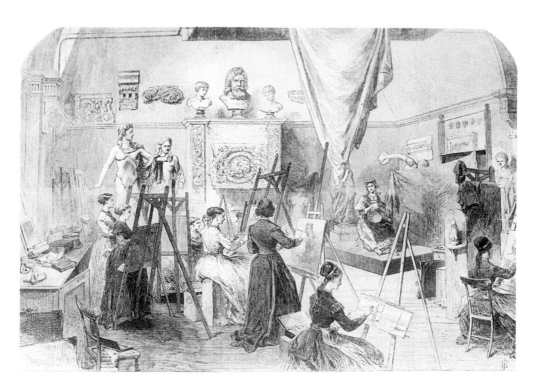

12. Anonymous engraving, 'Female School of Art', 1868. The *Illustrated London News* Picture Library. (Photo: Julie Phipps)

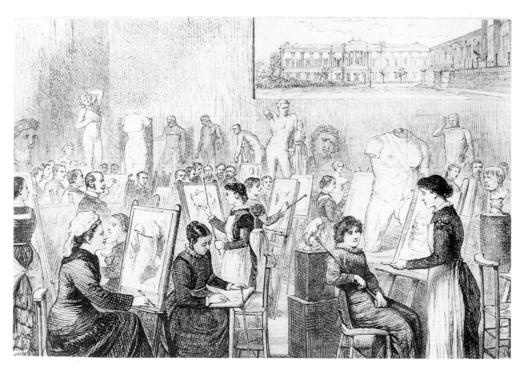

13. Anonymous engraving, 'Mixed antique class, Slade School', 1881. The *Illustrated London News* Picture Library. (Photo: Julie Phipps)

could get on at the Slade. Poynter paid them special attention in his first address:

> There is unfortunately a difficulty which has always stood in the way of female students acquiring that thorough knowledge of the figure which is essential to the production of work of a high class; and that is, of course, that they are debarred from the same complete study of the model that is open to the male students . . . But I have always been anxious to institute a class where the half-draped model might be studied, to give those ladies who are desirous of obtaining sound instruction in drawing the figure, an opportunity of gaining the necessary knowledge . . . It is my desire that in all the classes, except of course those for the study of the nude model, the male and female students should work together . . . .[68] [fig. 13]

Such attempts at equality were bound to attract women to the Slade – it was expressly made clear at the outset that the six three-year scholarships of £50 were open to women and to men – while other factors, too, rendered it more desirable for female students than either the Academy or the Female School. In Stuart McDonald's words:

> From its opening, the Slade School in Gower Street had great social advantages over the contemporary art schools. It was free from the regulations and restrictions of Cole's state system, it was on a sounder financial footing than any private school, and it had the additional status of being part of a university college. The surest confirmation of its respectability was made in 1871, when Edward Poynter, ARA, a lauded High Artist, was appointed to the first professorship. It was only to be expected that persons of the middle and upper classes, especially the ladies, would prefer to attend the Slade rather than the South Kensington Schools, where the course was tedious and some of the pupils of rather humble origin.[69]

During the early years of the School, women students out-numbered men, and an early proof of the conspicuous place women were allowed to take at the Slade is that the two scholar-ships given in 1872 were both awarded to women, Miss E. M. Wild and Miss B. A. Spencer; while one of the winners in 1874 was Evelyn Pickering [fig. 14] (who, along with Kate Greenaway [fig. 15], is

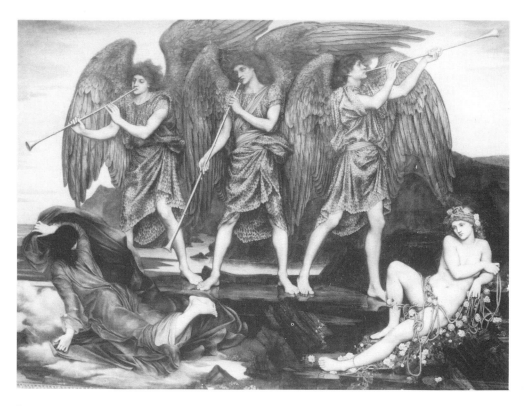

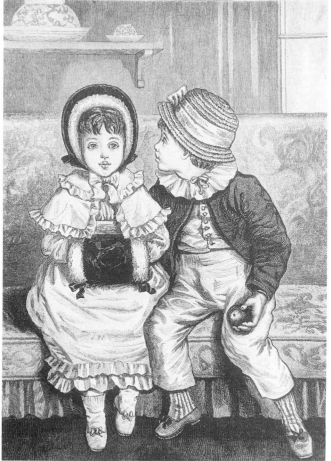

14. Evelyn Pickering DeMorgan,
'Aurora Triumphans', 1877/8.
Oil on canvas. Russell-Cotes Art
Gallery and Museum, Bournemouth.

15. Kate Greenaway, 'Little Loves',
1877. Etching. The *Illustrated London
News* Picture Library.
(Photo: Julie Phipps)

perhaps the most distinguished of the first batch of 'Slade girls';[70] she became a late Pre-Raphaelite of the Burne-Jones school, and Greenaway became an illustrator of children's books.)

The system of admission was paternal: no specific entry requirement was established, but the principal admitted a prospective student on examination of his or her work in interview. Poynter's sympathy with female students is clear – it is to be remarked that he was the sponsor of a number of female entrants to the Academy Schools – and his successor (in 1876), Alphonse Legros, came from a climate (mid-century Paris) of greater toleration of women in the arts than was found in contemporary London. The Slade's debt to French modes of art education was much discussed from its outset, but its continued adherence to the traditional hierarchy of genres and forms was the most ominous aspect of the School's continentalism, as far as female students were concerned. An article of 1883 on 'The Slade Girls' is, however, typically optimistic:

> The Slade Schools have from the first taken up an independent position as regards the method of instruction pursued. Mr Poynter, the first appointed Slade Professor at London University, came, as it were, to virgin soil. Bringing to his task a practical acquaintance with the Continental methods of teaching, as well as with those of the Royal Academy and South Kensington Schools, and having a strong conviction of the evils existing in the latter, he set to work to graft the good of the French method on to the foundation of the English . . . Here, for the first time in England, indeed in Europe, a public Fine Art School was thrown open to male and female students on precisely the same terms, and giving to both sexes fair and equal opportunities.[71]

The precise nature of those opportunities can be gauged from Poynter's annual addresses to the students. His approach combined academic criteria with a more modern (French) application of such ideals than was found at the RA, enlivened by a degree of Ruskinian appreciation of the animating spirit which an artist must evince in the face of nature. His prioritising of what he unapologetically called 'high' art, was fundamental to his teaching.

The system of atelier-based art training prevalent in France in the nineteenth century, whereby already established artists took students into their studios as apprentices of a sort, never had the same currency in Britain. However, a female artist often began her training by having lessons from a professional artist who might live near her, be a family friend, or an acquaintance of her father. Thus, Barbara Leigh Smith had lessons from William Henry Hunt, Elizabeth Thompson from Henry Standish, and numerous instances can be found of an aspiring female artist's early work being appraised by a famous artist whom her parents importuned for guidance as to their daughter's talent. As female artists became established in their own right, some turned to the provision of an art training which had not been available for them when they were younger: Louise Jopling and Henrietta Ward are the most obvious examples of female artists setting up their own schools. The assertion of a woman as a figure of authority, even if she deprecated the seriousness of her teaching (as Ward did), was a sign of the changing times: in the government design school system, the only head of school to be a woman was Louisa Gann (and subsequently Fanny McIan) who headed the Female School, while of course the Academy Schools would never have dreamed of asking a woman to act as a teacher. Even the Slade, for all its egalitarian rhetoric, was staffed by men well into the twentieth century.

However, whether as students or teachers, women were perceived to make great headway in terms of education generally, and art education in particular between 1850 and 1880. With prophetic optimism, Elizabeth Ellet had written in her significant book on women artists published in 1859:

> At the present time, the prospect is fair of a reward for study and unfaltering application in woman as in man: her freedom . . . is greater, and the sphere of her activity is wider and more effective than it has ever been. The general and growing apprehension of the importance of female education will gradually lead to dissatisfaction with the superficial culture of modern schools, and to the adoption of some plan which shall develop the powers of those who are taught, and strengthen their energies for the active duties of life. Many advantages besides these have encouraged the advancement of women as artists beyond any point reached in preceding years. We may thus find an increasing number of young women who, bent on making themselves independent by their own efforts, spare no pains to qualify themselves.[72]

Louisa Stuart, Lady Waterford, wrote in 1880 to Eleanor Boyle (EVB) – like her, one of the generation of women who had not had even the Female School to use when they needed a training: 'I get rather dispirited at my failures, and the want of that knowledge and *finish* I see in all women's work at exhibitions when they have had good training: there was none in my day.'[73]

The last word on education can go to the *Englishwoman's Review*, a consistent agitator for improved education for women in all spheres, discussing in 1877 the subject of art education, and optimistically summing up the ways in which it had changed for women in the recent past:

> Of course, women could always study art, and get admission to most of the great galleries, and copy the masterpieces there [fig. 16]; and they could win admission for their pictures to the annual exhibitions of academies. But it was very hard indeed until lately for a girl in England to get the real and thorough training which would enable her to do full justice to whatever artistic faculty she might have. The academies, too, when they received a woman's pictures, treated her much as the Universities until lately used to treat Dissenters – they witheld any title of honour for no matter what excellence. We cannot say that we have changed all that even yet, but we have certainly changed a great deal of it. The conditions of education in art are being rapidly equalised for men and women. It is no longer possible in this country for a girl to believe that there are twenty difficulties placed in the way of a real artistic career for her which are all carefully removed from the path of her brother . . . The girl student now goes in for hard work, thorough study, and what the whist-playing lady made famous by Lamb would have called 'the rigour of the game'.[74]

A sound art training was not, however, in itself, an answer to Hydra-headed convention, which could be just as strong as personal ambition. Anna Mary Howitt gave up painting for exhibition on her marriage to Alaric Watts in 1859, after very successful public shows in the 1850s;[75] Mary Severn gave up painting on her marriage to Charles Newton in 1861 to copy his archaeological discoveries; Florence Claxton stopped exhibiting at the Academy when in 1868 she became Mrs Farrington, continuing her work only in less conspicuous areas like the Society of Female Artists. That marriage was, in fact, expected to put an end to any activity which took a woman beyond the domestic sphere is implied quite concisely but clearly in the *Art Journal*'s obituary notice of the painter, Anna Charretie (née Kenwell): 'She was married, in the year 1841, to Captain John Charretie, formerly of the Hon. East India Company's service, but continued her study of Art.'[76] The conflict involved in women trying to be artists as well as 'proper' women led sculptor Harriet Hosmer (though not British, an example to British women artists of the period) [fig. 3] to declare:

> . . . an artist has no business to marry. For a man, it may be well enough, but for a woman, on whom matrimonial duties and cares weigh more heavily, it is a moral wrong, I think, for she must either neglect her profession or her family, becoming neither a good wife nor a good artist. My ambition is to become the latter, so I wage eternal feud with the consolidating knot.[77]

Hosmer's chosen single status can be suspected in the case of other women who enjoyed long, successful careers as painters: Emily Mary Osborn was artistically active for over 50 years, and remained unmarried; the sisters Martha and Annie Mutrie never married, and could claim 25 and 30 exhibiting years respectively. Other women of the period who did marry (and almost inevitably became mothers) have expressed their realisation of the deleterious or, at least, debilitating effect which the circumstances had on their careers. Henrietta Ward reflected on her early works:

> So far, as may be seen, I had not specialised – at least not to any great extent – in historical painting, confining myself instead to domestic subjects, which was surely natural, as all my leisure moments were of necessity spent in looking after my children.[78]

She recalled the advice of a friend's mother who said, 'I was very wrong not to make my child's clothes and give all my time to domestic matters, and . . . if I did my duty to my husband and home there would be no time left to paint.'[79] Louise Jopling was driven, with two children and an errant husband, to remark that 'Only abroad can a working and domestic life be carried on simultaneously with little effort.'[80] A woman's enforced domesticity, as Ward indicated, had certain consequences for her subject matter, and contributed greatly to a stereotype of 'female art'.

Despite the obstacles to becoming and remaining an artist which have been discussed here as peculiar to women, the number of women active in the fields of painting, sculpture and illustration

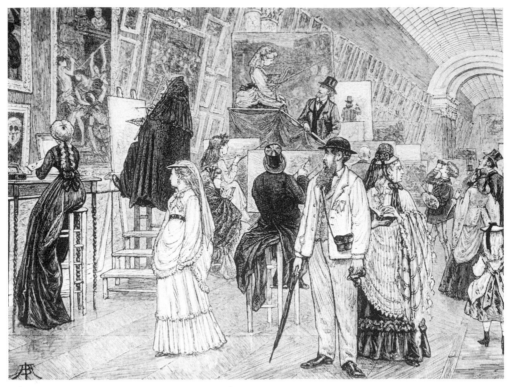

16. Anonymous engraving, 'Art students in the Louvre', 1872. *The Graphic*.
(Photo: Julie Phipps)

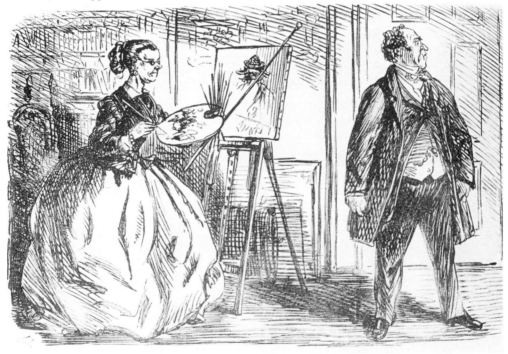

17. Anonymous engraving, 'Shocking Incident in Real Life', 1864. Reproduced
by permission of *Punch*. (Photo: Julie Phipps)
'Bachelor Brother: That confounded organ again! Although I told him to go! But
– phew! – my dear Rebecca, what dreadful odour is this in the room? (The truth
is, Rebecca, who is passionately fond of the Fine Arts, and of everything Italian
in particular, has had the Pfifferari and a Grinding Ruffian to sketch from.)'

did increase conspicuously during the nineteenth century (see p. 3 above), and the female artist emerged as a recognisable [fig. 17] though maligned figure. She earned public respect far more slowly than the female writer, though the two were sometimes linked, as here by Harriet Martineau in an article, 'Female Industry', in the *Edinburgh Review* (1859):

> There remain the classes which speak so well for themselves as to leave others little to say; – artists and authors. Here nature indicates the path of action; and all that we are practically concerned with is that her behests are not disobeyed, – her guidance not perverted, – her elect not oppressed, through our mismanagement. A Jenny Lind cannot be stopped in her singing, nor a Siddons in her dramatic career, not a Currer Bell in her authorship, by any opposition of fortune: but none of us can tell how many women of less force and lower genius may have been kept useless and rendered unhappy, to our misfortune as much as their own . . . The artists have an unlimited field before them; and the annual exhibition of the works of female artists prove the disposition to occupy it . . . the female artists can take very good care of themselves. Music will be listened to, if it is good; and sculpture and painting must assert their own merits . . .[81]

And they did: at the start of the period under discussion, women's participation in art was seen to be fit only to be mentioned in passing, but as the 1850s merged into the 1860s, the tide changed in a way that demanded recognition. George Eliot reported in 1859, after visiting the summer exhibitions: 'David Roberts was in the gallery at the time, and I heard him say, "If ever one sees a fine picture now, it is by a woman." '[82] While the 1862 Academy show elicited the following effusion from the *Critic*'s reviewer:

> There will be one feature in the Exhibition which will raise the enthusiastic admiration of foreigners for Englishwomen to a higher pitch than ever – that is, in the pictures by English ladies who have made art their profession. At least four pictures we can speak of that will, at any rate, do a good deal to annihilate the dogma that no woman ever made an impression on the world of art or religion . . . This is as we might anticipate from an age which is . . . the most aspiring in the history of womanhood.[83]

Notes

1.   John Ruskin to Sophia Sinnett, 1858, quoted in Cook and Wedder-burn, *The Life, Letters and Complete Works* (1903), vol.14, p.308, n.2.
2.   Ibid.
3.   Ibid., vol.33, p.280.
4.   See Pamela Gerrish Nunn, 'Ruskin's Patronage of Women Artists', *Woman's Art Journal*, Fall/Winter 1981/82; and for Ruskin's correspon-dence with two women artists, Anna Blunden and Louisa, Lady Waterford, see Virginia Surtees, *Sublime and Instructive* (1972), and vols. 36 and 37 of Cook and Wedderburn (*op. cit.*) for his correspondence with sundry others, including Jemima Blackburn/Wedderburn.
5.   'Women's Rights, the new starting point', *Spectator*, 8 March 1856, p.271; see also Strutt, *op. cit.*, p.78 ff., for discussion of the nature of female capabilities.
6.   See George Romanes, 'Mental Differences between Men and Women', *Nineteenth Century*, vol.21 (1887), p.654 ff., for an instance of this frequently aired point.
7.   *Illustrated London News*, 6 June 1857, p.545.
8.   *Athenaeum*, 9 February 1861, p.200; *Spectator*, 6 June 1857, p.594.
9.   'Rosa Bonheur', *Spectator*, 17 January 1857, p.71; her work became a standard indication of female artistic achievement, such that her name was used as a standard of excellence; thus, Barbara Bodichon was called 'the Rosa Bonheur of landscape' and Martha Mutrie by 1858, was 'becoming quite the Rosa Bonheur of azaleas' (*Athenaeum*, 8 May 1858, p.597).
10.   'The Future of Englishwomen', *Nineteenth Century*, June 1878, p.1028; the writer was the former Alexandra Leighton (1828-1905), distinguished chiefly for her *Life & Letters of Robert Browning* (1891). For a reply to this article, see Millicent Garrett Fawcett, 'The Future of Englishwomen', *Nineteenth Century*, August 1878, p.349.
11.   Simone de Beauvoir, *The Second Sex* (1953), Introduction. Writers did, in fact, often use the phrase 'the other sex' to indicate women or men, depending on which gender was their principal subject.
12.   *Athenaeum*, 8 May 1858, p.596; *Athenaeum*, 5 May 1866, p.603; *Illustrated London News*, 9 May 1863, p.518; *Illustrated London News*, 7 May 1864, p.455.
13.   *Spectator*, 26 May 1855, p.555; in this periodical's obituary notice, the artist was called 'the Elizabeth Barrett Browning of Painting' (20 July 1861, p.783).
14.   *Athenaeum*, 20 July 1861, p.89.
15.   See, for instance, the magazine *Woman*'s report of the Royal Academy exhibition of 1872, 'Women's Pictures at the Academy', 18 May 1872, p.333, and the *Englishwoman's Review*, 24 April 1858, p.569, where positive discrimination in the reviewing of exhibitions is called for.

16. Elizabeth Fries Ellet, *Women Artists in all Ages and Countries*, (1859), p.2.

17. Françoise Basch, *Relative Creatures: Victorian Women in Society and the Novel* (New York, 1974).

18. 'Girls . . . are brought up to think their education of no consequence, except as fitting them to take their place in their own social sphere. They are taught explicitly, or implicitly, that marriage is the only career open to them, and they learn but too quickly that success in that career does assuredly not depend on their efforts at self-improvement,' Maria Grey, *On the Special Requirements for Improving the Education of Girls* (1872), p.24; in contrast to this was the stern reality of mid-Victorian society's demographic state: 'There is . . . an actual ratio of thirty per cent of women now in England who never marry . . . The old assumption that marriage was the sole destiny of woman, and that it was the business of her husband to afford her support, is brought up short by the statement that one woman in four is certain not to marry, and that three millions of women earn their own living at this moment in England,' Frances Power Cobbe, 'What shall we do with our Old Maids?', *Fraser's Magazine*, November 1862, p.594, a pro-woman piece on the 'redundancy' question; for statistics, see Wanda Neff, *Victorian Working Women* (1929).

19. 'The Wild Women', *Saturday Review*, 1 January 1870, p.14: 'The economical objection to the indiscriminate influx of women into the labour-market, whether as shopkeepers, clerks, preachers, journalists, or doctors, is found out to be that they hardly ever become skilled artisans in any employment which they take up. In America it has not been found to answer to give employment to any decent-looking girls. They always pursue business as a stop-gap, not as their work in life. They know that to marry, bear children, and keep the house is the female *raison d'être*, and that ledgers, watch-making, and compounding medicines are merely taken up in default of a legitimate business for life.' The author is, Eliza L. Linton.

20. Martin Archer Shee, *My Contemporaries* (1893), p.299; the entry is from December 1865.

21. Ruskin to Mme Roch, editor of *L'Espérance*, a feminist journal based in Geneva, 8 May 1873, quoted in Cook and Wedderburn, *op. cit.*, vol. 34, p.509.

22. 'Lectures to Ladies on Practical Subjects', *Saturday Review*, 15 December 1855, p.116: 'Again, looking at the matter in another point of view, it seems very doubtful to us whether anything which draws women away from their own firesides may not, in the end, be more productive of harm than good.' This was hopelessly out of touch with the changes that were actually taking place in women's situation in the late 1850s, which bore fruit in the next two decades in the form of numberless ranks of women working outside the home in jobs additional to those which

working-class women had long laboured at; see, for instance, Ray Strachey, *The Cause* (1928) ch.12, where she recounts the entry of women into nursing, teaching, shop and clerical work; and Frances Martin's account of the progress of the College for Working Women in *Macmillan's Magazine*, October 1879, vol.40, p.483.

23. Sarah Tytler, *Modern Painters and their Paintings* (1874) p.300. The author's real name was Henrietta Keddie.

24. Clayton, *op. cit.*, vol.2, p.34 of Agnes Bouvier Nicholl and J.L. Roget, *The History of the Old Watercolour Society* (1891) vol.2, p.426 of Mary Lofthouse.

25. Christopher Wood, 'The Artistic Family Hayllar', *Connoisseur*, May 1974.

26. The *Spectator* critic, reviewing the Dudley exhibition in 1875, remarked with some asperity: '. . . we wish that artists, with whose names critics cannot always be expected to be familiar, would afford us some means of knowing by their designation whether they belong to the category of Mr, Mrs or Miss.' Typographical errors in catalogues were commonplace, but it is quite probable that some contributors to the Dudley gallery – which was known as an outlet for the young and the female, especially – withheld their titles deliberately, thinking it less important than the critic did that he should know their sex and marital status.

27. *Art Journal*, 1 May 1861, p.139; *Times*, 15 April 1850, p.5.

28. *Spectator*, 21 May 1853, p.495; *Times*, 29 April 1854, p.12; *Spectator*, 31 May 1862, p.606; *Times*, 7 May 1863, p.7; *Saturday Review*, 23 May 1863, p.662; *Illustrated London News*, 8 June 1867, p.578.

29. On dependence and originality, see George Moore, 'Sex in Art' (Appendix).

30. See, for instance, Francis Palgrave writing on 'Women and the Fine Arts' in *Macmillan's Magazine*, 1865, p.119.

31. On 'A Children's Summer'; *Spectator*, 29 January 1853, p.109.

32. *The Times*, 14 January 1863, p.9; the exhibition was the Lancashire distress show.

33. 'Women as Artists', *Spectator*, 29 July 1876, p.956.

34. *Spectator*, 7 June 1851, p.547.

35. Martin Hardie, *Watercolour Painting in Britain* (1968), vol.3, p.245.

36. George Eliot, *Middlemarch* (1950), ch.7 and ch.16; though published in 1871/2, the novel is set in the late 1820s and 1830s.

37. Anne Brontë's *The Tenant of Wildfell Hall* first appeared in 1848; another literary heroine involved in art appeared in Dinah Craik's *Olive* of 1850, wherein the eponymous artist is an oil painter who exhibits at the Royal Scottish Academy.

38. 'Unladylike' covered any work which rendered her conspicuous outside the house and thus excluded her from work which brought her into contact with men; but, since it was unladylike for her to take money

for her activities anyway, her work was meant to be a labour of love, philanthropic and unrewarded by monetary gain.

39.   Surtees, *op. cit.*, letters B32 and B30, p.107 and p.105.

40.   *Dictionary of National Biography*, vol.4, p.426; it is important to remember that engraving connoted the artisan and the sweatshop – quite inappropriate for a respectable female.

41.   Ibid., vol.2, p.68.

42.   H.G. Adams, *Cyclopaedia of Female Biography*, 1866.

43.   *Dictionary of National Biography*, vol.7, p.1247.

44.   *Art Journal*, February 1876, p.47; the *Athenaeum*, reporting the artist's death in 1875, went into more detail: 'she married, in 1814, Mr Harrison, a gentleman in easy circumstances. He, unfortunately, as his family increased, was induced to enter into a partnership that proved disastrous. He became a broken-spirited invalid, and the duty of providing for a family of twelve children devolved upon Mrs Harrison. This duty she bravely performed, and it is interesting to know that many of her loveliest groups were what Thackeray has called pot-boilers' (*Athenaeum*, 4 December 1875, p.758).

45.   Louise Jopling, *Twenty Years of my Life* (1925), p.5.

46.   See, for instance, 'Woman, and her chance as an artist', *Magazine of Art*, April 1888, p.xxv; 'Women at Work: their functions in Art', *Magazine of Art*, March 1884, p.98.

47.   Clayton, *op. cit.*, vol.2, p.299. A later generation was to be much more forthright about the need for sound training: 'This put an end to my Art studies, as never after this had I the leisure, or the money, to continue them. I had to become my own instructor. Does not someone say that, if you teach yourself, you have a fool for a master?' (Jopling, *op. cit.*, p.8).

48.   Ellet, *op. cit.*, p.218. Corbaux was sometimes credited with having led women to attend the Royal Academy students' lectures: see *Englishwoman's Review*, 8 August 1857, p.12 and *Art Journal*, 1 July 1857, p.215; although Ward later claimed that she had done this: for Ward, see below, Chapter 6, and Ward, *Memories of Ninety Years* (1924), ch.4, p.58.

49.   In the 1840s and 1850s, the most obvious way for women to help themselves was to attend lectures for ladies; the *Athenaeum* often carried on its front page such notices as: 'Fine Art – Practical Lectures for Ladies Only. No.1 Torrington Square. Mr. George Scharf, Jun. FSA. FRSL, will lecture, at 12 o'clock on the following days: Tuesday, March 4 – "On Ancient Painted Vases, their Varieties, Ornaments, and Uses". Thursday, March 6 – "On the Muscular Structure of the Hand and Forearm, as far as necessary for Artists." Saturday, March 8 – "On Medieval Art, the Successors of Giotto, the Age of Rienzi, and Expulsion of the Greeks from Constantinople by the Turks"', (*Athenaeum*, 1 March 1856, p.1). Even more frequently advertised were series of lectures in theoretical art, that is to say, in art history: see, for instance, the advertisement on the front of the

Athenaeum, 7 January 1860, for 'Dr Kinkel's lectures for Ladies, on the History of Art'. He also offered German, History, and Geography! Later on, the means for self-help were closer to hand: the *Athenaeum* reported in 1875 a proposal that 'female artists desirous of mutual improvement, and who hope to gain by the criticisms of a qualified painter' should meet for mutual criticism, under the eye of W.H. Fisk, who 'acts as Examiner, and is likely to do his "spiriting" wisely and kindly'; the location was to be the Society of Lady Artists' gallery in Marlborough Street, but it is not clear whether the meetings are a Society function, as such (*Athenaeum*, 6 November 1875, p.616). It is indicative of how valuable to women were the private schools, that most of the women who achieved any note in the 1860s seem to have started out at one of these schools if they had been seeking training before 1861 (when women began to enter the Academy).

50.   *Art Journal*, 1 May 1858, p.143.

51.   See, for instance, 'Lady Art-students in Munich', *Magazine of Art*, 1881, p.343; 'The Girl-Student in Paris', *Magazine of Art*, 1883, p.286; 'An Atelier des Dames', *Magazine of Art*, 1886, p.152; 'How Working Women are trained abroad', *Englishwoman's Review*, January 1880, p.38.

52.   Howitt had already been in Germany with her family as a girl: her mother recalled: 'My eldest daughter, who desired to devote herself to art, had never forgotten the profit and delight which she had derived from our visits to the German capitals and their works of art. Our visit to Munich and the studio of Kaulbach had especially impressed her mind and imagination . . . Anna Mary felt that Munich and Kaulbach would afford her the most consonant instruction, and in May 1850 went thither, accompanied by a fellow-votary, Miss Jane Benham' (Mary Howitt, *An Autobiography*, ed. Margaret Howitt, 1891, p.56).

53.   See 'Art Education for Women in France', *Woman*, 20 April 1872, p.273 and 27 April 1872, p.290; comparisons between the situation of French and British female artists were made from quite early on in the period, usually to the disadvantage of Britain. The success of Bonheur in this country must have gone a long way to suggesting such a comparison, and in 1861 the inclusion in the Society of Female Artists exhibition of several French exhibitors encouraged critics to bring the comparison up again. The exhibitions at the French Gallery in Pall Mall, organised by the dealer Gambart from 1854 onwards, familiarised the public with the work of Henriette Browne, as well as with Bonheur and numerous male artists. The fine art establishment in France confronted the question of women artists some years earlier than its English equivalent did: in the *Athenaeum*'s report of the 1855 sitting of the Permanent Commission of Fine Arts in Paris, a stirring paragraph is devoted to Jeanron's championship of women artists in the face of the establishment's discrimination against them (*Athenaeum*, 6 January 1855, p.18). In the later part of the period under discussion here, when numbers of women had been to France for artistic purposes, the French influence showed itself additionally

in different ways: the *Art Journal* in 1871 carried a notice of a new school, 'conducted after the manner of the schools at Paris', run by a M. Yvon; while *Woman's Opinion* in 1874 had the Society of Female Artists exhibition reviewed by a Frenchman (28 March 1874, p.58 and 18 April 1874, p.68) and the Slade was modelled on French lines.

See also *Art Journal*, January 1872, p.10; *Englishwoman's Review*, 15 August 1877, p.379.

54.   The Society of Female Artists' establishment, two years previously, must be seen as adding credence to such a claim, despite its mixed reception: see below, Chapter 3.

55.   *Athenaeum*, 30 April 1859, p.581.

56.   *Englishwoman's Review*, April 1871, vol.6, p.101.

57.   G.D. Leslie, *Inner Life of the Royal Academy* (1914) p.42. See H.C. Morgan, *A History of the RA Schools* (University of London, 1968), App. IX, for the names of those men from the art world who did support female entry, by nominating them for admission.

58.   Royal Academy Council minutes, vol.12, 14 May 1863, p.138.

59.   Figures from Jeaffreson, 'Female Artists and Art Schools in England', *Art Pictorial and Industrial* vol.1, no.2, August 1870, p.72; the ins and outs of the RA minute-keeping are difficult to square exactly with Jeaffreson's figures, but certainly admitted before the clamp-down were Herford, Helen Mary Johnson, Emily Burford, Rosa LeBreton, Louisa Starr, Catherine Edwards (later Sparkes), Edith Martineau, Constance Phillott, Harriet Aldham, Janet Rolfe, Helen Thornycroft (daughter of the sculptor) and Annie Ridley. The list of their proposers gives an idea of whence male support was coming in the first flush of victory over the Academy's intransigence: Herford prop. Heatherly, Johnson prop. Heatherly, Burford prop. Heatherly, LeBreton prop. J. Williamson, Starr prop. Heatherly, Edwards prop. A. Cooper, Martineau prop. Heatherly, Phillott prop. J.H. d'Egville, Aldham prop. Cary, Rolfe prop. not known, Thornycroft prop. J. Foley, Ridley prop. M.W. Ridley. The reason given for the clamp-down – given only when the Academy's decision was widely publicly challenged – was lack of space (and, presumably, what would now be termed a 'last in, first out' process). This is evidently not truly the reason, for in the years immediately following the move to ban women again, the student intake – now exclusively male once more – was markedly no smaller than in the years immediately preceding 1863.

60.   Report on Commissions, 1863, vol. 27, p.302 (328)ff. and p.491 (517).

61.   F.D. Maurice, 'Female School of Art; Mrs Jameson', *Macmillan's Magazine*, 1860, no.9, vol.2, p.227. When this article appeared, it was one manifestation of the mobilisation of support for the School which, in 1860, was threatened with closure when the government subsidy which enabled it to function, was withdrawn; for others, see the *Spectator*, 31 March 1860, p.305 and the *Art Journal*, 1 February 1860, p.61.

62.   This is distinct from the Female School at South Kensington, which was the women's part of the South Kensington branch school, evolved in the 1852 rearrangements.

63.   *Builder,* 28 April 1860, p.268. For accounts of such events in the press (almost unanimously sympathetic to the cause and often condemnatory of the government's action), see the *Spectator,* 23 June 1860, p.601; *Art Journal,* 1 March 1861, p.62; *Illustrated London News,* 2 July 1864, p.17. In 1862, the Queen became the School's patron, followed by Princess Alexandra in 1863.

64.   For example: Stoke (1851) 69 m., 42 f.; Hanley (1851) 75 m., 23 f.; Worcester (1851/52) 114 m., 43 f.; Belfast (1851/52) 267 m., 29 f. (figures from *Art Journal* reports). No order emerges in the figures as the decade proceeds.

65.   Reported in the *Art Journal,* 1 February 1849, p.53.

66.   *Illustrated London News* carried a report on the progress of the Camden branch school in 1852 (17 January 1852, p.46): 'Associated with this subject there is an advantage which, to many persons, will appear of equal or greater importance than the cultivation of taste among men – we mean the opportunity which it affords to women for the lucrative employment of their time in a manner suited to their tastes and domestic character'; while the *Spectator,* writing on the Female School in 1860 under the title 'Employment for Women', reported that 'Since 1852, 690 students have entered themselves at the school, and the number at the present time is 118, of whom 77 are studying with the view of maintaining themselves. These are chiefly of the class who would otherwise swell the rank of governesses who oppress the tender-hearted readers of the *Times* advertising columns' (31 March 1860, p.305).

67.   E.J. Poynter, *Ten Lectures on Art* (1879), p.95.

68.   Ibid., p.111; although the *Illustrated London News* announced, in its notice of the school's establishment, that 'The structural arrangements allow for the separate admission and accommodation of female students, if such separation should be thought desirable' (2 September 1871, p.215). The *Art Journal* reported in 1874, that 'An evening life class has been established in the Slade schools, University College, under the sanction of Professor Poynter, ARA, to meet the requirements of lady artists whose professional engagements prevent them from attending the classes held during the day' (1 December 1874, p.373). Doubtless this was also of benefit to lady artists whose *domestic* engagements encroached on the time they could spent on art.

69.   McDonald, *op. cit.,* p.269.

70.   In her article on 'The Slade Girls' of 1883, in the *Magazine of Art,* Charlotte Weeks makes especial mention of Pickering, Greenaway, Hilda Montalba, Jessie McGregor, Edith Martineau and others as being former students of the Slade who had, by the time of writing, 'obtained a position of standing among the artists of the present day' (*Magazine of Art,* 1883, p.329).

71.   Ibid.

72.   Ellet, *op. cit.*, p.209.

73.   Waterford to Boyle, 23 February 1880, quoted in Augustus Hare, *The Story of Two Noble Lives* (1893) vol.3, p.400. The two artists were cousins and friends: see below, Chapter 4.

74.   *Englishwoman's Review*, 15 November 1877, p.510.

75.   William Michael Rossetti noted in his diary, 12 December 1870: 'she does not now pursue art, except under the form of Spirit Drawings'. *William Rossetti's Diary* 1810/13, ed. Odette Barnard (Oxford, 1977). An alternative but quite complementary reason is suggested, however, by the artist's mother: 'Our daughter had, both by her pen and pencil, taken her place amongst the successful artists and writers of the day, when, in the spring of 1856, a severe private censure of one of her oil-paintings by a king among critics so crushed her sensitive nature as to make her yield to her bias for the supernatural and withdraw from the ordinary arena of the fine arts.' (Quoted by G.B. Hill, *The Letters of D.G. Rossetti to William Allingham*, (1897), p.204.)

76.   *Art Journal*, January 1876, p.12.

77.   Letter of 1854, quoted in Cornelia Carr, *Harriet Hosmer* (1913), p.35.

78.   Henrietta Ward, *Reminiscences* (1911), p.88.

79.   Henrietta Ward, *Memories of Ninety Years* (1924), p.52.

80.   Jopling, *op. cit.*, p.5.

81.   Harriet Martineau, 'Female Industry', *Edinburgh Review*, April 1859, vol.109, p.333.

82.   Gordon S. Haight (ed.), *The George Eliot Letters* (New Haven and London, 1954/55), vol.3, no.134.

83.   *Critic*, 10 May 1862, p.468; this reviewer was not the only one to be so struck by the show women made at the Academy in the early 1860s: see below, Chapter 3.

3
Exhibition

Given the development in the mid-century of the status and scope of women's art, the field of exhibition illuminates that development in a vivid way. Baldwin's sketcher was not expected to display her work – except for the approval of eligible bachelors – nor to sell it; and, since showing and selling were understood to go together for the most part, she hardly ever broached exhibition. The commercial function of public exhibition was acknowledged by exhibiting societies and bodies to varying degrees but in fact underlay nearly all shows of artwork. (Even amateur exhibitions were often fund-raising, when not positively commercial.) So, despite the fact that the catalogues of, say, the Old Watercolour Society exhibitions did not include prices of exhibited works, it had always been the intention that visitors to those shows could purchase the works on show. Similarly, the British Institution catalogues did not carry prices of works before 1852, and the New Watercolour Society catalogues give prices only from 1853, yet all along the aim had been to sell the work on show. Since it was considered highly unbecoming of a lady to earn money from any of her activities, and even worse to *seek* to earn money therefrom, and indecorous to draw attention to herself in any public sphere, public exhibition was not the logical destination of her work, even were it considered 'good enough'. So professional female exhibitors, such as Margaret Carpenter [fig. 9] or Harriet Gouldsmith, were few and far between.[1] Amateur exhibition was a slightly different case, because it did not pretend to seriousness or commercialism, but still the condition of showing work might be decorous anonymity (as in the coy use of the title 'A Lady'). The amount of work from female hands which actually saw the public light of day, so to speak, in the rooms of the Royal Academy, British Institution, Society of British Artists (Suffolk Street), Old and New Watercolour Societies, and the halls of Norwich, Bath, York etc., was, therefore, undoubtedly only a small proportion of the work which women were producing. A combination of modesty, economic ease and lack of encouraging precedent destined them rather for the album or the parlour walls than for the exhibition room.

When, therefore, in 1857 a Society of Female Artists was founded, it demonstrated that not only were women engaged in painting, drawing, and sculpting, but also that they wanted to display their work in public and, furthermore, to sell it; that they were prepared, for the most part, to become not only visible but known; and that in some cases they even nurtured an unladylike desire to become famous. With the Society of Female Artists, the relation of women's work to men's, and women's relation to the defined standards of art became issues which had not seemed to exist when the numbers of visible women artists had been so small as to seem negligible. Exhibiting female artists, largely ignored in the madding male crowd, were treated (when they were noticed) by critics, *confrères* and each other, as a race apart, more so as they became an issue. Their work was reviewed in separate paragraphs (though some critics graduated from this debatably useful categorisation as the time went on), even though their work was not hung separately. Women's presence at art-world functions was neither desired nor missed. Neither did women artists – because of social convention – enjoy that social opportunity, outside the gallery and beyond the newspaper column, of self-exhibition, which supplemented so effectively an artist's showing in the exhibition room (an opportunity which male artists uninhibitedly had). Thus the woman artist's exhibiting was practically the only way in which she became visible – and before the Society of Female Artists, the level of that visibility was low indeed.[2] Those women who *had* been practising

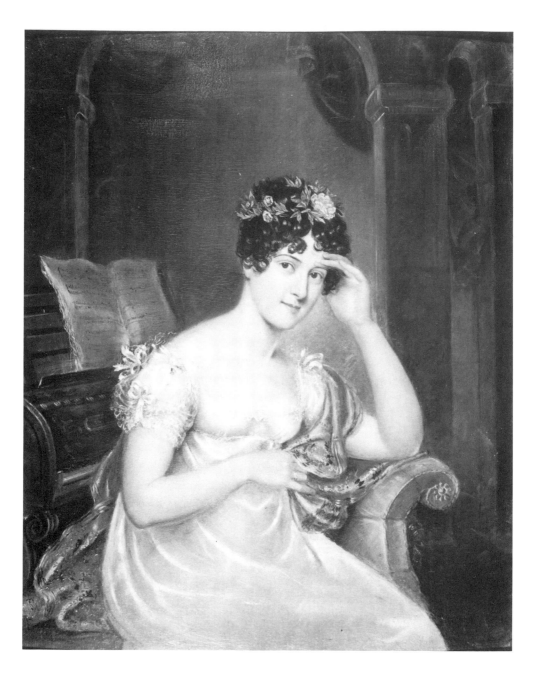

18. Rolinda Sharples, 'Self-portrait', 1820s? Oil on canvas. City of Bristol
Museum and Art Gallery.

as artists in the art world (as opposed to simply in the home or in the amateur aristocratic mode) before the 1850s became noticed in the mid-century as they had not before: they were few in number, and Margaret Carpenter is probably the only one easily accessible to us now. (Rolinda Sharples, though strictly speaking a Georgian artist – she died in 1838, the year after Victoria came to the throne – seems now in retrospect a prototype of the female artists who arose from the generations succeeding her [cover illustration and fig. 18].) Carpenter's pictures, both oil and watercolour, are mostly portraits or fancy pictures, and can be seen in the Victoria and Albert Museum among other places.

The competition of the art world was perhaps more manageable in the provinces, in one's home town (familiar territory) than in London, because less worldly. Before 1857 there were, by and large, more female participants in provincial shows than in any London show. Provincial towns established art societies, for both the practice and the exhibition of art, for a number of reasons. Trevor Fawcett accounts for the rising tide of regional art interest in the immediately pre-Victorian period thus:

> The players, the professional artists, wanted above all an exhibition. Not *any* exhibition, however, but one of modern British art, where they could set out their wares and hope for sales – or, if not always immediate sales, then at least the publicity and recognition that would gradually lead to future commissions and sales. They wanted the glamour of an exhibition, a point to which they could bend their efforts throughout the year, a display ground for their rival talents. Pride as well as the economic motive played a part; pride as a professional body of artists, a local analogue of the Royal Academy, as well as individual pride. The professional recognised too that exhibitions could raise personal standards and were of substantial benefit to the young artist.[3]

London, however, was the focus of exhibitions, despite the rise of centres such as Liverpool later on. The Society of Female Artists (SFA) must take pride of place in the following survey, since it was that body which was most significant for women artists in the period; the other exhibiting societies will be considered from the viewpoint of the female artist's situation, to put the SFA in context. It is worth noting at the outset, however, that in the middle of the century the general state of London exhibition was widely considered unsatisfactory:

> There is no foreboding the degree of badness to which with well-directed effort, an English exhibition may be made to attain [1853];[4]

> A long annual interregnum has hitherto prevailed in art from the closing of the Academy in July to the opening of the earliest exhibition in the succeeding February . . . for the public it is anything but desirable, more especially for visitors and foreigners, who would scarcely know in what direction to look for a compendious sample of living art . . .[5]

The Society was established in 1857, due largely to the efforts of Harriet (Mrs) Grote. Elizabeth Eastlake, writing in 1880, in her memoir of Mrs Grote, reported:

> It was owing also to her exertions and liberality that the Society of Female Artists was set on foot in 1857. She engaged the interest of many friends, both in the form of contributions and patronage. But Mrs Grote herself, with the late Mrs Stanley – not to omit Mr Grote, who became guarantee for the rent of the exhibition-room – were the main and indefatigable workers of an Institution which, however modest in its pretensions, remains active and useful to this day[6]

The genesis of the Society is difficult, not to say, impossible, to follow: Harriet Grote herself made little mention in her own writings of the growth of the project or its eventual achievement, restricting herself to a brief comment in the year after the Society's debut (1858):

> The month of January saw us established in London, where we stayed until May. At this date after having started my Female Artists' second Exhibition of Paintings, I took my departure for the Continent, to avoid the further fatigues of the London season proper . . .[7]

The archives of the Society (which continues to the present day as the Society of Women Artists) were destroyed in the Second World War, and we have therefore no further insight into the actual creation of the Society, from primary sources. Despite the absence of immediate documentary evidence, however, the Society's establishment can be seen as a reflection of the growing numbers of women anxious to show their work but dissatisfied with the conditions of exhibition which prevailed (which discriminated against them) and as a move to extend women's working (and therefore earning) possibilities. But why the instigator should have been Harriet Grote, and why the scheme came to fruition in 1857 rather than earlier in the decade when the row over the Water-colour Society's unfairness to women erupted, for example, can only be speculated upon. It is the case, however, that discontent with the Royal Academy, which had been rife since the beginning of the decade, reached a particularly outspoken level in 1856, and a letter published in the *Builder* in May that year, from 'a very estimable artist', went so far as to suggest specifically that a solution to that institution's dominance for artists who felt themselves hard done by (this would obviously include female artists) was to organise for themselves:

> . . . the answer is, that bold and united efforts must be made to break down the long-established usages to which the Academy clings . . ., that the large body of artists who stand without, must combine for their universal safety and success, and seek some means to take the tide of patronage while at its flood, hoping it may yet last long enough to bear them on to a permanent haven.[8]

Once established the Society and its progress become easier to chart. The first exhibition was held at 315 Oxford Street, from 1 June until 18 July, opening hours were 10 a.m. to 7 p.m. daily, with an admission price of one shilling, and a charge of sixpence for the catalogue (standard charges on the London circuit).

The exhibition contained 358 works, submitted by 149 artists.[9] It had been anticipated in May by the *Art Journal*:

> *Lady Artists' Exhibition.* – Arrangements are in progress for opening an exhibition of paintings and drawings by ladies, professional and amateur. It will be, we understand, of a high order and manifest a truth which is becoming every day less questionable – that in the Fine Arts women are capable of great achievements. All our exhibitions of late years contain abundant proofs in support of this belief; and although it may be expedient to gather their works into one collection, we cannot consider that they have been unfairly or even 'ungallantly' dealt with in any of

the existing exhibitions. We shall probably be, ere long, better enabled than we now are to report on this novel project – a project which cannot fail to be interesting and agreeable.[10]

The *Spectator*'s anticipation of the opening, in the same month, was forthright in its politics, placing the notice under the heading 'More Employments for Women':

> The admission of female artists to the established exhibition societies is limited; and although it may be true that the sex has produced no great painter, with only one Rosa Bonheur, it is equally true that it has produced a Lady Waterford, a Mrs Donovan, and a Mrs Boyle . . . The new exhibition will afford to professional ladies an opportunity both of showing their competency and of selling the pictures and drawings that they may produce; and in order to render the collection yet more attractive, several ladies of known taste and proficiency have promised to contribute their own works.[11]

Two issues fundamental to the existence of the Society, which were to prove consistently contentious throughout the SFA's career, were raised in these pieces: namely, the standard of the art produced by women, and their treatment by the art establishment; in other words, the grounds on which women artists declared themselves separate from male artists.[12]

It is through critics' appraisals of the SFA that the issues it raised can best be discussed, for the Society itself hardly ever raised a voice in print to argue its case or explain its activities. Also, of course, critics' writings were very influential and expressed, in their different organs, a range of dominant perceptions which facilitated or hampered women's progress in the arts, and indeed generally in society. Reviews of the first show, in 1857, indicate the spectrum of critical attitudes which the press consistently applied to the Society over the years. In the beginning a gallant encouragement, often couched in very patronising terms, was the order of the day.[13] As time went on, petulance and impatience crept in as if a just punishment for the critics' disappointment, and the Society's very existence was brought into question. A recurrent niggle was whether or not autonomous exhibition was either necessary or beneficial, in face of the fact that many female artists shunned the Society's facilities. From the start, critics complained of the artistic standard of the shows, some ostensibly kindly and others plainly gleeful.[14] All of the journals examined here, it must be said, served the middle classes, and it is interesting to note the variety of positions thus shown to exist within these ranks of society. The mid-Victorian middle class was, it will be seen, by no means a monolithic and unified entity: a church magazine, for instance, might carry exhibition reviews which would be informed by a substantially different ethic from the reviews in a liberal and polemical periodical like the *Spectator*. Criticism which analysed the ideological issues raised by the Society of Female Artists' existence was, nevertheless, quite rare, and since most of the reviewers were male and most wrote anonymously, their engagement with the questions was oblique and their accountability very slight. Unsurprisingly, reformism was the most radical reaction to the SFA that these journalists summoned up.

Among male critics, the *Art Journal*'s reviewer did engage in some analysis:

It was a bold experiment of these ladies to challenge, on behalf of their sex, a title to public favour as an associated body of artists, able to produce works which might fairly be worthy of notice. Yet it is quite evident that they did not over-estimate their own powers, nor need they appeal to the forbearance of the critic to deal leniently with them, nor to his gallantry for his approbation and encouragement . . . It has been too much the custom with a certain class of connoisseur, real or pretending, to speak disparagingly of the productions of female artists – to regard them as works of the *hand* rather than of the *mind* – pretty and graceful pictures, but little else. Yet when a Rosa Bonheur, for example, astonishes the world with a 'Horse-Fair' [Plate I], or a herd of half-wild oxen, then we hear from the same lips some such exclamation as this: 'Clever – very clever, but *decidedly unfeminine!*' so that these lady artists often have occasion to sing, in the words of the old ballad – 'What shall we poor maidens do?' Between the absence of due appreciation of the one side, and the sneers of the other, it is difficult for them to hit the right mark. Moreover, the obstacles which lie in the way of their receiving an Art-education that will qualify them to undertake works of a higher order are not sufficiently taken into account by those who assume to be their judges . . .[15]

Such well-meaning analysis was to be characteristic of the way in which the *Art Journal* treated the question of women artists in all

75

its ramifications during the next two or three decades. The paper's editor, Samuel Carter Hall, and his wife Anna Maria, were great friends with Henrietta Ward, which no doubt influenced the way in which the subject was covered. In contrast, *Punch*, though proud then as it is now of its iconoclastic and independent-minded image, displayed the commonest prejudices against women in the crudest manner, in its 1857 review:

> Those who are fond of 'The Society of Ladies' will rush to No. 315 Oxford Street, and there enjoy an exhibition that is the result of female handiwork. It is not an exhibition of stitching or embroidery, such as shirts made at home, or anti-macassars, or floral smoking-caps or butterfly braces, or sporting slippers with a series of foxes running helter-skelter over the toes. It is not an exhibition of Berlin-wool work, or potichomanie, or any other mania that occasionally seizes hold of young ladies' fingers, and makes them, for the time being, excessively sticky to squeeze, as though you were shaking hands with a Sub-Editor in the full agony of paste and scissors. It is not an exhibition of jams and jellies, or marmalades, or preserves, or much less, pickles. You must not expect you are about to be invited to a choice collection of pies, or tarts, or cakes, or puddings, of a most marvellous sweetness, such as is generally imparted by white-looking hands that are more in the habit of playing with the keys of the piano than the keys of the storeroom. Nor is it wax-work with its mossy baskets of blooming fruits, such as would certainly tempt birds to come and peck at them, nor vases of paper flowers, so faithfully rendered as actually to cause maidservants to water them. It is nothing to eat, nothing to play with, nothing to wear, nothing that you can adorn your magnificent person with. It is simply a collection of 358 works of art, that have been contributed exclusively by the talent and genius of English ladies.[16]

Clearly, for *Punch*, women's creativity was home-bound, and infinitely trivial in its possible manifestations. As so often, women's rights was simply an excuse for a joke. Women evidently had nothing to do with art at all: that was men's work, as the *Illustrated London News* critic showed:

> Strength of will and power of creation belonging rather to the other sex, we do not of course look for the more daring efforts in an exhibition of female artists: but observation, taste, or the art of

selection, and various other qualities adapted to the arts, are to be found in this Oxford-Street display.[17]

The Times' critic followed the same line:

> Such a revelation of artistic enterprise on the part of the fair sex is, of itself, a remarkable fact, and there is no apparent reason that it may not prove the beginning to a great result. Nor have the artists confined their energies to the more ladylike branches of art – to the production of fruit and flower-pieces . . . [See Table p.118] That we had lady-artists of course everybody knew, but that we had lady-artists who could fill a large room in Oxford Street with creditable works is a fact that is now made known for the first time.[18]

The *Art Journal* declared at the show's close: 'If the first season of the existence of this society may be accepted as an augury of its future, the institution may be said to be established'; but ended on a note that proved prophetic: 'We earnestly hope that no "apple of discord" may impair its utility.'[19] The *Illustrated London News* demonstrated, in its greeting of the second SFA show, that the Society's progress was not going to be untroubled by any means. The basic conflict between what one could term the establishment and the female avant-garde was then articulated quite clearly:

> Why a Society of Female Artists? In the field of Art, as in that of Poetry,[20] one would think that the two sexes might hold their ground on equal terms, without any fear of unfair dealing. And is it just the best way of maintaining the 'rights of women' for them to withdraw in this declared manner from association and competition with their brother artists? . . . Many ladies send agreeable contributions to the exhibitions in Regent Street, Suffolk Street (Pall Mall), and Trafalgar Square, and find them well-treated there. Then why this exclusive exhibition of art – this petticoat republic? And what would the fair members think, if, in revenge, the gentlemen were to interdict them from their premises?[21]

The writer of this petulantly naive complaint was obliged to return to the field some ten days later, enlightened if not chastened:

> Some observations we made in the course of a former brief

notice, questioning the necessity for this establishment of female independence and exclusiveness in art, have called forth rejoinders and explanations from several correspondents who, we must admit, make out a very fair *prima facie* case in behalf of the ladies. It is alleged that the old-established exhibiting societies either wholly exclude female artists or admit them to an extent wholly inadequate to their requirements;[22] whilst none allow the favoured few admitted to have any share either in the management or the profits of the concern. Add to this that the works of female artists are to a great extent of a special class, and so small in dimensions as to run the risk of being lost amid the more obtrusive claims of a general collection,[23] and the occasion and purpose of a distinct exhibition appear to be satisfactorily established.[24]

Some interpreted the women's attempt at autonomy as secession from the field of exhibition through cowardice, believing that the women's complaints of sex discrimination at the hands of societies other than the SFA were either fallacious or exaggerated; and should not the alleged mistreatment be seen as more of a challenge than a discouragement?

It is questionable how many of the critics who ventured to express their opinions of the Society's shows understood its point of view, while their own points of view shifted throughout the Society's career, depending on an uneven logic that was obviously confused by the developments of feminism at large (which they recognised as bearing on the SFA). William Michael Rossetti, for some years reviewer for the *Fine Arts Quarterly*, illustrates this typical lack of coherence on the fundamental and the circumstantial questions the Society raised simply by its existence. He wanders around and around the points at issue, but never really gets anywhere:

To call this or others of the Ladies' Exhibitions satisfactory to the artistic or critical sense would be neither true nor really complimentary to the ladies themselves, who may at any rate be credited with sufficient appreciation of art to know what a success is, and consequently what is not a success. The policy of distinct female exhibitions might probably with little hesitation be pronounced altogether erroneous, were it not for the one practical consideration that, if the ladies did not exhibit by themselves, they would too likely be crowded out of other exhibitions, or so inconspicuously placed that the important fact of the effort that a certain number of women are making to establish a standing in art would sink out of public observation. Considering this, we are inclined to think that the ladies have a fair show of reason for starting and maintaining an exhibition of their own. On any other ground, we should decidedly deem it a mistake; and especially on the ground that art is a matter of capacity and attainment, not of sex; that such few women as have attained ought to come forward among their peers, who are artists of the male sex; and that the large number who have not attained, are scarcely, in a female exhibition, supplied with the great incentive of emulation. They can paint very indifferently indeed, and yet keep head above water according to the level of the separate Female Exhibition; and this is no shame for the present to the ladies, but a necessity of their case.[25]

Rossetti does show (more than many of his colleagues,) a willingness to sympathise with difficulty where it existed and to grant it, however contradictorily, special treatment. But the point which nearly all critics of the SFA stumbled on continually was the women's exhibitions' relation to other mixed exhibitions.

There was a continuing stream of reviews, starting in the early 1860s, pointing out the absence of some women artists who had achieved some recognition in other galleries. This factor was seen by critics as considerable proof that the SFA had little justification for its existence, or at least that its justifiability was thereby put seriously into doubt. Perhaps it was just a nest for lame ducks? The *Spectator*, for instance, on the 1861 exhibition:

> . . . it must not be forgotten that this exhibition does not fully represent the position of art amongst women; there are several distinguished lady artists whose works do not adorn the walls of the Society. Mrs E.M. Ward, Mrs Benham Hay, Miss Osborn, Miss Solomon, Miss Nasmyth, Miss Mutrie, and Miss Susan Durant in sculpture, are some of the names which occur to us as having a reputation in the Academy Exhibition, yet it is to be regretted that some pictures by these ladies do not lend their support to an exhibition which represents ostensibly the talents of the female artists of the day . . .

Interesting as is this fourth exhibition – one which any man may visit with pleasure, and without those references to 'sex' which are always so many covert assumptions of superiority – it still imperfectly represents the state of female art and amateurship in this country. Some of our known lady painters exhibit; but more are absent . . .[26]

Thus the *Athenaeum* on the 1860 show; and the *Illustrated London News*, on the 1865 show, demonstrates how this line of criticism provided a means of denying the SFA attention and status:

The visitor must, notwithstanding, still be cautioned against accepting this gathering as affording anything near a fair criterion of the capabilities of the female artists of this country, seeing that at least a dozen of the most eminent are absent . . .

A rejection of this line of criticism came from a source sympathetic to the SFA, the *Englishwoman's Review*:

Complaints are made that ladies of acknowledged talent send their best works to other exhibitions. These seem to us unreasonable. What should we say if a writer who can earn £5 to £10 by writing an article for *The Times* or *Pall Mall Gazette* were blamed for sending his articles there instead of to some penny newspaper? Writers begin by writing for penny papers and small magazines, and then if they have talent they rise, and are in time promoted to write for the best newspapers and magazines. A beginner, however, is glad of admission for his or her articles into the cheap newspapers and small magazines, and would rather earn 5s. a page than nothing at all. In the same way a young artist is glad of the opportunity of exhibiting her pictures in the room of the Female Artists' Society, and of the chance thus afforded of selling them. Some people like to read penny newspapers and sixpenny monthlies, and some people like to buy cheap pictures. For our own part we could spend a good deal of money with great pleasure in purchasing pictures in the Female Artists' Exhibition. If we had a limited amount of money and wanted to buy pictures to decorate our drawing-room we should go there to buy them. If our supply of money were unlimited we confess we should go elsewhere. If we wanted a newspaper and could afford it we should take *The Times*, but if we were poor we should take a penny print, and be glad there were such things as cheap newspapers. We make these remarks in consequence of several criticisms in the newspapers, showing that quite a wrong view is taken of the use of the exhibition, which is to assist and encourage youthful talent to develop itself, and at the same time to supply the public with what the public likes – i.e. cheap pictures. Here can be bought the works of rising artists, whose pictures ten years hence may be worth large sums, and whose early efforts, containing no small share of merit, will then be valuable not only for their own worth but also because they bear the name of a distinguished painter. It is, however, hardly to be expected that when these ladies have achieved celebrity they will continue to send their best pictures to the Female Artists' Exhibition.[27]

It is likely, given the sympathy that existed between the *Review* and the Society, that the view expressed here is that of the dominant sector of the SFA itself. However, admission of such an ambition did the Society's credibility as much harm as good, since it allowed outsiders to confirm their ill-concealed suspicions that the SFA was nothing but a collection of 'small-beer daubers' floundering with importunate shrieks in a mire of amateurship, dilettantism, and strong-mindedness. It also typecast women's work – whether oil paintings, drawings, or sculpture – as cheap or, to put it another way, not worth much money. It is ironic, too, that the writer here circumscribes the Society's exhibitions with a sign saying 'cheap art here', for it was through lack of revenue that it had stumbled along for such a long time rather than soaring to greater heights. If it had to price its exhibits low, it would never get enough commissions to be a going concern. Neither, of course, would its artists, and it is clear from exhibition records that many of the well-known female artists of the 1860s and 1870s had a lot of difficulty in selling their work, even though their output might be critically praised. Their exhibition, of sketches and studies supporting a major painting should be seen as an economic effort, I think (rather than, say, an avant-garde assertion of the sketch as a finished picture, as might be the case with Impressionist artists in France). An image of the SFA as a forum for beginners would deter an established artist from exhibiting there as her prices would presumably be unacceptably high. However, in some cases, a female artist who was failing to sell in higher-priced venues might show at the SFA in some desperation, at the Society's habitually low price-level. (Rebecca Solomon, for instance, showed at the SFA for the first time in 1874, having up till then preferred the Academy, and provincial academies if a work did not sell in London. Her career was effectively at its end at that point, and she did not exhibit again before her death.) The SFA's price range in 1868 (the time of writing of the above article) was 2 guineas to £52 10s, with £105 being asked for copies by two artists. By contrast, in 1868 Landseer got £4,200 for the large and much-admired painting 'Braemar, Deer'.

In practical terms, the Society led a chequered career: it moved premises yearly until 1860, after which it stayed at 53 Pall Mall, the galleries of the New Society of Painters in Watercolour, until 1862.[28] From 1863 to 1866, the exhibition was held just along the road, at 48 Pall Mall: this was seen as a consolidating move:

> The Society of Female Artists has entered a new and improved phase of existence this year; it appears, for the first time, as an independent body, having a gallery for exhibition of pictures, and also, we are glad to learn, for the holding of a drawing school, in the very convenient locality of Pall Mall, no.48. We may consider the body as adolescent, if not adult, and congratulate the ladies interested upon the success of their efforts so far.[29]

Despite impressions that the lease at 48 Pall Mall was for seven years,[30] the Society moved yet again in 1867, to the rooms of the Architectural Association, Conduit Street, where it remained for several further years. It is not possible to say whether the problem was lack of funds for permanent premises or lack of support from landlords. The commercial side of things also went through some experimentation: from 1859, prices of works appeared in the exhibition catalogue, making the intention to sell more frankly evident. Before that, the Society had had the not unusual habit of retaining a man[31] in the gallery with prices noted down, of whom one made inquiry if one wished to purchase. From 1859, too, the structure of the Society was made clear in the catalogue: names of the Committee (8), those of Members (24), and of Honorary Members (8) were listed. (Honorary Members were also exhibitors.) The Committee decreased in number progressively until there were only two Committee members in 1864 (Harriet Grote and Jenny Lind Goldschmidt, who had served since the Society's inception). It was for this reason there was a 'reorganisation' in the following year, 1865, whereby patronesses were introduced into the catalogue, headed by the Duchess of Cambridge and supported by a veritable panoply of the female aristocracy, including the Marchioness of Waterford and Lady Eastlake, who had a recognised link with the visual arts.[32] That this reorganisation was not, however, as effective as was perhaps hoped, might be inferred from the appearance in 1867 among the Members of a seven-strong Management Committee (this faded from sight after 1870, however). The need of a society, which failed to be self-supporting and which many regarded as an organisation to be patronised and humoured, for altruistic financial support was shown all too clearly from 1867 with the advent in the catalogue of a list of life subscribers:

> A Donation of 5gns. will constitute a Life Subscriber, entitling the Donor to admission for Self and a Friend to all the Private Views and Exhibitions of the Society. Life Subscriptions will be devoted to the formation of a Fund for the use of Professional Members in case of accident or temporary illness.

The male names outnumbered the female (nine men and seven women); and whilst the female subscribers were all exhibitors of the Society (prominent among them were Bodichon and Fox[33]) the men, necessarily, had had a much less intimate connection with the institution and therefore less identification with the spirit of the enterprise.[34] By 1872, these subscribers had swollen in number to 33, and the preponderance of men over women had increased. This was the most effective way, indeed, in which a man could express his sympathy with the Society: by sharing his (economic) power and by lending his credibility – a credibility which derived not only from his gender but also from that economic power. The declaration of charitable status did nothing, though, for the common perception of the Society's artistic standard: the *Art Journal* wrote in its 1869 review:

> Partly philanthropic and partly artistic, it has obtained, as it deserves, considerable sympathy and support. Its funds are replenished by subscriptions and donations, its exhibitions receive contributions from both artists and amateurs. An association constituted for these good ends has a claim to be treated with tenderness, and the works sent to the gallery may be received with kindliness, rather than judged by strict critical standards. Yet among the 483 drawings and paintings here on view, there are many which need no apology.

The mingling of 'professional' with 'amateur' work has already been remarked upon, and this in itself was against the grain, for it called into question the dividing-line between those two precious categories. Another aspect of the work which seemed problematic were the copies. From 1861 they were officially disallowed.[35] The role of copying in women's art education was central, but the admission of copies was seen to lower the standard of the exhibition immeasurably, and there was a general critical sigh of relief when copies were no longer allowed to sully the walls of the exhibitions. The *Athenaeum's* critic wrote in 1861:

> . . . the ugly copies have totally vanished, and hideous transcripts from Correggio or Turner offend not the public eye on these walls. This is a relief. All the pictures, however bad the mass of them may be, are the independent perpetrations of the artists, for which no-one else, except perhaps the fathers, husbands, or brothers, who have been the types for imitation frequently chosen, is responsible.

It was always the case that *some* other agency would be seen as responsible for women's efforts, as has been emphasised already, since originality was held by many critics to be beyond their powers. What was apparently particularly offensive in these copies was the travesty of a great name which was perpetrated by the presumptuousness of the female beginner. It is clear that critics brought male-defined standards of what was good and what was bad to bear on the Society's shows. The standard generally accepted in other exhibitions was seen, as has been evident above, to be the one that women should be willing to be judged by, even though at the outset it was a widely held belief that women's art was appreciably different from men's. It was as if as long as women artists stayed on mixed ground – which is to say, as long as they were content to be second-runners – they would be judged by a special (that is, a lower) standard; but once they tried to establish their own ground, they had to meet the general standard. This process had the effect, reassuring to the prejudiced male, of explaining why women were ignored in mixed artistic company and why they could be ignored when in segregation: in neither case were they 'good enough'. Thus, it is not surprising to read this sort of verdict on the Society:

> This society shows a persistence worthy of the best of causes. Undaunted by discouragement, it ever renews virtuous efforts, and whatever may be wanting in point of Art finds compensation

in good intentions . . . The beneficent managers of the 'Society of Female Artists', though they rightly spurn commiseration, deserve, indeed, encouragement.[36]

It obviously failed to command respect as an artistic body, because it did not obey the rules of the game. One can recall, too, Lady Eastlake's apologetic verdict on the Society quoted above.

What, then, if anything, did the Society of Female Artists achieve? Most obviously, it increased the opportunity for exhibition and sale that women artists might enjoy. At the time of the Society's inception, there were six other principal exhibiting bodies in London: the Academy, the British Institution, the Old and New Watercolour Societies (the latter of which became the Institute), the Society of British Artists (Suffolk Street), and the National Institution (originally the Free Exhibition). These were variously discriminatory towards women, as will be described below.[37] There were, too, the charitable amateur shows (and had been the amateur exhibitions), the various winter exhibitions which were sometimes related to and sometimes independent of the Societies, and the Crystal Palace exhibitions from 1856, while the role of dealers such as Gambart, Wallis and Flatou as exhibitors was increasing. Later in the period, the setting up of the Dudley and the Grosvenor Galleries increased the exhibition space available to women. But there was no establishment, among all of these, which treated women equally with men, in terms of the numbers of works shown and the amount of administrative or policy-making power given. During the period considered here, none of the foregoing exhibitions (either on average or in particular) showed as many female artists as did the SFA, which in its peak years included in single shows over 200 women artists.[38]

The Society provided an outlet for the work of artists who felt unable to show anywhere else in London, thus increasing the total number of both artists and female artists showing their work. The incidence is high, in its shows, of artists whose interest in or attempt at exhibition was erratic or short-lived, and an exhibition space which allowed for that unevenness was particularly valuable to women, with their routines subject to sudden changes caused by childbirth, marriage or widowhood.[39] Because it was a specifically female arena, for many who made art either casually or seriously it presented an opening which they found more attractive (either in terms of propriety or of competition or of ideology) than other exhibiting bodies. During the period 1850 to 1879, there were nearly 300 women who exhibited at the SFA while appearing to have shown nowhere else in London (except perhaps at the less publicised charity shows); that is to say, 300 artists whose work appears to have surfaced only with the Society. The selection of exhibits was, undoubtedly, conducted on a liberal and amicable basis that was ill-informed about professional standards and perhaps uncertain as to how rigorous to be, neither plumping wholeheartedly for the beautiful nor the true. This was one of the main dissatisfactions which gave rise to the reorganisation of the Society in 1865, though it can be read as a positive disregard for established evaluative hierarchies. There were, too, many women who, exhibiting first or early with the SFA, later spread their wings in the other London societies, the SFA thereby providing a springboard for women wanting to enter the art establishment. Thus the Society led to general reform in exhibition.

The Society also brought into discussion, as has been demonstrated, issues concerning women's participation in the visual arts which previously had been scarcely articulated. Not only the particular issue of unfair treatment by other exhibiting bodies, but also questions about 'female art' or femininity in art and, ultimately, about artistic standards (what is great or even good art, and how is it recognised?) and about art education. In 1857, critics displayed their established opinions about women artists uncritically, but their continuing contemplation of women's art, brought about simply by having to review the SFA show each year, made them more aware of women's art appearing elsewhere, and to reassess (or modify in some cases) their prejudices, and their aims. So over the years comments like these became ever more frequent in the art press: '(This is). . . a very spirited work – we were about to say, for a lady; but ladies now paint with as much power as the other sex . . .' (Elizabeth Jerichau's 'Danish Shepherd with dogs and sheep', 1859); 'Though by a female hand, it is essentially a *masterly* picture. It has all the general excellence which skilled *male* Art could have brought to its illustration . . .' (Ward's 'Queen Mary quitting Stirling Castle', 1863 [fig. 8]; '. . . worthy, we will not say, of a "female artist", now a term of contempt – it holds its place strongly by its genuine pictorial merits' (Osborn's 'Lost'. 1870, [fig. 6]).[40]

Another indirect effect of the SFA consequent on the points noted above – was to bring attention to individuals who would not otherwise perhaps have achieved much notice, and certainly not their fair share of attention. For in fairness to the majority of critics who concerned themselves with these matters, it should be noted that they often obviously strived to notice a creditable woman's work or a laudable female artist from a mixture of gallantry and patriotism if not from any more progressive motive.[41] In terms of artistic opportunity in general, the Society's artistic significance was felt, too, in its efforts to improve women's training in art.

Given that the SFA related to the women's movement as well as to art, and was seen to do so, the Society's ideological importance must not be overlooked. It was certainly seen, at the start, as a feminist movement – if by that is meant that it was seen to be a blow struck for women's rights – and, although the names associated with its establishment do not read as a list of front-line 'women's righters', and one should not assume that any woman who supported the Society necessarily supported the feminism of the late 1850s, the fact that the SFA's woman power included Harriet Grote (who was one of the speakers at the first public meeting on women's suffrage, in 1869), Bodichon, Mrs Roberton Blaine (whose husband was one of the few witnesses to the Royal Commission on the Royal Academy to recommend increased rights for women),[42] and that it counted among its exhibitors Bessie Parkes and Ellen Blackwell, indicates that the Society had the blessing of progressive women of the mid-century. Later writers documenting this period have also seen the Society as part of the women's liberation movement of the time:

Women were finding duties for themselves in the most diverse spheres of life. They were asking themselves questions which would never have occurred to their grandmothers. Why, for example, were so many of their children sickly? Why was there so much prostitution? So much hysteria and hypochondria? What were the hereditary diseases, and how could they be checked? What were the conditions of women in factories, Poor Law institutions, and lunatic asylums? Why were there no women supervisors in all these places? Seeking the answers to these questions, they formed themselves into committees for Sanitary Reform, for Moral Regeneration, for Factory Inspection, and every other kind of social improvement. And when society was exhausted, the arts and sciences unfolded new fields of conquest. Why were there so few women artists,[43] and so many poor commercial designs? Why were there no women doctors, and so many women's ailments? The Society of Female Artists was formed. The Women's Medical School in America was studied with increasing interest and envy . . .[44]

Yet it would be ultimately impossible to infer from the running of the Society, the work displayed, or its manner of self-presentation, any precise political, let alone, militant premise; the evidence for such a conclusion is not apparent, however much such a conclusion would seem probable.

The impression remains – and, in the absence of the Society's records, it can only be an impression – that the intention at the time of the Society's inception, was for a body of a more militant character than the SFA did actually express. Even so, Lady Eastlake did the Society less than justice when she encapsulated it as 'an Institution which, however modest in its pretensions, remains active and useful to this day'. Perhaps as an aristocrat – albeit a woman – she could not regret the limitations of its achievement more.

The other contemporary exhibiting bodies in London will now be considered in a roughly chronological order of establishment, (rather than in order of status) in order to expose women's relationship to them.

The Royal Academy (est. 1768) enjoyed a monopoly of the fine arts not only throughout the mid-century but beyond. A letter in the *Builder* in 1856, already referred to with regard to the SFA, is worth quoting at length for an indication of the vigour of its opposition and the degree of indignation which the Academy aroused:

> ... In the present collection, it is said, that 27 feet of the line are taken up by one member; as much by a second; about 30 feet by one associate, and nearly as much by another; and mainly, too, by works of a class much resembling each other, and not all tending to illustrate the high aim and purposes of art; while the works of striving men, out of the circle, are consigned to the cellar. Is it thus that art is to progress amongst us? Is it thus that England is to hold up her head among the schools of Europe, or to maintain her position as foremost among the patrons of the ennobling, and elevating, and refining arts of peace? Surely not: and it becomes a question of the highest moment to the artists themselves, whether they submit to a state of things so uncertain and so deceitful; or whether they cannot combine for action in such a way as to secure more certainty in the management of the public exhibition, which is nothing more than the fair opportunity of exposing to view what fair and intelligent means, and honest labour of mind, have produced ... the answer is, that bold and

united efforts must be made to break down the long-established usages to which the Academy clings, – that its administration, so cramped and illiberal, must be made to adapt itself to the requirements of the age in which we live; – that it must be aroused from that lethargy which makes its onward movement so tardy . . .[45]

Despite such fulminating (or perhaps in proof of it), the Academy predominated over the other exhibiting bodies, over-shadowing them in size and duration of shows, and remaining their exemplar, although the Free (later the National Institution), the Old Water-colour Society[46] and the SFA, were set up specifically in opposition to certain elements of its policies. Its annual shows were the biggest in the country by far, the total number of works in any one show frequently exceeding 1000. Its hegemony was inescapable:

Art: the great advent of the year in pictorial art is coming upon us, and all lovers of the brush and pencil are looking forward towards next week for the sight of new indications of our artist-talent . . .[47]

Work by members of the Academy (Academicians and Associates) was automatically given a place in the exhibitions, but work by outsiders ran the gauntlet of selection by a panel of Members, works being submitted anonymously; and hanging was also expedited by Members.

Within an Academy show, Members were preferred to non-Members to a degree far surpassing the distinction made in other societies: Members' works were hung on the line or in the best positions and were treated as the principal interest of the show, so that outsiders played the also-rans to Members' front-runners. Bad hanging was a frequent focus of complaint with artists and reviewers, alike: if a work was hung near the floor, or 'skied' at the top of the wall, or put in a dark room, the work might be noticed by very few and *seen* by even fewer [fig. 19]. Critics frequently complained that bad hanging prevented a fair assessment of a work, and when the victim was female, additional complaint could be made against the insensitivity of the hangers:

This picture had two claims upon the [Royal Academicians] who distributed the pictures; first, because it is a very commendable work; and next, that it is the production of a highly talented and

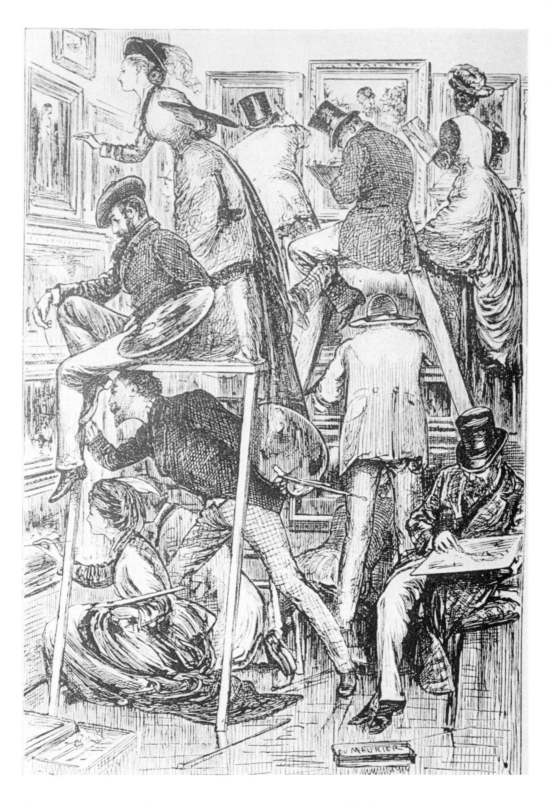

19. George DuMaurier, 'Varnishing Day at the Royal Academy', 1877. Engraving.
Reproduced by permission of *Punch*. (Photo: Julie Phipps)

assiduous lady. Perhaps they have hung it so because they have a professional pique against E.M. Ward esquire, RA, her husband and their brother member. Who knows? anyway, and whatever the motive, it is very unfairly hung . . . [this] is by some thought to add want of gallantry to want of taste . . . Looking at the unmitigated rubbish which has been hung upon and near the line in other parts of the exhibition, it would be absurd to urge as an excuse for the 'hanging committee' that there was no room for Mrs Ward's picture, and we cannot but think that kindness to the wife of a fellow Academician, if not the common politeness due to a lady, should have secured her better treatment.[48]

Outsiders' work, however, was always conspicuous by number, if not by placement, for numerically non-Members nearly always exceeded the Members, so that the bulk of a show would consist of outsiders' work. To take a random example, in the 1862 exhibition there were 1142 exhibits, of which 146 were by Academicians and Associates, and 996 by outsiders. It was sometimes protested that Academicians rather neglected, in fact, to show work at the shows, the implication being that they were content to rest on their laurels and not actually 'produce the goods', relying on outsiders to provide the substance for an exhibition.

Louise Jopling recalled what a rat-race it all was:

I was busy . . . on a picture of two girls, which I called 'Consolation'. When it was finished, I bravely sent it up to the forthcoming RA Exhibition. It was neither accepted nor rejected. It was in the 'Doubtful' class. For the benefit of the uninitiated, I will explain that when the Council is sitting in judgement on the pictures sent in by outsiders, a few are accepted, and are bound to be hung, and they have the magic letter 'A' chalked by one of the assistants on the back of the canvas; others are summarily rejected, and have an ugly cross marked on them. The rest – more than could possibly be hung – are marked with a 'D', and are utilized to fill any vacant space. In these 'Doubtful' pictures, Luck is a dominant factor. Sometimes, an inch too much in the size of a frame, preventing a vacant space being found for it, will ruin the artist's chance for that year. My picture was eventually not hung . . .[49]

Thus there were not infrequently, too, complaints by artists that their work had neither been rejected *nor* hung. This added to the suspense and uncertainty surrounding exhibition at the Academy for outsiders.

Works were selected for exhibition anonymously, therefore sexlessly, so that the discrimination which excluded women from the RA Schools and from membership of the Academy did not, in theory, prevent their work from appearing in the exhibitions of that august body. There are no records which permit us to know what works in any year were submitted but not accepted, so it is only from passing remarks in memoirs or autobiographies that we can know to what degree submission meant exhibition for any artist.

Membership was for life, so the surprises and freshness of an Academy show came often from the outsiders' work rather than from that of the Members, who could easily become repetitious and tediously predictable to observers, before their membership (and they) expired. Such was the superior position that the Academy assumed for itself, that no Member was allowed simultaneously to be a member of another artistic body; and such was the superior position that the Academy had, that artists often resigned their membership of other societies in anticipation of entry into the hallowed ranks of the Academy. There were supposed to be 40 Academicians, 20 Associates, 2 engraver Members and 4 engraver Associates (until 1864). The exclusivity of such an arrangement as this was seen to extend to the mechanics of exhibition, to the scepticism and chagrin of many non-Members. In the mid-century, the number of female exhibitors at the Academy varied from 48 to 108, the low years being 1860, 1861, 1862 and the peak being reached in the year before the SFA started, 1856. 1869 was an exceptional year, in that a supplementary exhibition was held of works which had been selected for showing but not hung, giving two totals for that year, 56 female artists being in the exhibition proper, and an additional 67 in the supplementary show. It is, sadly, unsurprising that more women appear in the latter total than in the former.

The obstinacy of the Academy on the question of women, and its self-image as a gentlemen's club (an inheritance from Reynolds' day), continued to vex and frustrate women artists' efforts throughout this period, but did not, it seems, greatly diminish the covetability of a place within it, whether as a Member or simply as an exhibitor. This meant that the Academy was, at the same time, the field in which women most wanted to succeed and the principal barrier to their achieving success, despite its waning power.

The British Institution (BI) was set up in 1805, its professed aim to:

> ... encourage the talents of the Artists of the United Kingdom; so as to improve and extend our manufactures, by that degree of taste and elegance of design which are to be exclusively derived from the cultivation of the Fine Arts.

Further, to do this by a particular means: 'to open an Exhibition for the sale of their productions'.[50] It was headed by Governors (derived by subscription), from whom a Committee was formed to run the organisation; there was no membership scheme. All the officers at the time of the Institution's formation were male, but there was a note in the rules to the effect that 'Ladies, who shall be governors, may vote by proxy'. This recognition that, though the polite conventions were to be observed, women might have some role in the Institution's survival, is vindicated later in its existence by the emergence in the 1850s of such persons in the lists of its various supporters. These could be a Governor (50 guineas subscription); a Hereditary Governor (100 guineas subscription), Annual Subscriber (5 guineas annually), Life Subscriber (3 guineas annually); the only category of supporter who needed no financial qualification was that of Honorary Member (elected by the Committee Directors) and that of Exhibitor. The likelihood of women participating in the last guise was the greatest, of course, but some wealthy females, including Angela Burdett-Coutts, Mrs Egerton Leigh and Mrs James Harrison, served as Hereditary Governors in the 1850s and 1860s; while the roll of Life Governors included, in the same two decades, the names of Miss Atherton and Miss Middleton; and several female names appeared among the Subscribers, too.

As for their part as exhibitors, however: in the first exhibition, in 1806, the only female names out of a total of 82, were Miss Andrus 'modeller in wax', Olivia Serres and the Misses Spilsbury (Maria and E. Ashe).[51] (Their male colleagues included George Stubbs, J.M.W. Turner, Benjamin West, James Ward and Paul Sandby.) Pictures were selected for inclusion in the show by a group of seven chosen from among the Directors. The rules in the mid-century advised intending contributors that 'No Picture or other Work of Art, will be received which has already been publicly exhibited', and that 'Portraits, Drawings in Watercolours, and Architectural Drawings, are inadmissible'. These regulations, though devised to encourage a standard of 'high' art, effectively excluded large numbers of women, since (as was recognised) they very often exercised their skills solely in watercolours, and their subjects were frequently only or mostly within the genre of portraiture. It is not surprising, then, to find the numbers of women exhibiting with the BI rather low; but it *is* surprising that their number is low when one reflects that the consequence of an exclusion of portraits meant a predominance of landscape, and that was another genre in which women habitually worked. However, the numbers were low, ranging from a lowpoint of 17 (out of 500) in 1850 to a highpoint of 36 (out of 399) in 1866.

Perhaps the experience of Anna Mary Howitt in 1854 was typical. The *Athenaeum* reported in March that year:

> A story is going about, curiously illustrative of the taste and judgment displayed by the mysterious and irresponsible power which sits enthroned in Pall Mall, dispensing its ignorance in matters artistic very much at its ease. On several occasions lately we have been compelled in the interests of Art to use sharp words against the British Institution, – but nothing which we have said in the way of condemnation can have carried home the sting of censure like the fact we have now to state. It is positively said that the gem of the Portland Gallery, Miss Howitt's 'Margaret returning from the Fountain', the finest picture so far of the year, and one of the best pictures – both as to the conceiving imagination and the executing hand – ever painted by a woman, was rejected as unworthy of a place on the walls of the British Institution!

The BI exhibitions, indeed, commanded more complaint than praise throughout the 1850s and 1860s from critics and artists alike, its reputation declining inexorably.

To do the Institution justice, it had always laid as much emphasis on its summer exhibitions of works by deceased artists and on the educational facilities it offered from study of these (old and new) master-works, as on its so-called winter exhibitions of living artists' works.[52] Also, its own confidence was undermined by its awareness of its subservient relationship to the Royal Academy, which had started with its inception.

Given the unsatisfactory reputation, then, of the BI shows in the period, it would be understandable if for many women it was not an attractive arena to try to enter, unless one could hope to shine brighter there, among dim lamps, than at the RA. But some women did choose it, and not because they could find entry nowhere else. Mary Thornycroft showed at the BI between 1840 and 1864, although she was being accepted at the Academy in the same period; Carpenter, in her long career, showed 50 works at the BI, in the same period when she was being hung at the RA (although her RA total was three times that of her BI exhibits); Mrs Mary Harrison showed at the BI between 1845 and 1861, when she was also being received at the Academy, Suffolk Street, the New Society of Painters in Watercolour and the SFA; Eloise Stannard only resorted to the Academy once the BI had closed (29 works at the Institution, 30 works at the Academy, between 1856 and 1893).

In 1867, the Institution's life was terminated when the lease on its premises expired. Throughout that year, the art press discussed the success or failure of the body over the years; by the November, it concluded: 'The character of the winter exhibitions had of late years so much deteriorated, that, in the final closing of the Institution, there is little left to regret save the annual summer collection of old pictures.'[53] It was suggested by the writer that the setting up of a life school might have prolonged the Institution's usefulness. Had this occurred, it would have made a difference to women's situation fascinating to contemplate (always assuming that women had access to it). As it was, the British Institution did contribute to women's art education through its collection of old masters,[54] and provided an exhibition space that offered a less stringent (but therefore less prestigious) place for the artist who wanted to work and succeed on conventional terms. The Institution was not a gallery to which the 'modern' woman would send (Howitt and Fanny McIan preferred the Free, Bodichon supported the SFA) and neither was it the gallery with which the academically ambitious woman bothered – Ward, Blunden, Boyce/Wells, Robbinson, Solomon, etc. all persisted at the Academy. But it was evidently valuable to women at large, simply because it provided another exhibition room for them to try.[55]

Despite the traditional linking of women with watercolour painting, its related connections with amateurism, its secondary status, and its typically modest physical attributes, a French reviewer of the Old Watercolour Society's 1855 exhibition could comment: '*L'acquarelle est, pour les Anglais, un art national... Ce genre de peinture, que nous abandonnons volontiers aux pension-nats de demoiselles, est cultivé en Angleterre par les artistes de premier ordre.*'[56] This impression (surely, in fact, erroneous, in spite of Turner) was what the Old Watercolour Society (est. 1804) had worked towards: this meant that it had striven to eschew anything and anybody that suggested the amateur or the secondary. Women, in the Society's view, seem to have come into both those categories, to judge from the discrimination they received from this exhibiting body. Perhaps prophetically – since it was to be the Watercolour Societies which so antagonised women artists that their treatment by exhibiting bodies became an issue – the Society discriminated against women from the start, when it was set up by ten men for 'the revelation it made of the strength acquired by an imperfectly recognised school of painting, as well as . . . the opportunity then given to amateurs and collectors of choosing and acquiring examples of the rising art'.[57] The following extracts from the rules tell their own story:

1.   The Society . . . shall consist of 24 Members. There shall also be an additional number (not exceeding six) of Ladies, and twelve Associate Exhibitors. They shall all be of good moral character, and resident in the United Kingdom . . .

27.   Ladies, Members of the Society, may send their Pictures, not exceeding eight in number, for exhibition. They shall be admitted according to the regulations expressed in clause 28 ['Any Person desirous of becoming an Associate Exhibitor, shall be proposed by a Member, and admitted by ballot; two-thirds of the votes, including proxies, shall be the majority necessary for the election of the Candidate.'], and shall be liable to the provisions expressed in clause 52 ['Every Member shall send annually one finished picture at least, for Exhibition.'] They shall not be called upon to take any share in the management of the Society's affairs, and they shall be exempt from all contributions towards the expenses of the Society.

Roget interpreted this legislation in the following way, when discussing Anne Byrne, the only woman in the Society during its first five years: 'The special provisions applicable to her class, which are in modern times less rigidly insisted on, were not wanting in chivalrous generosity'; and he quoted the following commentary from 1808:

Ladies associate-exhibitors, as they can never share actively in the management of the Society's affairs, are not eligible as Members;

but from the moment of their election they become entitled to partake of the *profits* of the exhibition in the same proportion as the members, while they are exempt from the trouble of official duties, and from every responsibility whatever on account of any *losses* incurred by the Society.[58]

Although the writer quoted by Roget seemed to have been patting the men of the Old Watercolour Society (OWS) on the back for their generosity, these regulations protected the Society rather than the women to whom it claimed to be condescending, since very few women had money of their own that would enable them to assist in making up any losses the Society might make. So these rules simply ensured that those who commanded the resources to be respons- ible for losses, *were* responsible for the same. The logic on which the ruling is based has a circularity which is almost impossible to penetrate – the ladies may not be Members because they may not be Members, seems to be the message; this was to irritate the strong-minded women of the 1850s beyond bearing.

The first exhibition took place in 1805, consisting of 275 works by 16 artists;[59] thus, the shows provided a place where an artist could display a representative selection of work, not being restricted to being judged on one or two pieces. No previously exhibited work was admitted, even when it had been shown only out of London. For a short period (1813–20) oils were admitted, but their 'extended scope had not rendered them more successful in attracting public support than were those which had been confined to watercolours',[60] so the autonomy of watercolour was reasserted. In 1823, the step was taken of excluding amateurs, militating, however incidentally, against women with considerable effect. At the time this ruling was made, there were four women in the Society (Barrett, Byrne, Fielding, Scott[61]) and, although the number of women in the Society fluctuated over the years, there were still only four female participants at the middle of the century – Maria Harrison, Mrs Criddle, Eliza Sharpe and Nancy Rayner – who had been showing with the Society as Associates (and now called Honorary Members) since 1847, 1849, 1829 and 1850, respectively. (Women who had been associated with the Society in the intervening years were Harriet Gouldsmith, a Member since 1812; and Eliza Sharpe's sister, Louisa, who had been elected in 1829.) At this stage (1850) there were 26 Members and 17 Associates (all, of course, male). Only these people exhibited with the Society: that is to say, no outsiders were admitted as exhibitors. The move to re-categorise the women, terming them Honorary Members, and further distinguishing them from legitimate Members of the OWS, provoked the following letter, signed 'ONE FOR THE LADIES', and appearing in the *Art Journal* in June 1850:

> Sir, – Let me call your attention to a subject alluded to in the *Athenaeum* of today . . . the Annual Committee of Arrangement at the Old Watercolour Society have thought fit, *for the first time*, to put the ladies down in the catalogue as *honorary members*, which they are not. It is not necessary now to prove that the committee possessed no power to do this, nor to throw any light upon their object in doing it; it is enough to assert, that no such term as *honorary member* occurs throughout the laws and regulations of the Society. As you know, this is a title implying that the possessor of it is but an amateur, and no professed artist – the public so understand it, and would estimate accordingly the works of the said most unjustly and heedlessly, so-called honorary members. In short, the interests of the ladies have been placed, for a time, in great and serious jeopardy; virtually, their names have been struck out of the list of members, without cause assigned . . .

The *Athenaeum* piece referred to by the writer was probably its review of the OWS shows, in which the critic said:

> There is a new addition to the list of what we perceive the Society now denominate 'honorary' members – meaning thereby lady members. This title is calculated to mislead the public into the idea that these are amateurs. The young aspirant in question is Miss Nancy Rayner – and she gives great promise.[62]

The oldest Rayner sister was, of course, in no degree an amateur. The following year, the catalogue showed that the female members had been reverted to 'Ladies', and in 1860 they became subsumed into the 'Associate Exhibitor' category. By 1891, Roget was able to refer to 'the "Associateship" of the Society of Painters in Water-colours, which had long since been adopted as the equivalent title to "Lady-membership" '.

The numbers of women did not increase, however, and in 1870 the number was still only four: Criddle, Sharpe and Harrison still, with the addition of Gillies (since 1852). However, the fortunes of female painters improved at the OWS in the later 1870s, with some of the strongest of the younger generation of watercolourists being called in, in the persons of Clara Montalba (1874), Helen Allingham (1875), and Helen Coleman (Angell) (1879). Montalba, one of four artist sisters, was a landscapist, Allingham specialised in domestic and rural scenes, and Coleman produced still life.

In general, admission of women into the Society's ranks seems to have been very much a contingent affair, the women's suitability deriving from their relation to another Member whose place, more often than not, the incoming woman filled. For instance, Maria Harrison was accepted on the death of her brother George; Maud Naftel (elected in 1887) was daughter of the Member P.J. Naftel; Miss M. Scott (later Brookbank), who had been elected in 1823, was the daughter of the Associate William; Nancy Rayner's father Samuel had been an Associate since 1845.

It is ironic – or perhaps self-explanatory, given the jealousy which male artists were accused during this period of the rising woman artist – that in the very field which traditionally was supposed to be womanly, even feminine, female painters figured so slightly. The Old Watercolour Society, in fact, seems to have adopted much the same stance towards women as the RA, whom it tried to parallel in its own medium. (Its winter exhibitions betrayed the same bias, stemming as they did from the same body.) The OWS's stance on women can be seen as one of the chief reasons why the Dudley, or General Exhibition of watercolours, beginning in 1865, was so welcomed: the Dudley was often noticed as giving a good place to women, who in their turn were often noticed as doing good work. By that time, largely due to the OWS and New Society, watercolour was a medium which was accepted as having a life of its own. This was however at the expense of the traditionally feminine qualities of watercolour, which had to be denied if such status was to be attained.

The New Watercolour Society – later to become the Institute of Painters in Watercolour – despite initial differences from its predecessor, had in common with it (unfortunately for women) its disdain of female artists. The New Society was set up in 1832, distinct from the Society of Painters in Watercolours (which became known therefore as the Old), and started as a free exhibition showing in Bond Street.

The record of the New on female representation, like its parent's, is not glowing. The finite nature of the exhibition opportunities offered by it – it had a members-only policy, like the elder society – was a considerable factor in the slight appearance women made numerically in the exhibitions. Of a membership of 57 artists in 1850, only 8 were women; these were Fanny and Louisa Corbaux, Jane Egerton, Fanny Harris, Mary Margetts, Mrs William (Emma) Oliver, Sarah Setchell and Fanny Steers.[63] The number only rose on the election of an additional member, in 1854, to 10 (Emily Farmer was the new recruit) and in 1861 to 12, on the election of Mrs William (Mary) Duffield and Elizabeth Murray; while there was a similar accession in the 1870s as there was in the Old, with the advent of Thompson/Butler (1874), Coleman (Angell) (1875), Marion Chase (1879) and Mary Gow (1875). Comparative numbers of men in the Society ranged between 30 and 50 (Members) and between 17 and 24 (Associates) in the period under discussion. Women were listed distinct from the men in the catalogues from 1856 (1859 in the case of the winter exhibition) as 'Ladies' or 'Lady Members', in contrast to 'Members' and 'Associates'; this, together with the comparable move on the part of the OWS, makes it disingenuous for some parts of the press to welcome the SFA in 1857 with such words as 'we were surprised to hear that a new Exhibition had been started in consequence of the unjust exclusion of ladies from our Watercolour Societies'.[64]

There was another small way in which women infiltrated the male ranks of the New, however, and this was in the guise of Honorary Members, among whom Bonheur (1866) and Henriette Browne (1868) found themselves; though no British women were included in the lists (which also contained Millais, Maclise, Madou and Fred Goodall). Though women's work was slight in number at the New's exhibitions, it was often seen as the most interesting. The names of Steers and Farmer were often cited in this way: 'The best bits of landscape in the Gallery are two little sunny English views by Miss Fanny Steers, thoroughly charming and artist-like'; 'At the junior Society no landscape pleased us so thoroughly as the "Lock-hampton Church, Sunset" of Miss Fanny Steers'; 'We fix unhesitatingly upon Miss Fanny Steers as the author of the two best things in the Gallery: "An Autumn Evening" and "A Woodland Scene" '; and, indeed, the *Critic*'s reviewer observed in 1862 that 'The lady artists take a very high position in the New Watercolour Society'. The women who showed with the New were of various character. As is obvious here, Steers was a landscapist and Farmer a painter of domestic genre; Margetts painted birds, animals and still life, while Harrison and Harris were fruit and flower painters, and Duffield produced landscape, along with Oliver; Murray and Fanny Corbaux tended more to the figure, while Egerton specialised in fancy portraits. There was, seemingly, no prescribed number of works that should or might be exhibited by each artist, and Harrison, Margetts and Oliver would sometimes show ten or eleven works in one exhibition.

It took the New (or Institute) a long time before it stood out from under the shadow of the elder watercolour society, but it eventually achieved the character of a somewhat more progressive counterpart to its staid parent, though it lost some of its best exhibitors to the Dudley, after 1865 (among them Coleman, whose work everywhere attracted notice).[65] As with the OWS, too, the Institute suffered, as far as its women were concerned, from the Dudley's greater liberalism, although the *Athenaeum* had been able to say of the New in 1852, 'There is no exhibition-room in which female talent and genius figure to such good effect as in this.'

Despite the watercolour societies, most of the London exhibitions did not professedly favour any one medium over another, although in practice such an open policy meant the predominance of oil painting. The Society of British Artists (SBA) was the gallery in which oils and watercolour seem to have mingled perhaps the most democratically. Formed in 1823, the Society of British Artists' original purpose was to extend and improve exhibiting opportunities for artists in London. It 'was not to rival the existing societies since every member was to "be at liberty to assist and support any other Society" '[66] and every opportunity seems to have been taken by the Society to stress its wish to be seen as not unfriendly to other exhibiting bodies.

The Society was supported by a subscriber system, and drew its members, as did the Academy, from elections; non-members could exhibit along with members. To give up membership, however, cost £100![67] Women were admitted as Honorary Members, and allowed to exhibit free of charge (that is to say, without having to pay a commission to the Society). The number of women connected with the SBA (often referred to by the name of its gallery's location, Suffolk Street) increased steadily over the years, from a situation where no women at all appeared in the exhibitors' book, to the 1850 show including 46 women, the 1857 exhibition featuring 62, and the 1869 show boasting 98 female contributors. No members, however, in this period were women, though by 1858 the membership had risen to 28.

The Suffolk Street shows suffered from critical abuse quite as strong as that endured by the BI, though not perhaps so prolonged. During the 1850s and 1860s, however, the following was not untypical, especially if the source in question was the *Athenaeum,* the *Spectator,* or *The Times*:

> We thought the British Institution poor enough this year, but it was beaten by the National, and now the British Artists come to dispute the prize – not without solid claims. (*Spectator,* 1853)

> Every man at his worst is the character of the Exhibition of the Suffolk Street Society which opened to private view on Saturday last. There is a peculiarly sodden and exhausted air about it – a flavour as of re-boiled tea-leaves. We have seen the same thing 50 times before, and not only the same, but less bad of its kind. (*Spectator,* 1858)

This does not say much for any of the artists who exhibited at Suffolk Street, but the women do not seem to have been outstandingly bad among the other contributors. In fact, in some shows a reviewer will specifically commend the female exhibitors (who seem, from the following passage, to have been hung separately):

> A high average of merit is maintained in the room containing the works of female artists by such pictures of well-known excellence as Rosa Bonheur's great cattle-ploughing subject, 'Labourages – Nivernais' and portraits by Henriette Browne; Mrs E.M. Ward's 'Children in the Tower'; Mrs Benham Hay's illustrations of scenes in the narrative of Tobit and the parable of the Prodigal Son; and Miss Osborn's 'Christmas' [fig. 20] [of the SBA Winter Exhibition, 1865][68].

> Among the animal painters ... in this class, the watercolours of a lady with whose name we had not yet been familiar, Mrs Withers, stand supreme. These are not only the best here, but would be extraordinary anywhere.[69]

From the early 1830s, the SBA had held winter exhibitions and shows of deceased artists' works, as well as the annual summer exhibitions, and in 1847 it set up a school which included classes for ladies, involving models 'classically and picturesquely draped'.[70] The size of the shows increased during the period here being discussed (the 1850 show had 345 contributors, the 1870 show, 545), but it grew not at all in status. For women, though, it proved more accessible than any other of the London galleries, for it showed a higher proportion of female exhibitors in the period than

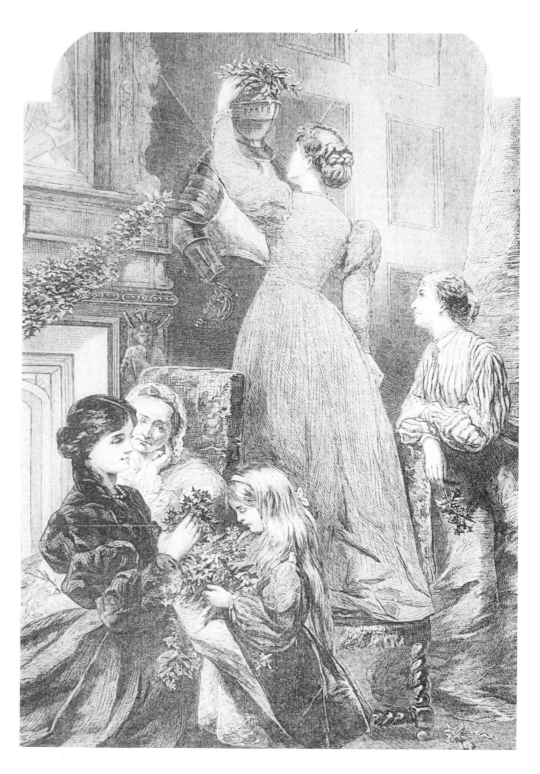

20. Anonymous engraving after Emily Mary Osborn, 'Christmas Time', 1865.
The *Illustrated London News* Picture Library. (Photo: Julie Phipps)

any other regular exhibition, with the exception of the SFA. This reflects its usefulness to women as a sort of refuge from the rigours of the Academy, which yet was a reasonably respected arena for both oil and watercolour artists.

Artists tired of the hegemony of the Academy, and willing openly to disdain Academy-inspired or Academy-related exhibiting policy, however, could show with the Free Exhibition, from 1848, at Portland Street. It was as the Free Exhibition that the National Institution was set up in 1848: 'The objects here sought to be attained are, as far as possible, *Freedom* for the Artist, *Certainty of Exhibition* for his [sic] works, and the *Improvement* of *Public Taste*', according to the catalogue. It was chiefly, quite evidently, in opposition to the hierarchical and exclusive principles on which the Royal Academy exhibitions were mounted and the casual and high-handed way in which those same exhibitions were expedited. Meant as a radical move, it was heartily greeted as such in some quarters – the *Art Union* wrote:

> Various causes have operated to render this project advisable, indeed, absolutely necessary. It is notorious that nearly three thousand works of Art are annually rejected by the Royal Academy, the British Institution, and the other Societies, for 'want of room'. Every year the catalogues record this startling – may we not say this appalling – fact. The Society of British Artists are famous for taking care of themselves, and for giving little or no chance to mere contributors. The two Watercolour Societies hang no pictures but their own; while the charge for admission to each of our Exhibitions is a serious bar to their utility; keeping effectually out of the reach of their influence the humbler orders, and rendering even the comparatively rich content with the enjoyment and instruction to be derived from a single visit.[71]

The catalogue of the first exhibition asserted the character of paintings and statues as commercially viable products of a person's labour, while the catalogue of 1850 emphasised the wish to put an end to jealousies, rivalries and disappointments which arose through the artist himself having no control over the fate of an exhibited work. It was explained, at the time of the 1850 exhibition, that the original intention of holding the shows open free of charge had proved to be unviable but that, although an entry charge henceforward had to be made, the exhibition would remain open 'free of charge, for the benefit of the working classes' for a fortnight at the end of the season. The other significance of the exhibition's name – the Free Exhibition – had been, the year before, commented on rather sourly by the *Illustrated London News*, whose correspondent was glad that that original intention had had to be modified in the light of experience:

> The first [exhibition] was rather a hurried affair, in order that a year might not be lost; and the second was done on a very erroneous principle, of allowing every exhibitor to purchase so many square feet of wall for the arrangement of his own works after his own manner. As may be readily imagined, the Exhibition, though fair to the exhibitors at first sight, was highly injurious to them, and very unfair to the visitors; for the Gallery, by this disinterested kind of arrangement, was made a very motley affair to the visitor.[72]

The conditions of exhibition were, that no copies might be shown, nor any work that had already been shown in London. As with all the other societies here surveyed, there was a commission on sales (5 per cent; by comparison the SBA, for instance, charged 10 per cent) and a deposit required of purchasers. Unlike its companion exhibitions, however, the Free recognised in its catalogues the artist's membership of other exhibiting bodies. The officials of the Free's organisation were 26 Proprietary Members, whose number included Trustees, an Honorary Secretary, a Treasurer, and a President; these were all male, at the Free's inception.

Exhibitors in 1848 numbered something short of 100, of which 12 were female.[73] This proportion went down over the years although the number rose: in 1861 (the latest year for which figures of exhibitors are available) the total of exhibitors was 166, of whom 16 were women.

On occasion it was the work of these artists that redeemed the National from its apparently generally unsatisfactory position; the *Athenaeum* critic greeted Howitt's 'Margaret returning from the Fountain' of 1854 thus:

> From a crowd of smooth incarnations of smug vanity and complacent ugliness, – from portraits of self-applauding nobles and portraits of very common commoners that very few applaud, – from widows at Nain and widows who are inane, – from firework phantasmagorias and ballet-dancing angels, – from sketches from Nature that look as unreal as imagination, and imaginings

much more sober than Nature, we turn with pleasure to 'Faust's Margaret returning from the Fountain' . . . by Miss A.M. Howitt. It is like stepping out of the glare and noise of a country theatre into the soft lustre and dewy freshness of a May morning . . .

How many artists supported the National on ideological grounds is almost impossible to say; as far as the women there were concerned, it offered a less overtly discriminatory situation, though as long as opportunity was based on monetary resources, they were bound to be at a disadvantage. The women who did exhibit there were so various as artists, that no generalisation can be made as to why they found the National attractive. The *Builder* of 1857 observed: 'the advantages offered by this institution are palpable to newcomers', and the small ratio of women at its exhibitions can only be explained by the fact that, at the start, it very properly had a radical character which, just as it appealed to such as Howitt, would have frightened off other women; and by the fact that the payment required for one's space could have put women off who, ironically, therefore, would have been better able to show (free of charge) at the Academy, which in other respects was much more opposed to their interests than was the National Institution.[74]

The London exhibition scene was expanded and enlivened in the later 1860s and early 1870s by additional galleries: the General Exhibition of watercolour work started in 1865, eventually becoming the Dudley when it took up residence in the gallery of that name. It was an auspicious development for women, as has already been implied; the *Art Journal* observed in its second year:

> . . . the rights of women are fully recognised within these walls. No other gallery, with the single exception of that occupied by the Society of Female Artists, contains so formidable an array of lady-exhibitors . . . We are glad to say that woman's work ranks on an equality with that of man.

This equality, consequent of a generally liberal policy which some found refreshing and others found amusing, eccentric and fit only to be ridiculed, lasted (unlike the Free's good intentions) beyond the first few years of exhibition. In 1868, the *Saturday Review* reported: 'Lady-artists, we are glad to observe, are seen in the Dudley to advantage – all the more so because content to be simple, and in the small.' While the *Art Journal*, without displaying such qualifications, observed in 1871:

The Dudley Gallery has from the first been a favourite resort of the ladies: a dozen ladies, at the very least, here distinguish themselves: there is, in fact, a greater display of female talent in this room than in the gallery in Conduit Street, exclusively set apart for the benefit of ladies . . .

The Dudley Gallery is further distinguished by the best flower-painting now to be met with, and again we have to acknowledge our obligation to the ladies.[75]

They tended to belong to the younger generation, and to exhibit elsewhere as well, although to less conspicuous effect than at the Dudley, where it is evident they were given some prominence.

The same generation benefited from the establishment of the Grosvenor Gallery in 1877, though here the opportunity was more limited since it depended on the invitation of the Gallery's instigator, Sir Coutts Lindsay. The Grosvenor therefore had a somewhat exclusive basis, deriving its exhibitions as it did from the invitations of one person, although, in the words of the *Athenaeum*'s reviewer in 1877:

An examination of this Exhibition will convince the visitor that a noble and cultivated taste has been at work in the task of selection, that invitations have been issued in a generous and liberal spirit.[76]

Female exhibitors in the first show reflected the mixture of the fashionable, *recherché* and avant-garde which was to characterise the shows both for its supporters and for its detractors. They included Louise Jopling, Marie Spartali, (by then Mrs Stillman), Helen Coleman (by then Mrs Angell), and Margaret Gillies, and amounted to nine, among a total of 64 artists. The next year, women numbered 11 out of 96 contributors, and included notably Sophie Anderson [fig. 21], Lady Waterford and Princess Louise, while those already mentioned were again represented. A similar pattern showed in the third year (1879), when the female contributors – additionally among them Louisa Starr, Anna Lea Merritt [fig. 22], Clara and Henrietta Montalba and Evelyn Pickering [fig. 14] – numbered 22 of 131 artists, mostly painters. The Grosvenor favoured the Aesthetic school and a form of classicism which was highly decorative and sensual, pseudo-historical and often very titillating, though elegant. Thus the so-called Olympian artists (such as Frederic Leighton and Laurens Alma-Tadema) were its

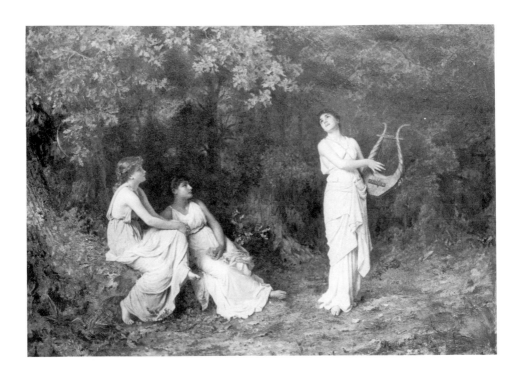

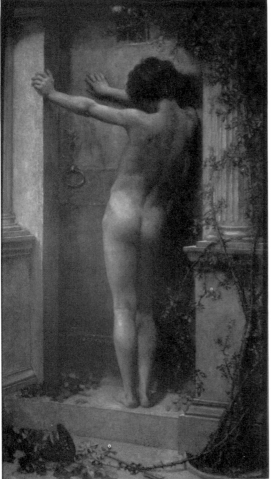

21. Sophie Anderson, 'The Song', 1881. Oil on canvas. Wolverhampton Art Gallery Collection.

22. Anna Lea Merritt, 'Love Locked Out', 1889. Oil on canvas. Reproduced by permission of the Tate Gallery, London.

lions, along with Edward Burne-Jones who was enjoying a new lease of life as a Symbolist hero, especially once D. G. Rossetti was dead. Of the female artists just mentioned as Grosvenor contributors, Pickering and Spartali could represent the Burne-Jones trend, Lea Merritt and Anderson the Neo-classical.

The various enterprises of Ernest Gambart greatly expanded the opportunities for exhibition in London also, from quite early in the period. The French gallery opened in 1854, devoted to the work of artists from Gambart's native country, but it became beneficial to British artists with its winter exhibitions which began in 1853. The proportion of women shown here was low at the start, and remained so (e.g. 1858: 12 out of 71; 1868: 3 out of 124), but most of the more prominent female artists of the time showed there at some time or another. (The French Exhibitions, themselves, were often dominated by one woman, of course: Rosa Bonheur. The *Builder*'s review of the opening show observed: 'Perhaps the greatest attraction of the Gallery will be considered by the public generally to be the cattle pictures by Mlle. Rosa Bonheur. As the productions of a lady, they are perfectly astonishing...') And it was Gambart who gave Bridell Fox and Bodichon their own shows, in 1859, 1861, 1864 and 1866.[77]

The Crystal Palace exhibitions, though difficult to find information on, must be included in the proliferating exhibition arenas of the 1850s. Annual catalogues of the paintings and sculptures shown in this gallery, after it moved to Sydenham, are not available, but among the women who evidently showed there, to judge from specific press mentions, are Bodichon, Ward, Osborn, Margaret Robbinson, Brownlow, Rebecca Solomon, Howitt, Annie Mutrie, Kate Swift, Jane Bowkett, Jessie McLeod, Charlotte James, Margaret Backhouse and Charlotte Babb. The first four won prizes at these exhibitions in (respectively) 1873, 1872 and 1873, 1864 and 1869.[78] A report in the *Illustrated London News* of the Crystal Palace show of 1865 noted a roll of contributing artists which included six female exhibitors out of 77: the writer does not comment upon this proportion.[79]

The amateur exhibitions, erratic though they were, supplied many women with an exhibition opportunity which they had not before enjoyed, but which became redundant once the SFA was established. The first amateur exhibition was held in 1850, to critical enthusiasm, and women predominated in this and in the few subsequent shows: in reviewing the third show, the *Builder* noted that 'The ladies take the lead, indisputably....'. Gambart took over the gallery in which these exhibitions were held in 1853 or 1854, and it is not unlikely that this is why they ceased as a regular event (i.e. because they were not very profitable).

The exhibition season expanded, too, as well as the exhibition space: the concept of a winter exhibition had been presented first by Grundy's 1849 attempt, and in 1852 the *Builder*'s critic declared that 'The Winter Exhibition may now be considered as established . . .'; while a decade later the same pages offered the observation that:

> Winter exhibitions of pictures, drawings, and sketches have become so much in vogue of late, that they may now be as confidently expected in their turn as their more important precursors of earlier date . . . thanks to these offshoots of after-growth, the distance between August and February is most pleasantly relieved and shortened. Cornhill and its neighbourhood have become the Pall-Mall of the east . . .

The SFA was in the minority in holding no winter augmentation to its regular show, but then its regular show opened so early in the season as to almost qualify for such an appellation. However, women were given a particular winter place by the efforts of Henry Wallis, to whom Gambart handed over the management of the French Gallery in 1861, and who bought the lease of that gallery in 1867. In 1865, Wallis arranged a winter show at the Suffolk Street gallery 'with a section representing French, Flemish, and female practice in particular as a special adjunct',[80] while his first winter show as lessee of the French Gallery featured a woman's work as its special attraction (Jane Benham Hay's 'Florentine Procession').

The mid-century period saw a rich and varied expansion of exhibition opportunities in the capital, perhaps originally inspired by the Great Exhibition of 1851 or the feelings and ideas that went with it, from which artists generally benefited. An expansion in exhibition opportunity would not necessarily, in itself, have proved beneficial to female artists, but given that this expansion took place in the period of increasing ambition on women's part and of developments in the range of activities for them to explore, it evidently greatly assisted their rise to a position of notice in the Victorian art world. The first phase of increasing numbers of exhibitions in the early 1850s, coupled with the persistence of anti-Academy feeling, followed by the addition of regular exhibition galleries to the London circuit in the 1860s and 1870s,[81] all

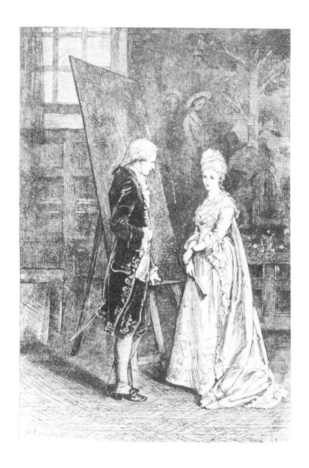

23. Helen Paterson Allingham, 'Angelika Kauffmann
in the Studio of Joshua Reynolds', 1875.
Wood engraving. (Photographer unknown)

exemplifying a certain commercial spirit built upon that anti-Academy feeling, gave women varied exhibition opportunities from which – to go on the evidence available – they derived equally varied benefit (see Table opposite). This is the age of the rise of the one-artist exhibition, also, and it is reflective of the marked but still moderate progress which female artists made in the field of exhibition in this period that there were some one-woman exhibitions in London during the period, though they were very few and little publicised.[82] Even at the end of the period, it seems that the only female artist who was seen as strong (and lucrative) enough to stand quite on her own before the public would be not a British one, but a French (Bonheur or Browne), although Elizabeth Thompson's [fig. 4] and Helen Allingham's [fig. 23] popularity went some way towards ameliorating that situation at the end of the century.

It must, finally, be pointed out in considering the state and institution of exhibition in the Victorian age from women's point of view, that I have been discussing only those creative activities traditionally associated with exhibition, but that other artistic forms such as embroidery and lacework began to be promoted in exhibition during this time as more properly women's work. This was encouraged by the annual exhibitions of the Government Schools of Design, which suggested that it was not only paintings and sculpture that could be displayed and consumed through formal exhibition, but 'craft' work also. This line was tacitly and strongly motivated, when applied to women's work, by women's persistence in those 'fine' fields of creative endeavour traditionally monopolised by men. In the 1880s, indeed, critics overtly welcomed exhibitions of women's traditional activities as a relief from displays of female attempts at fine art. Exhibitions of embroidery, lacework, household design and 'handiwork', which became a feature of the 1870s and 1880s, have as much to do, I would contend, with the question of women and art as with the rise of the Arts and Crafts movement in which context they have already been explained by others.[83] In an era when women's work within the fine arts was expanding and becoming ever more visible, movements towards eroding the primacy of oil paintings and statuary as the archetypal art objects must be seen as a mixed blessing, very much tainted with the self-interest of men which jealously guarded the status which went with the production of fine art, and wanted nothing more than to see women embrace once again their traditional and 'lesser' crafts.

Female Exhibitors in the Shows of London Societies, 1850–79

Year	SFA[1]	RA	SBA	OWS	New[2]	BI	NI[3]	Dudley (water)	Dudley (oil)
1850			46	4	9	17	6		
1851		61	42	4	7	20	7		
1852		84	43	5	8	23	10		
1853		79	54	5	8	26	13		
1854		84	48	5	9	28	15		
1855		90	69	?	8	25	14		
1856		108	63	4	9	25	15		
1857	149	91	62	4	8	28	13		
1858	275	99	52	4	8	26	15		
1859	246	93	61	4	8	28	22		
1860	200	48	63	4	6	26	18		
1861	165	49	60	4	8	23	16		
1862	133	55	70	4	9	24			
1863	111	65	60	4	18	32			
1864	100	60	76	4	9	30			
1865	113	63	70	4	9	29		31	
1866	158	60	89	4	9	36		54	
1867	168	76	81	4	10	34		59	11
1868	164	75	88	4	10			56	19
1869	183	56*	98	4	5			83	13
1870	211	61	73	4	8			76	20
1871	198	59	76	3	8			79	34
1872	186	79	73	3	9			91	43
1873	216	93	86	3	5			85	42
1874	284	92	95	4	7			83	36
1875	301	75	85	4	9			73	34
1876	?	97	56	5	8			68	39
1877	257	110	76	5	9			92	52
1878	403	95	44	5	7			107	43
1879	429	103	82	6	6			105	45

Notes:
1. Changed to SLA 1872
2. Later the Institute of Painters in Watercolour
3. Formerly the Free Exhibition
* In supplementary exhibitions: 67

*Female artists patronised by Art-Union prizewinners, in
descending order of popularity*

Artist	Year	Work	prize	price	gallery
Emma (Mrs William)	1849	'On the Dart'	£15	£15	RA
Oliver	1850	'At Rowe, North Wales'	£15	£17	NI
	1851	'The Brathay'	£15	£15	RA
	1855	'Wargrave on the Thames'	£10	£10	NI
	1858	'Near the Lake de Garda, Tyrol'	£20	£21	New
	1859	'Wabash on the Moselle'	£15	£15	SFA
	1861	'Bouvignes on the Meuse'	£15	£21	New
	1863	'Trabach from the Moselle'	£15	15gns	New
	1876	'The market-place, Verona'	£10	10gns	New
Caroline F. Williams	1865	'Wargrave Ferry, Evening'	£10	£10	SBA
	1865	'Morning on the Medway'	£10	£10	SBA
	1873	'Summer Evening on the Thames'	£10	£10	SBA
	1875	'A Troutstream, Cumbernauld'	£10	£10	SBA
	1877	'Margate, night'	£10	12gns	SBA
	1878	'Summer's Night, Scarborough'	£10	£10	SLA
	1878	'Autumnal Evening'	£10	£10	SBA
	1879	'Night on the Medway'	£10	£10	SBA
Eloise Stannard	1852	'Fruit from Nature'	?	£31.10	BI
	1853	'Fruit from Nature'	£10	12gns	BI
	1855	'Fruit'	£20	£31.10	BI
	1860	'Fruit'	£25	£25	RA
	1862	'Fruit from Nature'	£25	£25	BI
	1866	'Fruit'	£50	£50	BI
Sophy S. Warren	1865	'A Lane in Oxfordshire'	£20	£20	SBA
	1866	'Distant View of Exeter Cathedral'	£25	£25	SBA
	1869	'Beech Hill Common, Hants'	£10	10gns	SBA
	1871	'A Berkshire Watermill'	£20	£21	SBA
	1875	'Evening'	£30	£31.10	SBA
	1878	'On the Avon near Burpham'	£25	18gns	SBA
Emma Brownlow	1859	''Tis an old tale oft told'	£10	£10	SBA
	1860	'Preparing the Village Guy'	£20	£20	BI
	1863	'The shortest way Home from School'	£10	£10	BI
	1867	'The Beggar's Story'	£10	12gns	SBA
	1867	'Waiting for the Boats'	£30	£30	SBA
Emily Desvignes	1862	'Sheep'	£10	£10	RA
	1863	'Sheep'	£10	£10	SBA
	1874	'Sheep, evening'	£10	£10	SBA
	1874	'Cattle, morning'	£10	£10	SBA
	1878	'Cattle, evening'	£10	£10	SLA
Jessie McLeod	1849	'Interior, Fisher's Cottage'	£25	£25	BI
	1853	'The Arrest of Effie Deans'	£60	£60	BI
	1856	'Highland Courtship'	£20	£25	SBA
	1867	'The future home'	£30	£30	SBA
	1877	'The Escape of Prince Charles Edward'	£60	£50	CP

Artist	Year	Work	prize	price	gallery
Jane M. Bowkett	1873	'Venus! Looking-glass'	£10	10gns	CP
	1876	'What's o'clock?'	£15	£15	CP
	1877	'Rustle Vanity'	£20	£20	CP
	1878	'A Shepherdess'	£25	£25	CP
Anna (Mrs J.) Charretie	1871	'Little Goody Two-shoes'	£30	£31.10	SBA
	1871	'Lady Russell'	£10	£10	SBA
	1873	'Queen Guinevere'	£15	£15	CP
	1875	'Lady Betty at Home'	£35	£45	SBA
Mrs L. Leroux	1877	'Sunset on the Wye'	£10	£10	CP
	1877	'Llanberis Lake'	£15	£15	CP
	1878	'Sunrise, lake scene'	£10	£10	CP
	1879	'Lake scene near Dolgelly'	£15	£18	CP
Mary Margetts	1852	'Roses'	£15	17gns	New
	1853	'Bacchanalian Hunting Cup'	£40	£40	New
	1858	'Still Life'	£25	£30	New
	1864	'Grapes'	£10	£20	RA
Frances Stoddart	1858	'Lower End of Loch Tummel'	£20	£20	SBA
	1858	'On the Bank of the Mousse'	£15	£15	SFA
	1865	'Valley near Oban'	£10	£15	RSA
	1866	'Southwick Water, Dumfriesshire'	£10	12gns	RSA
Agnes Bouvier (Nicholl)	1870	'Under the Cliff'	£10	15	SBA
	1876	'Our Kitties'	£10	£12	SBA
	1876	'The task performed'	£20	£20	SLA
Marian Chase	1876	'In the Greenhouse'	£25	£25	OWS
	1877	'A November Nosegay'	£25	£25	New
	1879	'Blackcurrants and Cherries'	£10	12gns	New
Mrs H. Criddle	1857	'Children in the Wood'	£25	£25	OWS
	1860	'Auld Robin Grey'	£30	£30	OWS
	1866	'Ophelia'	£40	£36.15	OWS
Mrs Wm. (E.) Duffield	1864	'Spring Flower'	£15	13gns	New
	1867	'Fruit'	£15	£26.50	New
	1870	'Flowers'	£30	£30	New
Kate Swift (Bisschop)	1858	'The Gleaners'	£20	£22	SFA
	1863	'The Past'	£20	£20	BI
	1864	'Opportunity was the Thief'	£20	£20	SBA
Linnie Watt	1878	'Meadowsweet'	£15	£15	SLA
	1879	'Buttercups and Daisies'	£10	£10	SLA
	1879	'Summertime'	£20	£20	RA
Margaret Backhouse	1869	'Tattered and Torn'	£10	£10	RA
	1872	'In the Woods'	£15	£52.10	RA
Isabel Bennett	1874	'Summertime'	£10	£10	RA
	1876	'Early Summer in the River Lea'	£10	£10	SBA
J. Bertha	1877	'Evening on the Thames'	£15	£15	CP
	1878	'Sunrise near Capel-curig'	£15	£15	CP
Mary Ann Cole	1854	'The Youthful Hairdresser'	£15	£15	RA
	1858	'Hagar and Ishmael'	£10	£12	SFA

Victorian Women Artists

Artist	Year	Work	prize	price	gallery
Jane Egerton	1847	'The Nut brown Maid'	£25	£25	New
	1847	'Hush thee, Hush thee, Baby dear'	£15	15gns	New
Mary Gow	1873	'The Morning of the Fair'	£10	£10	BI
	1876	'Out of Date'	£35	£31.10	New
Elizabeth Hunter	1865	'The tiniest One'	£10	£10	BI
	1869	'My Neighbour Opposite'	£10	10gns	SBA
Jane Nasmyth	1853	'Near Dumfries'	£10	£11	SBA
	1855	'Putney Heath, Surrey'	£10	£10	SBA
Mrs J.F. Pasmore	1877	'Home lessons'	£10	£10	SBA
	1877	'You wild Flowers . . .'	£20	£20	SBA
Elizabeth Phillips	1849	'The ancient Rathaus Koblentz'	£15	£15	RA
	1868	'Junction of the Moselle and Rhine'	£30	£45	SBA
Mrs Profaze	1871	'Maiden Meditation'	£10	£10	SBA
	1872	'Sweet Seventeen'	£10	£10	SBA
E. Redgrave	1877	'Three Playmates'	£35	£35	SBA
	1879	'The Dairy, Cowdray'	£10	£10	RA
Margaret Robbinson	1864	'The rocky Chair'	£20	£20	SBA
	1866	'Happy Idleness'	£100	£100	RA
Helen Thornycroft	1870	'The Winner won'	£15	£15	Dud.
	1878	'Portia pleading'	£10	£10	SLA
Marcella Walker	1878	'The Wanton Troopers . . .'	£50	£50	SBA
	1879	'The Sailor's Sweetheart'	£40	£50	RA
Augusta Withers	1856	'Wild Flowers'	£50	£50	SBA
	1856	'Goldfinch, etc.'	£20	£20	NI
Kate Amphlett	1878	'Cottage near Gilvel'	£10	11gns	SBA
Anna Blunden	1862	'Weston Village, vale of Honiton'	£20	£20	SBA
Eleanor Brown	1858	'Near Temple Lock, Marlow'	£10	£10	NI
G.P. Brune	1879	'Portocotham Bay, North Cornwall'	£10	£10	SBA
Ellen Clacy	1873	'The missing Playfellow'	£25	£25	RA
Ellen Connolly	1878	'My Model's Opinion'	£45	£36.15	CP
Helen Coode	1867	'La fille bien gardée'	£10	10gns	RA
Fanny Corbaux	1849	'Hagar'	£40	£63	New
Louisa Corbaux	1862	'Afraid of the big Dog'	£15	16gns	New
Helga Cramen	1879	'Castle of Chillon'	£40	£40	RA
Mrs Crawford	1875	'Priscilla'	£40	£42	RA
Mrs A.G. Dawborn	1879	'Dover Castle'	£25	£25	SBA
Kate Edwards (Sparkes)	1878	'Mother and Child etc'	£40	£42	RA
Mary Ellen Edwards	1879	'I'm so happy'	£20		RA
M.E. Edwards	1876	'On the Common, Leytonstone'	£15	£21	RA
Edith Elmore	1877	'Spring Flowers'	£15	15gns	RA
Jane Escombe	1870	'A Backwater of the Wey'	£20	£20	RA

Artist	Year	Work	prize	price	gallery
Emily Farmer	1860	'Stringing Eggshells'	£15	£15	New
Mary Forster	1878	'Summer Morning, Coed-y-ffynon'	£15	15gns	RA
Eliza Bridell Fox	1863	'The enchanted Frog-Prince'	£25	£42	RA
Annie French	1864	'St. Saviour's Church, Jersey'	£10	10gns	SBA
Margaret Gillies	1867	'Judge Croke'	£60	£80	OWS
E. Glover	1876	'My Wintergarden'	£10	10gns	Dud.
Eliza Goodall (Wild)	1848	'The idle Nurse'	£10	£10	RA
Mrs. Curwen Gray	1864	'The Seamstress'	£35	£35	SBA
Georgina Greenlees	1878	'Corner of the Forest, Inverary'	£40	£40	RA
Kate Greenaway	1877	'Dorothy'	£10	£10	Dud.
E.S. Guinness	1879	'Sweet Seventeen'	£20	£20	Dud.
Sarah Hewett	1852	'Children at Play'	£10	12gns	NI
M. Hipwood	1868	'Spring'	£10	£10	SBA
H.H. Hopkins	1876	'The Reaper's Task is done'	£15	£18	RA
Ambrosini Jérôme	1857	'Gleaners'	£25	£26	BI
Fanny Jolly	1876	'Mateless, November 1875'	£10	£12	Dud.
Louise Jopling	1876	'Lorraine'	£45	£45	RA
Frances Keys	1871	'Evening on Dartmoor'	£15	£15	SBA
? Lauder	1867	'Idling'	£10	£10	RSA
Jessie McGregor	1874	'The old Terrace Steps'	£10	£10	RA
Fanny McIan	1849	'Soldiers' Wives awaiting the Result of Battle'	£80	£80	Free
E. Manton	1875	'By the sad sea waves'	£10	£10	CP
Maria Margitson	1875	'Fruit'	£15	15gns	SLA
M. Mason	1876	'The Path through the Beechwood'	£10	£10	SLA
Lois Mearns	1879	'The Solo'	£20	£26.50	RA
Eliza Mellville	1864	'Child of Joy'	£10	£10	SBA
F. Moody	1878	'Roebuck and rough Hounds'	£10	£10	SLA
M. Murray	1854	'Waiting for the Carriage'	£10	£10	RA
Martha Mutrie	1859	'Camellias'	£20	£26.50	BI
J. Naftel	1876	'Olive'	£15	£14	SBA
Barbara Nasmyth	1854	'Loch Katrine'	£10	£10	SBA
? Neumann	1863	'Grandmother's Lesson'	£10	£15	SBA
C.M. Noble	1875	'A common Friend'	£20	£20	SBA
E. Partridge	1879	'Through the Woods, Bavaria'	£15	£15	SLA
E. von Perbandt	1878	'Landscape and Cattle'	£40	£40	CP
E. Percy	1868	'Elaine'	£15	£15	SBA
Kate Perugini (Dickens)	1878	'A competitive Examination'	£30	£35	RA
Louise Rayner	1877	'High Street, Ludlow'	£40	£40	RA

Artist	Year	Work	prize	price	gallery
J. Russell	1870	'Waiting, watching, hoping still'	£15	£15	Dud.
Mrs Rymer	1857	'A Nook in the Conservatory'	£20	£25	SBA
Kate Sadler	1879	'Satisfaction'	£15	£15	Dud.
A.J. Salter	1876	'Young Squirrels at Home'	£10	10gns	CP
Rebecca Solomon	1867	'Giovannina Roma'	£35	£35	RA
Helen Stigand	1870	'Beeches in Knowle Park'	£15	£15	RA
Mrs G.F. Terrell	1879	'A Daydream'	£30	£30	RA
Florence Thomas	1868	'The New Book'	£15	15gns	SBA
Elizabeth Thompson	1873	'Missing'	£60	£80	RA
L. Tiddemann	1875	'Il Penserosa'	£15	£15	RA
Emmeline Vallentin	1869	'In the Market'	£15	£15	SBA
Emma Walter	1874	'Summer flowers'	£10	10gns	SBA
Eva Ward	1875	'Absent'	£15	£15	RA
Flora Ward	1875	'The Lesson'	£35	£35	BI
Henrietta Ward	1860	'The first Step'	£75	£75	RA
M. Wilson	1876	'Folkestone Harbour'	£30	£31.10	SBA

Analysis of Types of Work in SFA shows 1857–70 in
Approximate Genre Categorisations

Year	F&F*	Animals	Portraits	Copies	Land-scape	Sculpture	Totals pics	artists
1857	55	9	50	37	108	14	358	149
1858	85	19	38	79	162	21	582	277
1859	38	11	15	34	102	4	311	145
1860	40	5	9	64	132	2	319	150
1861	54	16	23	1	160	6	333	165
1862	35	10	25	3	136	5	283	133
1863	39	12	13	0	100	11	269	111
1864	49	14	13	1	105	0	253	100
1865	54	7	12	12	95	8?	276	113
1866	65	13	22	5	205	5	403	158
1867	50	9	16	14	167	6	400	168
1868	58	17	12	14	200	1	413	165
1869	57	8	28	17	213	1	484	183
1870	54	13	20	16	232	0	473	208

* F&F = fruit and flowers

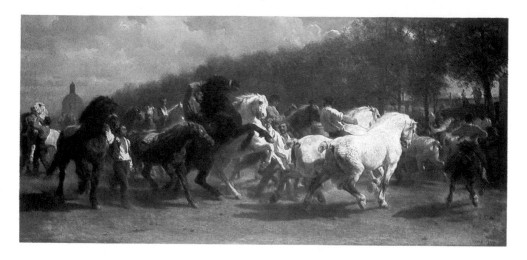

I. Rosa Bonheur, 'The Horse Fair', 1854. Oil on canvas. Autograph replica with
Nathalie Micas of original now in Metropolitan Museum, New York.
Reproduced by courtesy of the Trustees, The National Gallery, London.

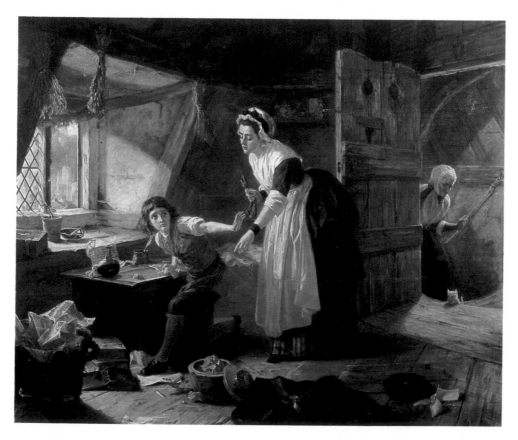

II. Henrietta Ward, 'Chatterton', 1873. Oil on canvas. City of Bristol Museum and
Art Gallery. (Photo: Julie Phipps)

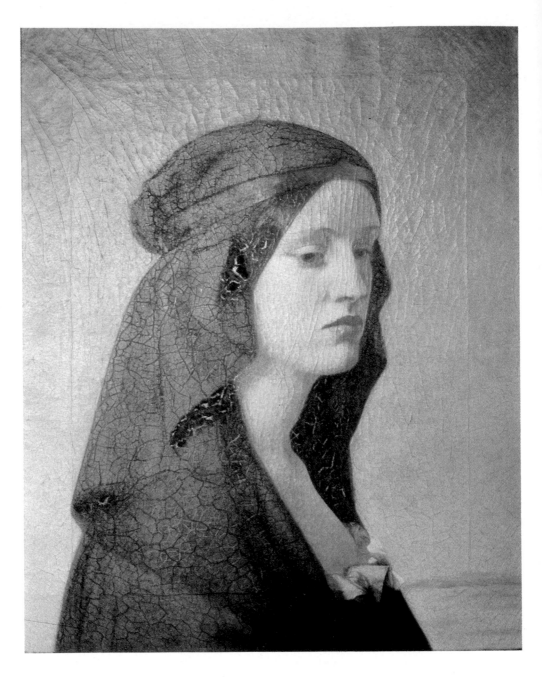

III. Joanna Boyce Wells, 'Elgiva', 1855. Oil on canvas. Private collection.
(Photo: author)

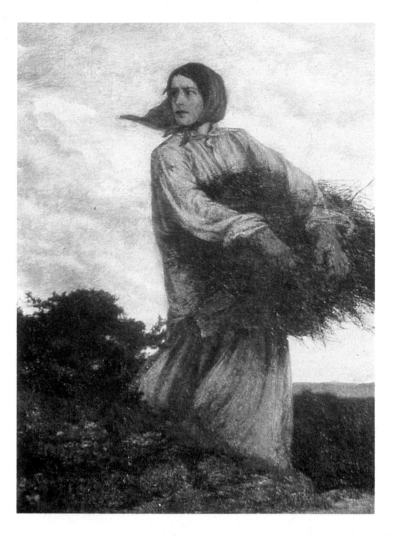

IV. Joanna Boyce Wells, 'The Heathergatherer', 1859. Oil on canvas. Private collection. (Photo: author)

V. Joanna Boyce Wells, 'Sidney', 1859. Oil on canvas. Private collection. (Photo: Julie Phipps)

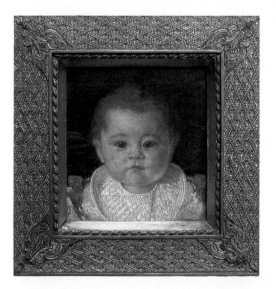

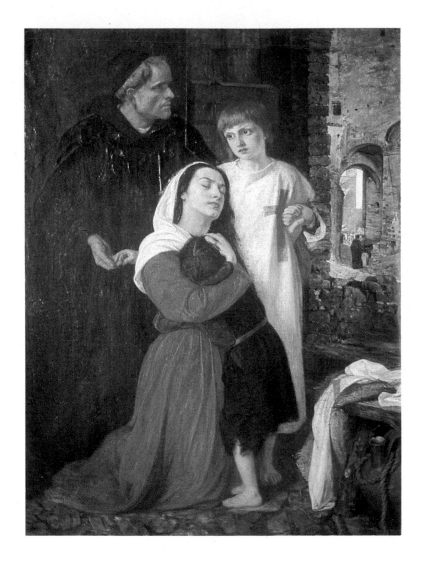

VI. Joanna Boyce Wells, 'The Child's Crusade', 1860.
Oil on canvas. Private collection. (Photo: author)

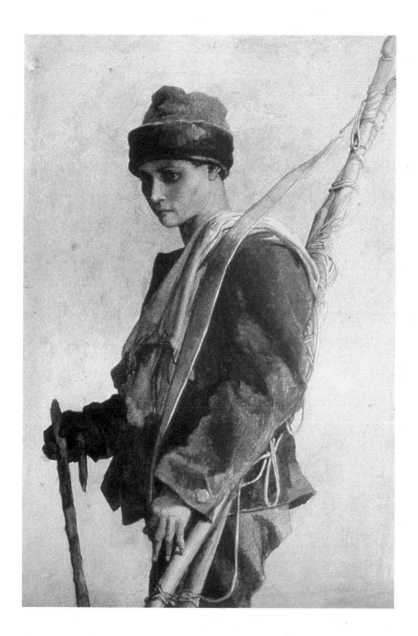

VII. Louisa, Lady Waterford, 'Mentone Fisherman', 1838.
Watercolour on paper. Reproduced by courtesy of
the Board of Trustees of the Victoria and Albert Museum.

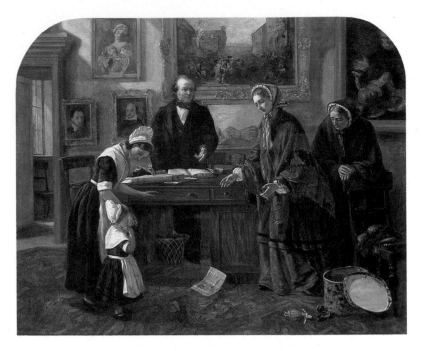

VIII. Emma Brownlow, 'The Foundling restored to its Mother', 1858.
Oil on canvas. The Thomas Coram Foundation for Children.

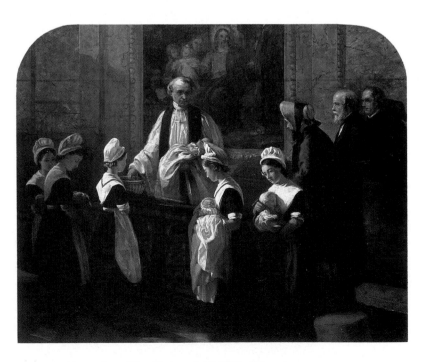

IX. Emma Brownlow, 'The Christening', 1863. Oil on canvas.
The Thomas Coram Foundation for Children.

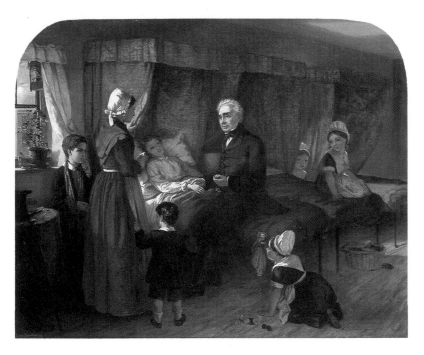

X. Emma Brownlow, 'The Sick Room', 1864. Oil on canvas.
The Thomas Coram Foundation for Children.

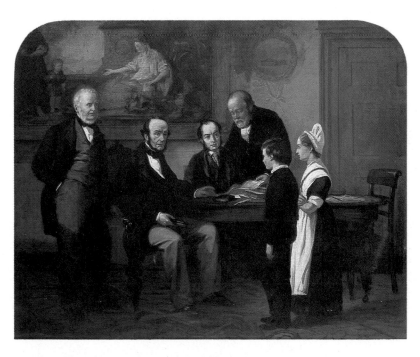

XI. Emma Brownlow, 'Taking Leave', 1868. Oil on canvas.
The Thomas Coram Foundation for Children.

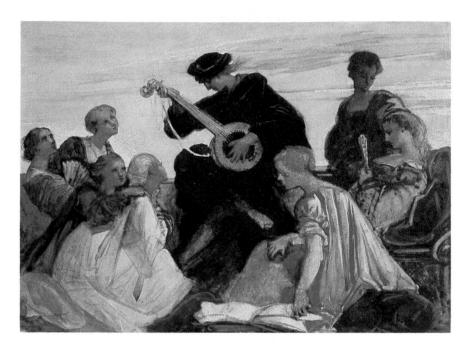

XII. Louisa, Lady Waterford, 'Sweetest eyes were ever seen', undated.
Watercolour on paper. Reproduced by courtesy of
the Board of Trustees of the Victoria and Albert Museum.

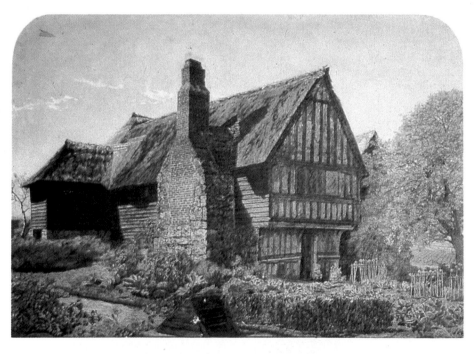

XIII. Rosa Brett, 'The Old House at Fairleigh', 1862. Oil on canvas.
Private Collection. (Photo: author)

Notes

1.   The former had exhibited in London from 1819, the latter from 1807; other early venturers into the field of public exhibition in London included Fanny Corbaux (from 1829) and various Sharpe sisters: Charlotte (from 1817), Louisa (from 1817), Eliza (from 1817) and Mary-Anne (from 1819).

2.   William Michael Rossetti wrote in 1864: 'The one useful result of these exhibitions has been to call attention to the art-movement among the ladies . . .' (*Fine Art Quarterly*, vol. 3, October 1864, p.33).

3.   Trevor Fawcett, *The Rise of English Provincial Art* (Oxford, 1974), p.3.

4.   *Spectator*, 2 April 1853, p.326.

5.   Ibid., 23 November 1850, p.1122: this notice congratulated the instigators of the first winter exhibition.

6.   Elizabeth Eastlake, *Mrs Grote, a sketch* (1880), ch.5, p.98.

7.   Harriet Grote, *Personal Life of George Grote* (1873), p.241.

8.   *Builder*, 10 May 1856, p.257; the letter was not published in the *Art Journal*, nor the *Athenaeum*, nor *The Times*, neither was such a communication even reported in these organs. It was referred to in the *Builder* as part of that paper's review of the Academy exhibition that year.

9.   I have not discovered precisely how the Society advertised for exhibitors, apart from the anticipatory notices such as the one mentioned immediately below. If this were known, it would give a clue as to what sort of women the Society meant to attract.

10.   *Art Journal*, 1 May 1857, p.163; truly, 'all our exhibitions of late years' contained increasing proof that women were capable of artistic achievement, but scant critical acknowledgement of it can be found before this point.

11.   *Spectator*, 9 May 1857, p.496.

12.   Such separation only recognised openly the tacit categorisation of women in a different class from men which prevailed generally in the period. Some critics saw nothing to object to in such a move (*Builder*, 3 April 1858, p.237; *The Times*, 25 May 1857, p.12), while others found it a threatening affront to a belief in male equitableness. Among women who objected to the open segregation, Jameson saw it as rather unnecessarily hostile (Letter 220 to Ottilie von Goether, c.1847, in *Letters of Anna Jameson*, ed. G.H. Needler (1939), p.233 and Introduction to *Social Life in Germany*, (1840)) although she recognised that men made such moves necessary (Introduction to *Sisters of Charity and the Communion of Labour* (1859), p.xvii); while Anna Howitt had an optimistic faith in men which made such moves repellent to her (*An Art Student in Munich* (1853), preface to first edition). For a modern discussion of what such segregation meant, see Parker and Pollock, *Old Mistresses* (1981), ch.1.

13.   See *The Times* review of the first exhibition, most unpleasantly condescending, and apologetic and defensive of the work to be seen in that and any future shows (25 May 1857, p.12) and the *Builder*'s review in

1859, indicating that the exhibitions were to be supported, not for artistic but for social reasons: 'The society, as likely to open a wider field for the independent striving of women, demands our best support' (26 February 1859, p.154). Both these reviews show the low expectations which many brought to their evaluation of the Society's exhibitions.

14.   Some papers stopped reviewing the exhibitions after a while. *The Times*, for instance, was erratic in its coverage, and the *Critic* seems not to have bothered, after a first flush of interest.

15.   *Art Journal*, 1 July 1857, p.215.

16.   *Punch*, 18 July 1857, p.27.

17.   *Illustrated London News*, 6 June 1857, p.545.

18.   *The Times*, 1 June 1857, p.9.

19.   *Art Journal*, 1 October 1857, p.326.

20.   This is probably an indirect reference to Elizabeth Barrett Browning, whose 'Aurora Leigh' had been published late in 1856.

21.   *Illustrated London News*, 3 April 1858, p.351.

22.   See p.95ff. on the Old and New Watercolour Societies.

23.   The idea that women necessarily worked on a small scale died hard, and often surfaced in critical appraisals; for instance, 'Miss Steers [has] contributed clever bits of landscape provoking in their smallness, and womanly in the old-fashioned acceptation of the epithet as implying that they must be sought for – so unobtrusive is their scale' (*Athenaeum*, 23 April 1853, p.504, reviewing the exhibition of the New Society of Watercolour Painters).

24.   *Illustrated London News*, 24 April 1858, p.423.

25.   *Fine Arts Quarterly*, October 1863, p.340; Rossetti, of course, knew several female artists, both who supported the SFA (Bodichon) and who did not (Howitt).

26.   *Spectator*, 16 February 1861, p.165; 11 February 1860, p.211.

27.   *Englishwoman's Review*, vol.7, April 1868, p.467; the tone here is reminiscent of that first *Times* review which the EWR so objected to, but an important difference is that the point is here being made in the light of experience and by the women themselves, not as a prejudgement and by a condescending male.

28.   The moves were not dictated by the scale of the exhibitions: after the expansion of the second year, numbers dropped to around 300 pieces (1859, 311; 1860, 319; 1861, 333), dropped into the high 200s in the mid 1860s (1862, 283; 1863, 269; 1864, 253; 1865, 276) then soared into the 400s for the rest of the decade.

29.   *Athenaeum*, 25 April 1863, p.559.

30.   *Illustrated London News*, 25 April 1863, p.463.

31.   *Punch* noticed this with glee: 'we have one great fault to find. We do strongly object to the Secretary and Check-takers. We have nothing to say against those gentlemen, excepting that they are gentlemen. They should have belonged to the opposite sex. That round collar, that black coat,

those Wellington boots, have no right to be in a room that, as they write over railway carriages, is "Engaged for Ladies". They are an intrusion, a living anachronism, two black spots on the uniform beauty of the picture. Away with them! Turn them out!' (18 July 1857, p.27).

32.   For Waterford, see below Chapter 4; Elizabeth Eastlake, as well as being 'married into the arts', and a writer on aesthetic matters, was an amateur artist.

33.   Two of the Society's most stalwart supporters; the former exhibited there 1858/59, 1866/75, 1877, 1880/81 and the latter 1857/58, 1867, 1869/74, 1877/79, 1886.

34.   The men were: Arthur Ashpitel, Leonard Collmann, Arthur B. Cook, Henry Bohn, Henry Gibson, Thomas H. Hills, Arthur Lewis, William Tite.

35.   Though they continued to appear!

36.   *Art Journal*, 1 March 1871, p.90.

37.   It is interesting that *The Times* review of the first exhibition included a specific disclaimer on the point of discrimination against women in the galleries: 'It is no wise intended as a rival exhibition to those already before the public, nor do the female artists wish to imply that they consider themselves unfairly treated by the older societies . . .' With its tone of quotation from a press release, this might be a reflection of some politic conservatism on the part of the Society's organisers.

38.   It is notable that the peak year at the RA was the year before the SFA began, and that the Academy's number of women (which had been climbing) began to drop erratically after the SFA's establishment. By contrast, numbers of women at the SBA, BI and Free (NI) seem to have been boosted by the Society's founding.

39.   Much was made of regular exhibition in other venues, an artist's absence from an annual show being commented on by critics and reputations depending on keeping in the public's view.

40.   Respectively, *Art Journal*, 1 June 1859, p.170; ibid., 1 May 1863, p.97; ibid., 1 June 1870, p.168.

41.   See the reviews of the 1861 SFA show, when French contributors had been invited.

42.   See above, Chapter 2.

43.   This begs comparison with the contemporary discussion, 'Why have there been no great women artists?', begun by American art historian Linda Nochlin in 1971 ('Why are there no great women artists?', *Woman in Sexist Society*, ed. Gornick and Moran (New York, 1971), p.480; and 'Why have there been no great women artists?', *Art and Sexual Politics*, ed. Hess and Baker (New York, 1973), p.1) and answered by, among others, Eleanor Tufts, *Our Hidden Heritage* (New York, 1974) and Parker and Pollock, *op. cit.*

44.   Burton, *op. cit.*, p.139.

45.   *Builder*, 10 May 1856, p.257.

46.   'The formation of the Society of Painters in Watercolours was a

protest against the RA's treatment of the medium as a subordinate branch' (T. Boase, *English Art 1800 – 70* (Oxford, 1959), p.30).

47.   *Victoria Magazine*, 26 April 1873, no.1, p.5; this was a woman's magazine, but such reports as the one quoted may have been written by a male correspondent.

48.   *Critic*, 7 May 1859, p.447.

49.   Jopling, *op. cit.*, p.11.

50.   Thomas Smith, *Recollections of the British Institution*, (1860), pp.4, 9.

51.   See H.T. Wood, *The History of the Royal Society of Arts* (1913), p.163 for more on Andrus, also Redgrave's *Dictionary of Artists* (1874), p.10; ibid., p.368 for Serres; ibid., p.389 for Spilsbury.

52.   A letter to the *Art Journal* in February 1867, defending the Institution against possible closure, made this point, saying: 'It was not merely an exhibition-room for the sale and display of pictures; for the exhibitions of the works of the old masters, chiefly from the collections of the Directors, afforded a field for the study of the highest class of works, an opportunity presented by no other Art-body in the country' (*Art Journal*, 1 February 1867, p.52); the letter was signed 'An Exhibitor at the "British" '.

53.   *Art Journal*, 1 November 1867, p.245.

54.   For instance, biographical accounts of Fanny Corbaux always mention the benefit she derived from study at the Institution.

55.   The 'New British Institution' was set up in 1870, continuing for several years.

56.   'Watercolour is for the English a national art. This type of painting that we willingly abandon to young ladies' schools is cultivated in England by artists of the first order.' The reviewer is Edmond About, the source unknown.

57.   Roget, *History of the Old Watercolour Society* (1891), p.1.

58.   Ibid., p.210; in the minutes of the meetings of 15 and 22 July 1807, further resolutions concerning women are reported.

59.   See Roget, *op. cit.*, book 4, ch.1 (p.201 ff) for a detailed account of the first exhibition.

60.   Ibid., p.397.

61.   These artists entered the Society in 1823, 1805, 1821, and 1823 respectively.

62.   *Athenaeum*, 11 May 1850, p.510.

63.   These artists had joined the Society in 1839, 1845, 1846, 1835, 1842, 1849, 1841 and 1846, respectively.

64.   *Athenaeum*, 27 June 1857, p.825.

65.   See, for instance, *The Times*, 24 April 1865, p.12; *Spectator*, 4 March 1865, p.244.

66.   Hesketh Hubbard, *An Outline History of the Royal Society of British Artists* (1937), p.11.

67.   Presumably, with the intention of deterring defection to the Academy.

68.   *Illustrated London News*, 11 November 1865, p.463.

69. *Critic,* 1 July 1850, p.335, of the National Institution show.

70. *Art Union,* 1 November 1847, p.389.

71. *Art Union,* 1 January 1848, p.28.

72. *Illustrated London News,* 31 March 1849, p.211.

73. These artists were Mrs Paulson, M.A. Barker, Cleaver, Mrs Pratt, Mrs McIan, Mrs Robertson, Mme. Mühlenfeldt, Mrs Oliver, Sutherland, Mrs Bessett, Nancy Rayner, Nicholls.

74. Catalogues for the exhibitions of the Institution, kept in the V. and A. library, cease in 1861, as do reviews of the exhibition in the periodicals which had theretofore shown a consistent interest in the gallery; none of these papers (which include the *Builder,* the *Athenaeum,* the *Art Journal,* and the *Critic*) make any mention in 1862 of the gallery's ceasing to function, but one must assume that it did.

75. *Art Journal,* 1 March 1871, p.85; in 1865, the Dudley show included 53 works by female artists, in 1866: 63, in 1867: 83, in 1868: 82 – these rising figures occurred within shows that on average totalled a number in the upper 600s. Companion exhibitions of oils began in 1867, which were smaller shows, containing about half the number of works in the watercolour shows.

76. *Athenaeum,* 5 May 1877, p.583; extraordinarily, this review ran to two pages, waxing particularly enthusiastic over Burne-Jones (who was represented by 'Venus' Mirror', 'The Days of Creation', and 'The Beguiling of Merlin'). Of the female exhibitors, only Spartali/Stillman is mentioned, and then cursorily.

77. For accounts of these shows, see the *Art Journal,* 1 May 1861, p.159; *Illustrated London News,* 16 July 1864, p.55.

78. Bodichon for an unidentified watercolour (gold, 1873); Ward for 'Going to Market, Picardy' (silver, 1872) and for an unidentified historical picture (gold, 1873); Osborn for 'Half the world knows not how the other half lives' (gold, 1864); Robbinson for 'Summer Afternoon at Strawberry Hill' (bronze, 1869).

79. *Illustrated London News,* August 1865, p.118; the women in question were Brownlow, Fox, Swift, Osborn, Solomon and Blunden.

80. *Builder,* 4 November 1865, p.778; see J. Maas, *Gambart* (1975) for Gambart and Wallis's business relationship.

81. In addition to those new regular shows already mentioned, the Black and White shows, at the Egyptian Hall, from 1872, should be noted as giving a particular exhibition opportunity to graphic artists. EVB was prominent here in the latter part of the decade.

82. Bodichon and Fox have been mentioned; Mrs F. Thomas had a show at 20, Cockspur Street, in December 1867 (see the *Chromolithograph,* 7 December 1867, p.46); Osborn had a show at Goupil's in 1887 (see *Daily News,* 2 December 1887); for an account of the joint showing of Thompson's 'Roll Call', 'Quatre Bras' and 'Balaclava' at the Fine Art Society galleries in 1876, see the *Art Journal,* 1876, p.190. See further on this

question in Chapter 5, below.

83.   See the excellent accounts of women's craft work in the Victorian period given by Anthea Callen, *Angel in the Studio*, (1979) and Rozsika Parker, *The Subversive Stitch* (1984), which nevertheless make no link with the women's art movement of the time.

4
Case Histories

Among the many female artists evidently active in the middle of the Victorian period, some have proved easier to study than others, for reasons which do not necessarily correspond to the stature, popularity or importance of the artists. For instance, Rebecca Solomon was prominent in her own time as one of the most conspicuous of the new breed of female artists attempting 'higher' art and exhibiting regularly at the Academy, and attached to an artistic family, yet surviving material relating to her work and her life has proved very scanty, and remaining works that are identified are very few.[1] Similarly, the sisters Annie and Martha Mutrie were highly esteemed in their own lifetime, yet material that would illuminate their careers beyond the critical encomiums they consistently received and the evidence presented by the handful of identified works which survive, has not come to light.[2] That obscurity is not simply related to the alleged importance of an artist's genre is proved by the fact that Solomon clearly eschewed traditionally womanly or humble genres such as still life, concentrating instead on figure pictures of modern life and literary subjects, but has become as obscure as the two Mutries, who produced flower and fruit paintings and nothing else. For female sculptors, the situation is no better, for unless a sculptor has work installed in a public space or national collection, it can easily become lost or obscured. Thus those artists who were evidently considered the best female artists of the period under discussion here – Ward, Osborn, Carpenter, Mutrie, Solomon, Benham Hay, Boyce/Wells – are not necessarily those whom it is possible to document in detail. Though fame is a great preserver, it has not served these women thus. However, two of those 'best' female artists of the period will be examined in detail here: Ward and Boyce (Mrs Wells), both of whose descendants have preserved their memory, though art history has not.

To set beside those examples of contemporary success, it is instructive to place the 'good average' artist, she whom critics recognised but rarely rhapsodised, who consistently produced and sold and who was like many other artists, and therefore representative of a type which characterises the period. Emma Brownlow will serve as the example of that type here: a wide exhibitor, frequently chosen by Art Union premium winners from the London galleries, given a lukewarm reception by critics. In studying *female* artists it is important, if the authentic range of artists is to be suggested, that the amateur – or, rather, the non-professional – artist is considered. Important, too, is the artist who does not become famous, for her art is probably more instructive as to the dominant modes and trends of the time in which she was operating than is the art of the 'great' artists who, precisely because they are not typical of the period, because they are different and original, have become called great. Such an artist is especially important in the period under discussion here, because during the Victorian era the rise of bourgeois and popular patronage and the expansion of the exhibition field, along with such technological developments as photography and metal-tube oil paint, seemed to open up the possibility of success to any artist, and a range of creative production was given attention which brought many names into the popular, critical or commercial eye which a few decades before would have been quite ignored. This is, obviously, particularly relevant to women. Thus two artists who were by no means professional (by which I mean that they did not make their living by their artistic practice neither did they mean to) will be detailed here: Louisa, Lady Waterford and Rosa Brett (Rosarius). The former achieved some renown in her lifetime, the latter none beyond her immediate circle; the former was socially conspicuous and the latter quite 'ordinary'; but they were both implicated in the most significant artistic movement of their time – Pre-Raphaelitism.

The question of Victorian female artists' relationship to the movements of their time is a significant one. It has been stated that in the usual, movement-based art history female artists have been left out: is this because there were none in the movements into which art practice of the past is categorised? The most conspicuous movement of the period and place under examination here, Pre-Raphaelitism, attracted many female artists. Several sisters, wives and daughters of the much-fêted male proponents of the movement, as well as individual women artists up and down the country, took up what was seen as an invigorating and challenging trend in painting and illustration (and, eventually, the applied arts). Many more female artists could be included under the broader heading of Realism, which is the art movement which characterises the whole of the Victorian period in this country and others (markedly France). There were also more or less private groups of painters on the British scene, such as the Clique, to which women might have belonged: but, even if, say, a female artist's husband saw himself as a member of such a circle, it is highly unlikely that his wife would have been voluntarily included by the group of men or that she herself would have felt appropriate to such a band unless the group was a very progressive one (which the Clique, for instance, was not). The formation of artistic groups always has as much to do with social questions as artistic ones, fulfilling ambitions on the part of men about their will to individual identity as much as their wish to establish a different art form for its own sake. And this is surely something in which women play a different part, our personal ambition being shaped in such a different way from men's.

Where female artists have adopted trends or styles for which male artists are now famous, their articulation of those modes is bound to be more complex and challenging for they have joined a grouping whose rules were made up for others to practise. Thus, in all the tendencies of nineteenth-century art which Modernist and non-Modernist art historians alike have identified, female artists were present (Orientalism, Pre-Raphaelitism, Realism, Impressionism, Japonisme, *et al.*), but they are almost universally ignored, presumably because it is only feminists who can identify and see as positive the contradictory ways in which such artists engaged with these trends. Thus, Sophie Anderson's or Henriette Browne's harem scenes have still to be examined by scholars of Orientalism,

Elizabeth Siddal and Rosa Brett are still invisible Pre-Raphaelites, and the depiction of workers by Emily Mary Osborn, Louisa Starr, or Anna Blunden has not been considered by historians of Realism. In the survival of traditional forms and tastes, (notably Victorian Classicism), female artists have also featured, but have received no more attention than their sisters in progressive movements. This despite the prejudice which expects women to be more conservative, generally speaking, and which should therefore not be surprised to find them in safe areas of cultural practice. (The possible exception to this last generalised criticism is Harriet Hosmer, who has received a deal of attention from American art historians, though it must be said that more often than not this attention was to her discredit.)

The case histories of these five artists, then, will not demonstrate all the stylistic and thematic trends of their age but will provide a survey of the genres of the period. That said, however, it has to be appreciated that certain staple areas of work in the western tradition are derived absolutely from male experience and were practically inaccessible to women at the time: the nude (male and female) and marine painting are absent from these five oeuvres, for instance. It was only in the last two decades of the century that female artists began to produce nudes in any number, and then, of course, their work was largely inauthentic because they were working to a male-defined schema and premise. Up until then, child nudity was permitted as a supposedly asexual nakedness (not that this was explicity articulated, just hinted at). The oft-denied and obscured truth that the nude is the product of desire (not of aesthetic feeling) comes clearly to the surface in the women artists question. For if nakedness in the artwork were 'innocent', why should women not have been trained and practised in it? Yet it was a subject which was withheld from female students until it had fallen from the status it had previously enjoyed as the most prestigious source of study and pictorial achievement.

The degree to which these artists' work fits easily into our received notion of Victorian art or jar with it is, then, important for us to consider. Because western art practice and its documentation spring from a class-, race- and gender-bound perception of the world, they tend to exclude women's achievement or distort it, either through an inability to 'read' it at all, or a misreading of it. We would expect, therefore, when we do come to look at women's work, to be met with 'difference': and so we are, to a degree. But also we are met with attempts to 'pass' (as is said of pale-skinned

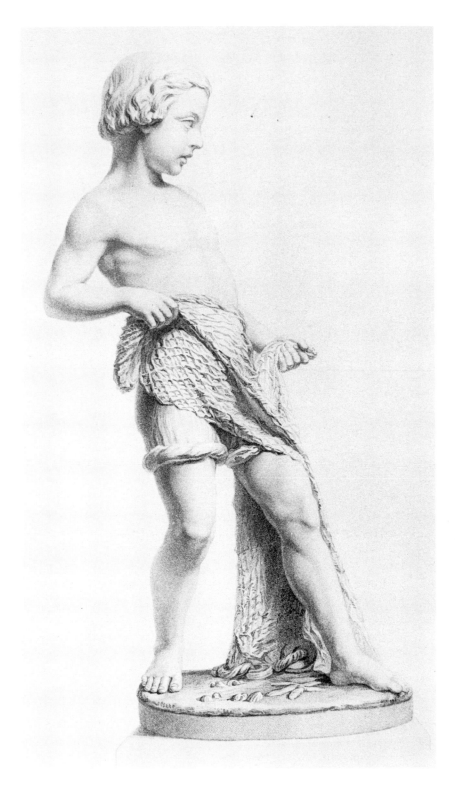

24. G.L. Stoddart after Mary Thornycroft, 'The Fisher (HRH Prince Leopold)', 1858. Engraving, 1864. *Art Journal*. (Photo: Julie Phipps)

blacks in a white-ruled society). Much women's work will be imbued with the attempt to be simply art and not women's work, as if such a thing as simple 'art' existed. Not surprisingly, many Victorian women artists sought conventional and established subjects and styles in order to make the grade: being a *female* artist was handicap enough, and to produce female *art* would have made success quite unattainable – or so the ideology went.

These five artists, then, must all be considered as women working within a male-dominated field and within a patriarchal culture, but they do not present us with a single unified response to that circumstance. Joanna Boyce wanted to be a radical woman artist, Rosa Brett wanted to be a Pre-Raphaelite, Henrietta Ward wanted to be an accepted woman artist, Emma Brownlow wanted to make a living, Lady Waterford just wanted to make art – and each of us, in turn, will make our own reading of each of these artist's work according to *our* positions. There are no female sculptors profiled here, because none of the admittedly fewer women sculptors of the day has left much mark behind for us to assess. Mary Thornycroft[3] [fig. 24] (or Harriet Hosmer) would be the most obvious candidate in this era, though her work is rarely seen these days. In graphics, the woman whose name loomed largest in the mid-Victorian period was Mary Ellen Edwards (later Freer, later Staples), also known by her initials as MEE [fig. 25]. She is even harder to throw light upon than Thornycroft, but her work was prolific in the galleries and the illustrated magazines throughout the years I am discussing.

A contemporary of the five painters profiled in this chapter, the mainstream painter William Frith, devoted a chapter of his autobiography to women artists (he calls them 'lady artists').[4] It is interesting to see whom he picks out at this stage (1887–8). He praises the Mutrie sisters, Elizabeth Thompson (Butler), Henrietta Rae, the Montalba sisters, Alice Havers, Rosa Bonheur, Helen (Patterson) Allingham, Helen (Angell) Coleman, Louisa Starr, Kate Dickens (Perugini), Henrietta Ward, Laura Alma-Tadema, Margaret Dicksee, Mary Gow, Marie Cornelissen, Anna Lea Merritt, Emily Osborn, Louise Jopling and Jane Dealy. Most of these are of the generation working at the time, rather than of his own generation.

What governs the memory of someone like Frith in the question of women artists? It can be supposed that he had never noticed Brownlow's work, had not even heard of the retiring Rosa Brett, would not have liked the work of Joanna Boyce, and scorned to introduce the name of Lady Waterford into a list of professionals.

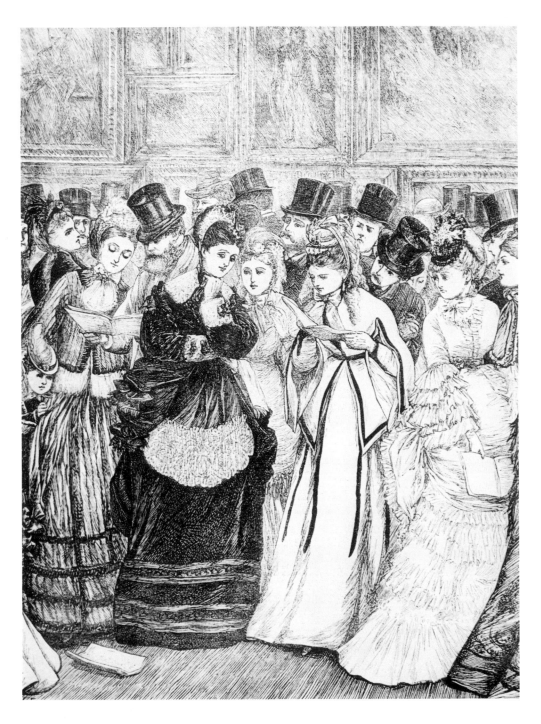

25. MEE (Mary Ellen Edwards), 'At the Royal Academy', 1871. Engraving.
The Graphic. (Photo: Julie Phipps)

Regrettably, the fame of women in male-dominated fields must always be dependent on the memories of men, just as their initial success must have been dependent on men's prejudices, and it is salutary to recall that William Frith was the sponsor of many female students at the RA and other schools in the 1870s and 1880s. It is telling of his own circumscribed view of art that the names he mentions here are all painters or watercolourists: he is only concerned with his own medium. Female sculptors he ignores, as he does graphic artists or workers in other media not considered fine art.

In comparison, to develop a perception of the contingent character of fame or reputation, we can consider from twenty years earlier a book that was intended to be, and became, a standard work: Ottley in his *Biographical Dictionary* had thought Mrs Annie Bartholomew, Carpenter and Martha and Annie Mutrie worthy of mention. While in 1874, Sarah Tytler (Henrietta Keddie), in her more modest volume *Modern Painters and their Paintings*, found room for Boyce, Ward, Carpenter, Jemima Blackburn/Wedderburn, the Mutrie sisters and Amelia Paton/Hill.[5] At the end of the century, Ernest Chesneau, in his account of *The English School of Painting*, described an all-male scene, with the exceptions of Thompson and Kate Greenaway.[6] The fluctuation in reputation that these examples represent is, of course, not exclusive to female artists; but women's fame is based on precarious ground in the first place, determined by how well they fulfil certain conditions which are not of their making. And it is thus conditionally held, as well as being subject to the tides of fashion and bias – a point which is relevant to those artists cited in glowing terms during the nineteenth century (Howitt, Thornycroft, Bodichon, Osborn) but whose reputation now is negligible or even non-existent, and whose careers cannot appear here as case histories due to the paucity or inaccessibility of extant material, despite their success in their own time.[7] The five case histories that will follow here, then, must represent many others, as well as the individual artists; they tell us, not only about themselves, but about others like them also excluded from the history of art; and, further, they shed a new light on the artists and the art that *have* been enshrined by history.

Henrietta (Mrs E.M.) Ward

Henrietta Ward, one of the most freely praised female artists of the mid-century, and yet the one most often coupled with her

inevitably more celebrated male relations, demonstrates resoundingly the immense hindrance to the achievement of an independent
reputation which sharing the name and pedigree of other artists
presented to the mid-Victorian woman. During her lifetime her
relationship, first to the James Ward family, and secondly to Edward
Matthew Ward, hung around her neck like a millstone. When she
died in 1923, an obituary notice in *Connoisseur* spoke first of her
male relations; while in the relevant edition of *Who Was Who*, she
is identified not as a painter or an artist, but as her father's daughter,
her grandfather's grand-daughter, her uncle's niece and her great-
uncle's great-niece.[8] A more constructive observation of the
relations she bore to the art world was made by Sarah Tytler in
Modern Painters and their Paintings (1874):

> I may observe, in proof of the difficulty which the technicalities
> of art must present to women, that of all the women painters
> whom I have chronicled, I am not aware of one, unless it be Suor
> Plautilla, or Mrs Wells, with whose antecedents I am only partially
> acquainted, who did not overcome the difficulty, by the
> advantage of an early familiarity with art, from having been the
> daughter of a painter, or, at least, of an engraver.[9]

As the most successful female painter of her day, Ward stands for
the progress that was made by women artists in mid-Victorian
times, but at the same time the very nature of her success displays
the limitations of that progress.

Henrietta Ward was born in 1832, the only child of George and
Mary Ward (a son having died in infancy some time before). Her
father, George Raphael Ward, was an established painter and
engraver; her mother, Mary, an invalid, was a miniature painter of
considerable accomplishment; Henrietta's grandfather was the
painter James Ward, whose connections brought the painters
George Morland and John Jackson into the family circle.[10] Growing
up in such a family, she naturally came into contact with many
people for whom art was not only a livelihood but also a first love,
and it is not surprising that she was encouraged to develop the
interest in painting which she already showed when young. Her
grandfather James, whose favourite she was, 'watched over my
budding intelligence, fortified and directed me towards an artistic
goal . . . I could draw and paint before I could read'.[11] The
favourable aspects of such surroundings for an aspirant artist were
made much of by later commentaries on Ward's career: the *Art*

Journal's James Dafforne wrote in 1864:

> Talent, or genius, is very far, as a rule, from being hereditary; yet, it would be strange indeed if it were not sometimes found descending from one generation to another when the individual is surrounded, even from the cradle, by everything that would be able to develop, if not create, it. Such was the case with the lady whose name appears at the head of this notice. She is grand-daughter of James Ward, RA, whose brother was William Ward, an eminent engraver, and whose sister married Morland, and whose daughter was the wife of J. Jackson, RA. Moreover, Henrietta Ward is daughter of Mr George Raphael Ward, the well-known mezzotinto engraver, and at one time a miniature painter, and a frequent exhibitor at the Royal Academy . . . It would therefore have been singular had she not shown powerful evidence of the influences which have on all sides surrounded her whole existence. Art was her inheritance, and amidst it she has 'lived, and moved, and had her being'.[12]

She seems to have been a spoiled and precocious child, spending most of her time in adult company brought to the house by the family's cultural connections. The artist herself describes the situation on the second page of her autobiography, the main source of information for this account:

> As I lay in my cradle, a great many 'giants' of art and literature bent over me, gave me their benediction, and professed an admiration, even if they did not feel it, for the little child about whom my parents were already building castles in the air. Later, these same men and women of genius were my devoted playmates.[13]

Landseer, Leslie, Tom Moore and the Chalon brothers were among the Wards' regular visitors at their home in Fitzroy Square, an area which boasted a large proportion of well-known names among its residents at that time. Henrietta seems to have been alarmingly capable of meeting the demands of such a life:

> My environment must have been totally different from that of any child I have known; my friends were all grown up, yet I never wanted children as companions. On the few occasions that I attended children's parties, their games and dances did not interest. I felt too superior to dance with them; frankly, they bored me.[14]

Her father regularly took her to Academy occasions and meetings of the Chalcographic Society, as well as insisting on her accompanying him on any social call or business errand, so one can well imagine that her manner and conversation and her awareness of the workings of the art world were mature even by the 'little adult' standards of bourgeois Victorian childhood.

Despite the tendency of such an upbringing to exaggerate a child's gifts, Henrietta possessed genuine artistic talent (in the field of music as well as in painting),[15] and she had a drawing accepted at the Academy in 1846 when she was only 14. This was a large black and white drawing called 'Elizabeth Woodville parting from the Duke of York', now in the possession of the artist's family. It shows the mother and son seated in a medieval interior, competently but not outstandingly rendered.[16] The 1849 exhibition showed a piece by her,[17] and she had her first oil accepted there in 1850, 'Results of an Antwerp Marketing', a theme which she treated in various forms ('Antwerp Market', RA 1852). She says that her mother first taught her drawing, and her father and grandfather encouraged her in art, but once she met the young artist Edward Matthew Ward, in 1843, it seems that he became her main preceptor. At the time, he was 27 and she 11.

> Finding that I was interested in Art, Edward Ward became my critic, my drawings were shown, and he gave me many valuable casts to help in my studies. He taught me much that was helpful in drawing... I worked very hard, beginning each day at six in the morning, every hour being mapped out till the afternoon, when Edward would arrive to criticise my work and set me fresh tasks . . . Nothing that was meretricious or showy in art could ever deceive him; he saw to the heart of things, and he used to say that the source of all design was in Nature, and a knowledge of it was to be obtained only through earnest study of Nature.[18]

It is important to consider the extent of E.M. Ward's influence on her at this impressionable stage of her career, since later on, as an independent artist, she was often said by critics to produce work very like his.[19] At this time, she would no doubt have become very strongly impressed with his own style and method, not only because he became her principal instructor in art but also because she sat for him for several of his own paintings, including 'Temptation' (1843), 'The South Sea Bubble' (1847), 'Doctor Johnson's Audience with Lord Chesterfield' (1845) and 'The Fall of

Clarendon' (1846), whose creation she therefore observed. That the young woman conceived a strong affection for the older artist, which resulted ultimately in their marriage, must be seen as a powerful factor in the degree of credibility and authority which he had in her eyes at this time. Germaine Greer[20] discusses interestingly the effect that love has on the formulation (and performance) of women artists (although she fails to consider the example of Henrietta Ward, for whom her generalisations are valid). She comes to the conclusion that its overall effect is, unfortunately, negative: Henrietta Ward however, claimed otherwise.

Her vocation established, Henrietta Ward was set up in her own studio in a room in the family house, and she was enrolled at Sass's for some training more formal than the advice and criticism which she received in the family circle. It is quite probable that this latter move was decided on at the urging of Edward Matthew Ward, who exercised a proprietorial interest over her. She credits him with helping her to maintain a serious attitude to art: 'By example he set me a high standard which I, who loved him dearly, ever strove to reach.'[21] Henrietta and Edward became engaged in 1847, their intention being to marry after two years, when Henrietta would be 16. The parents' misgivings at the proposed match, however, frustrated the couple's passion enough to drive them to a secret marriage in May 1848, with the connivance of Edward's friend, Wilkie Collins.[22] It was not until the August that the pair let out their secret, when they left their respective homes on honeymoon, and the estrangement to which this period of familial conflict gave rise continued more or less until the deaths of all the parents. Once these domestic stresses were settled, or at least abated, Henrietta settled down to enjoy building a career. She later wrote of this period in her life:

> The joy of following a profession entirely to one's own satisfaction is a privilege known only to a few. Art never bores, but offers always fresh vistas of delight and fascination. My husband was a rising man, broad-minded enough to take pleasure in the fact that I too was an artist. I worked on my own lines, but found him always the kindest teacher, the most unfailing friend I have ever known.[23]

However, the conventional demands of a married woman's situation soon made themselves felt – 'babies, that truly feminine impediment'[24] – and she had her first child in 1850, followed by a second the next year, eventually bearing six more.[25] She wrote in her autobiography, on reflection:

> In my young days most people would have agreed . . . that a wife and mother had no right to be a practitioner in paint, and I think in most households it would have been rendered impossible by the husband's and relations' combined antagonism to the idea . . . My work required great concentration, and orders were strictly enforced that I was not to be disturbed during certain hours of the day . . . But there were exceptions; I was occasionally confronted by an alarmed servant coming to tell me of a domestic tragedy, some knotty point that could only be solved by the mistress of the house.[26]

(One is reminded of Charlotte Brontë writing her novels in between the domestic tasks of the kitchen.) Throughout her career, however, she put to professional use the resources which her domestic circumstances did offer, frequently using her children and the home setting as subjects for her pictures (e.g. 'God Save the Queen!', (1857) [fig. 26], 'The Morning Lesson' (1855); 'The Bath' (1858) 'Flora, a nursery sketch' (1858)).[27] Her record of exhibited works in her first years of married life is a very varied one, ranging from the historical mode which her early Academy drawing had adumbrated, through the literary and the domestic, including some portraiture on the way. From the first, she received critical attention, usually favourable in the first decade of her exhibiting career. In 1851, the Academy saw 'The Pet Hawk' and 'Rowena' ('a very graceful work');[28] in 1852, 'Antwerp Market', which was bought by the Preston collector, Bashall.[29] Critical commentary on her work quickly adopted the stance that it was to retain until changing ideas rendered it unacceptable to claim that she was 'very good for a woman'.

As the 1850s proceeded and then gave way to the 1860s, skilled and confident works by women became more and more common, so the hitherto exceptional standard of Ward's work was less commented on. But certainly in the mid-1850s it was, generally, with impressed surprise that her anecdotal historical scenes and domestic vignettes were alike greeted: 'Mrs E.M. Ward in her very charming study, "The May Queen", has painted with an almost masculine vigour', wrote the *Athenaeum* critic on the RA in 1856. Her previous year's exhibit at the Academy brought similar responses: it was the 'Morning Lesson', which the *Art Journal* described as a work 'of great merit – sound and forcible to a degree we very rarely find in the labour of a lady's hand'. While the year before, her 'Scene from the Camp at Chobham' was praised thus in the *Art Journal*: 'as the work of a lady it exhibits great intellectual power. It is full of Art-knowledge of a matured order.'[30]

The *Athenaeum* critic raised the other point of criticism which was to remain consistent for the artist's works, that of her relation to her teacher and husband:

> A stout Highlander is teaching his child the use of the musket; while the mother who is watching in the background, watches him with a smile of interest. The rude fittings-up of the camp make a picturesque background and the details and faces are painted with a masculine firmness. The arrangement of colour, the red and black, and the tone of flesh, remind us of Mr Ward; and it is natural that the pupil of such a master would catch something of this mannerism and of his somewhat French colour. The affected sternness of the father's discipline, and the gravity of the soldier's child are exceedingly well given.[31]

The technical skill by which these early works impressed can be attributed in part to the fact that the artist kept up her basic education at this time, continuing at Sass's and having the resolution to attend the RA Schools' lectures for students, although women were unwelcome.[32] According to a later account, the instruction she sought in these years was primarily in the figure, an element on which, of course, many women's works fell down.[33] At the same time, it was inevitable that she should be advised and corrected by her husband.

Ward's singularity was that she was a female historical painter; but this subject-matter only gradually emerged as her speciality. The 1850s established her as a domestic painter, with some excursions into the literary ('Rowena' (1851), from Scott's *Ivanhoe*, and 'The May Queen' (1856) from Tennyson's poem) and, towards the end of the decade, a move towards a more substantial theme. In 1858, the *Athenaeum* reported, 'Mrs Ward, so rumour has it, makes an ambitious advance this year: – leaving the scene of domestic drama for the historical field. Her subject is said to be "Howard's Farewell" . . . a good subject in good hands.'[34] Such ambition, backed up in practical terms by exhibition, not only at the Academy but also at the SFA and in the provinces, was approved even by critics who feared 'masculinity' in women's works, and she went from

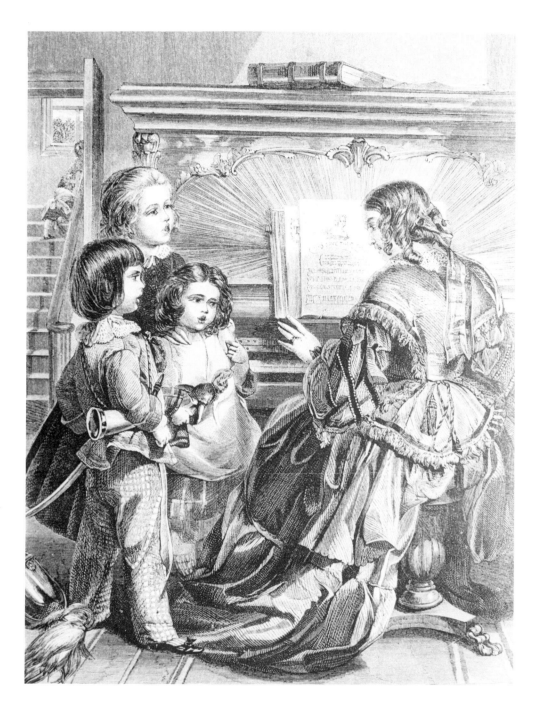

26. Anonymous engraving after Henrietta Ward, 'God Save the Queen', 1857.
Art Journal, 1864. (Photo: Julie Phipps)

strength to strength, gravitating towards a favourite subject area which could best be described as historical genre. Even without seeing all the works which she produced in this period of greatest success (1855-70), one can sense her increasing confidence and popularity from the continuing compliments of the never easily won art press. 'Howard's Farewell to England' (1858) was greeted thus by the *Art Journal*'s critic:

> . . . the most important work we have seen from the hands of this lady . . . it surpasses the productions of many of her masculine and even highly reputed contemporaries . . . in conception, arrangement, and execution, it leaves nothing to be desired.[35]

In reviewing the winter exhibition in 1862, the *Art Journal*'s critic concluded: 'This accomplished lady undoubtedly ranks among the best artists of our time.'[36]

The same year, the artist's status was reflected in being selected as the subject of no.77 in the *Art Journal*'s series 'British Artists, their style and character', articles published monthly in the magazine with two or three illustrations of the artist's work and on average two pages of biographical and critical commentary. The author James Dafforne concluded thus:

> Mrs Ward is still young, both in years and practice; we may therefore expect her future life to produce even richer fruit than any yet seen from her hands: we see no reason why she should not attain the highest position in historical painting.[37]

The favour with which this particular journal regarded Ward can be confirmed by the memoirs of its long-standing editor, Samuel Carter Hall, where he describes the artist as 'the accomplished lady whose works take rank with those of any painter of either sex which the age has produced'.[38] It must be pointed out, however, that S.C. Hall and his wife Anna Maria were close friends of the Wards: it was on such partiality that critical support depended, for the majority of artists.

Conservative voices put pressure on the artist to devote more attention to the less challenging domestic works which she frequently showed, and (the implication being) to leave to her husband the historical dramas in which he, unarguably, was skilled.[39] Her historical scenes, however, nearly always have some domestic content, or a familial context, although at the same time they stretched her powers of composition and expression visibly more than her homely subjects. The complexity of such scenes as 'Palissy the Potter' (1866) [fig. 28] at Leicester, 'Queen Mary quitting Stirling Castle' (1863) [fig. 8], 'Lady Jane Grey at Sion House' (1868) [fig. 27], or 'George III and his family at Windsor' (1872) at Liverpool, contrasts satisfyingly with the compositional simplicity and uncomplicated frontality of 'The first step' (1860).[40] Whether in a domestic scene or a historical one, Ward introduced an imaginative interest in accessory, in subdivision of space, and natural figural relationships into most of her works. One finds these qualities in equal measure in, say, 'Elizabeth Fry visiting Newgate' (1876) and 'God save the Queen!' (1857) [fig. 26] although the former remains a more interesting and consequential work because it challenges the artist's lived experience and demands more in terms of imagination and range of figural type and lighting effect.[41] However, the *Athenaeum* considered the 'Morning Lesson' in 1855: 'Though not perhaps equal to her picture of last year, in power, is superior to it – and to all her former works – in the delicacy of its sentiment.'[42] The same paper welcomed her 1862 'The Despair of Henrietta Maria' with: 'We trust Henrietta Ward will not abandon the painting of children. Who else will make the beauty of our little ones immortal?'[43] The same bias was expressed thus by the *Saturday Review*:

> Mrs E.M. Ward enters this year upon the domain of her husband, and produces a theatrically historical picture, 'Scene at the Louvre in 1649'. This picture purports to represent the 'despair' of Henrietta Maria on learning the fate that has befallen her husband at Whitehall. Can this demonaic countenance be taken for *despair*, or even as representing the beautiful queen of Charles I under the most unfavourable circumstances? Subjects of this kind are at best uninteresting, and least of all fitted for a lady's pencil . . . Surely it is better for a lady to paint the simple beauty of children, than to invest a beautiful Queen, when struck down by woe, with so extravagant an expression.[44]

The artist did not totally dispel the prejudice that she should be better occupied with domestic subjects as she continued to exhibit such pictures. While her principal exhibits treated historical themes, she treated domestic subjects as successfully, in technical terms, as she did the grander type of work. Some critical comment resisted for a long time the unwelcome notion that the latter might

141

be her preferred subjects: 'This year, as last, Mrs Ward has ventured on historical ground', wrote the *Times* critic in 1863, some five years after her first positively historical work had been shown at the Academy.

The artist's command of her medium can be but partially verified from remaining located works since they are so few, but it is interesting to set their evidence against the observations made in the 1860s and 1870s by critics, whose main theme always was that the picture in hand was the best that they had ever seen from the artist – although that did not prevent them making comments on the defects she displayed in the work. Her consistently strong points were not unanimously agreed upon, but her overall skill was often confirmed. Thus, 'In power of conception, arrangement of colour, and vigour of execution, this work may fairly claim recognition amongst the best efforts of modern Art' ('Episode in the life of Mary Queen of Scots' (1863); 'The picture is a thoroughly genuine work, easy in style and bright in colour' ('God save the Queen!' (1857)).[45] Her colour and her handling were most debated: 'These [pictures], if somewhat heavily handled, show much feeling for colour that ought to be refined and made brilliant' ('Two of my Pets' and 'The Toy Basket' (1862)); 'Mrs Ward's colouring is not factitiously brilliant; in truth, it is rather opaque and heavy; but it has been carefully arranged not to make a show of craft' ('Palissy the Potter' (1866) [fig. 28]); 'The execution has force as well as delicacy, the colour brilliancy; the realism of accessories could scarcely be more complete' ('Sion House' (1868)); ' "Morning Lesson" is crude and glaring at first sight, and in inspection wants refinement; yet the painting talent in it is very considerable' ('Morning Lesson' (1855)); 'excellent in drawing and colour, and the whole treatment of the subject shows both dramatic feeling and great technical skill . . . in parts, there is a certain garishness of colour and abuse of highlights' ('Sion House' (1868)).[46] The diversity of critical opinion does not, however, obscure her evident feeling for composition and, closely related, for clarity of narrative, perhaps more crucial features in her chosen genre than either colouring or handling. 'Chatterton' (1873) [pl. II], one of the few works from her heyday which survives, supports praise for her compositional abilities, while confirming that her drawing can be defective. While her touch is delicate it is not tentative, and the expressions of her characters interesting and true. 'Palissy' shows a tendency to melodramatic exaggeration in pose and a heavy use of colour, while affirming the frequent praise for

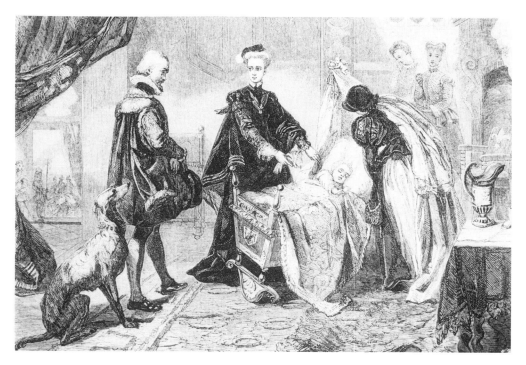

27. Henrietta Ward, 'Sion House, 1553', 1868. Oil on canvas. Private collection.
(Photo: Christie's)

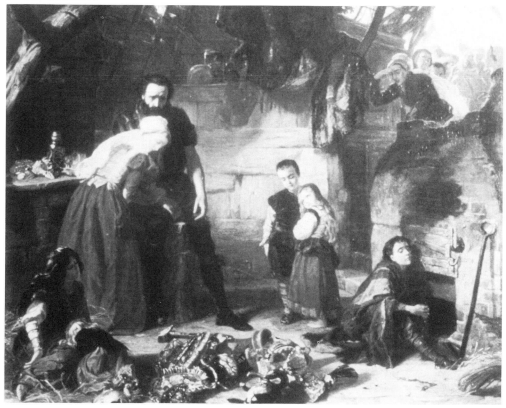

28. Henrietta Ward, 'Palissy the Potter', 1866. Oil on canvas. Leicestershire
Museums and Art Galleries, Leicester.

her eye for accessory, also to be noted in 'Chatterton'.

An element of Ward's artistic activity which contributed greatly to her prestige in her time was her connection with the royal family. She had many portrait commissions of royalty to her name and taught various of the royal children privately and later at her school in Lowndes Square. The Wards' connection with Queen Victoria began in 1854, when Edward received a commission for the new Palace of Westminster.

The royal couple, keen to invest this major event of public patronage with their personal support, made frequent visits to the Ward home and studio in Upton Park, Slough (as they did to the workplaces of other artists involved in the scheme) to express their interest in the progress of the fresco designs. An enduring relationship arose out of these beginnings, and Henrietta recorded in her autobiography that the royal pair 'often looked in on us as we worked . . . The Queen was clever at drawing and showed me most of her work.'[47] One wonders how the two women suited each other. Though no feminist, the artist had signed the 1859 memorial to the Council of the Royal Academy petitioning for entry for women to the Schools, and in recalling her attendance at the students' lectures in the early 1850s later wrote:

> Personally, I feel that the RA-ship should be open to women equally with men, for there is no sex in Art, and it is pure selfishness that has excluded women from this honour, with the exception of Mary Moser and Angelika Kauffmann.[48] [fig. 23]

But the professional discrimination she suffered on account of her sex, though it was recognised during her career on many an occasion by different quarters of the press,[49] does not seem to have outweighed her essential conservatism, which must have endeared her to Victoria. It is notable that her heroines were not women of her own day, and the modern women she did depict were shown in traditionally feminine roles: nurse, mother, wife. Although they are often shown executing those functions unsupported by men, it is apparent from their comfortable surroundings that they, like the artist herself for most of her life, had adequate male support in a conventionally respectable way. On her husband's death she received a Civil List pension 'in recognition of his Services to Art': though this may have been a way of approving her work too, it remained the only form of public recognition that women could receive for their involvement in art.

The death of the artist's husband in 1879, followed by that of her father in 1880, left her in her late forties with eight children to support, the eldest 30 years old but the youngest still a dependant. Her reputation was established but she was not the connoisseur's darling that, among women, Rosa Bonheur had proved to be.[50] She resolved the financial uncertainty of her situation by opening a school 'for the art education of young ladies' in Lowndes Square. She later claimed in her autobiography that there was no other similar establishment in London at the time; the great demand which apparently greeted it is, therefore, quite understandable:

> When I used to arrive in the morning from Windsor, I was soon accustomed to finding the hall full of parents and guardians, wishing to place their daughters under my charge. I was obliged to refuse many applicants, as well as offers of partnership in the school.[51]

Tessa McKenzie's *The Art Schools of London* of 1895, described the artist's school in the following terms:

> Although professional pupils study with Mrs Ward, her classes appeal most particularly to ladies who wish to have the moderate talent which they possess trained so as to be a source of interest and amusement to them, and not a means of earning a livelihood. Situated in Belgravia, the studio is chiefly patronised by the daughters of people in the higher ranks of society, and to encourage steadfastness of purpose in the youthful amateur mind is the chief aim in Mrs Ward's artistic instruction.[52]

In the original press accounts of her school, however, such exclusiveness was not implied. 'Parents whose daughters are anxious to pursue Art either as a profession or an accomplishment will be exceedingly fortunate in obtaining the aid thus brought within their reach', reported the *Art Journal* in 1879.[53] The artist, however, recorded that her patrons were the Duke and Duchess of Connaught, the Princess Louise, and the Duke and Duchess of Edinburgh, while her visiting tutors included Alma-Tadema, Briton Rivière, Horsley, Marcus Stone, Frank Dicksee, Fildes, Frith, Millais, Hook, and Calderon – a roll-call which guaranteed to recommend itself to conservative opinion. By 1887, an article in *The Lady* indicates that Henrietta Ward's school was established – 'her well-known and successful art classes', writes the author[54] – and a few months later in the same periodical, a review of an exhibition of the students' work hints at the sort of work which was done there:

> All the principal branches of Art were represented, from careful studies from the cast to portraits far beyond the usual point of excellence attained by the ordinary amateur, oil and watercolour painting from still life, and sketches from Nature.[55]

By this time, Ward's art was old-fashioned, and it is tempting to attribute her decreasing rate of exhibition in the 1880s, not only to increasing age and to the school demanding much of her energy, but also to an awareness that the latter decades of the nineteenth century demanded a different style and other themes than were the staple of her art. Her connection with the SFA (by now the Society of Lady Artists) continued until 1886, and her contributions to the Academy, though less and less frequent, continued until the year of her death.[56] Historical themes became a thing of her past, and the artist turned to landscape and domestic scenes, not necessarily animated. Her daughters, Eva and Flora, followed in their mother's footsteps, appearing at the Academy from 1872 and 1873 respectively, while the artist's son Leslie, became well known in another branch of art as the cartoonist 'Spy'. In 1911 the artist published her *Reminiscences* and the year after her death, another autobiography *Memories of Ninety Years* was published (Ward was 91 when she died in 1923).

Henrietta Ward, like many other prominent Victorians, lived beyond her time. In the words of the obituary notice published in the *Connoisseur* in 1924:

> The death of Mrs Edward Matthew Ward, which took place in July last, removes an interesting and noteworthy figure from the world of art. An artist herself, and coming of a family who for nearly a hundred and fifty years have always included distinguished artists among their members, she formed a link with long bygone generations of painters who had transmitted to her aesthetic traditions now forgotten.[57]

Joanna Mary Boyce (Mrs H.T. Wells)

Rather like Turner and Girtin, Ward's position as the foremost of British female artists in her day would have been almost certainly overturned if Joanna Mary Boyce had lived longer than she did. A review of Ward's 'Mary Queen of Scots' (1863) said, 'This fine work, firmly painted and drawn, and telling its tale with much clearness, seems to promise that the painter will supply the loss which we sustained lately in Mrs Wells.'[58] Boyce (who became Wells in 1857) died in 1861 after childbirth. The *Critic*'s obituary notice supports the suggestion that she was extraordinary:

> Seldom have the tidings of the premature loss of a gifted artist had so painful a significance for us, as those which abruptly struck our ear the other day, of the unexpected death on Monday the 15th inst. in her 30th year of Mrs H.T. Wells. In her, English art has lost more than it knows – unquestionably one whose works give intimation of qualities rare in any artist and in this case fated never to be developed in full . . .[59]

Behind the rhetoric endemic to obituary notices lies a compliment unusual for women artists of this period, and typical of the critical esteem in which Joanna Mary Boyce was held.

She had been born in 1831, the third of five children, the eldest of whom was George Price Boyce, who became a watercolour landscapist of the Pre-Raphaelite circle. Though the family was resident in London (her father carried on the business of wine merchant in the city until 1842, when he changed his occupation to that of pawnbroker), she spent her schooldays in Ramsgate and other places, and evinced an interest in, as well as an aptitude for, art at an early age – at 12 she was already copying with the encouragement of her brother. (After toying with the idea of adopting the profession of architect, he decided in 1849 to become a landscape painter.[60]) Like many women of this period who eventually chose art as their major activity, the girl seems to have been equally gifted in music, but her energies were evidently firmly channelled towards painting and drawing by the time she had reached her late teens, for the artist's descendants have sketch-books dated by her summer 1843, 1844 and 1845, showing sketches made at the seaside, in the country, of figures, cottages, etc.

In 1849 she entered Cary's, and on holiday that year other members of the family recalled, 'every day George and Joanna went out sketching'.[61] By this time George was 'in' with a certain artistic set, the result of being a student at the Royal Academy Schools. Although this involvement eventually drew him away from his sister, at this point in Joanna's development he was very useful to her. Joanna's closeness to George at this period led, not only to William Frith and his brother visiting the house to see Joanna's and George's sketches, but also to Joanna giving up her studies completely in June 1850 to nurse George through an illness from which he did not fully recover until November.

However, she returned to Cary's and at the beginning of 1852 started at Leigh's. During this period she was in the company of other artists – a letter of May 1851 describes a *soirée* at E.M. and Henrietta Ward's where the guests included C.R. Leslie, William Frith, Richard Ansdell, Augustus Egg, Charles Landseer and Frank Stone – attending lectures with her father, and making portrait studies. She sketched wherever she went – a crayon and chalk skyline study is inscribed 'Edgbaston August 51 JMB' – and was constructing an aesthetic which, to judge from her diary and sketchbook scribblings, was based to a degree on Ruskinian and Pre-Raphaelite thought. (Turner, she wrote in her notebook on 19 December 1851, was 'England's greatest artist' and her father took her and her brother to Turner's funeral on the 30th of that month.) Joanna Mary Boyce was, very apparently, an earnest and diligent student of her art, understanding the profession of painter to be one which required a whole person with an active mind and lively thoughts. Her sketchbooks of the early 1850s are teeming, not so much with drawings as with quotations, literary food for thought, notes of the books she is reading and the lectures she has attended. All these jottings tend to a serious and responsible attitude equally to life and to art:

> It is nothing in what ratio we get on comparative with another so that we work *honestly, constantly painfully ourselves this* if *we do* we shall never be behind. Keeping in mind we must work as *to God*, and not as to men and improve to the utmost the talent given the loins girt and the lamp burning.

> Know what you have to do and do it.
> Turner vide Ruskin.

> Books to read . . . life of Robert Wall, Fichte, Stilling [?], Pascal's letters, *Sartor Resartus, Lavengro,* Shelley, Hood's poems, Herbert's Poems.

> Genius is in truth nothing but a *strong desire of knowledge* and the *spirit* of *industry* is its *truest mark.*

Such intellectualism is a mark of the 'modern woman' which, in her

148

striving for a sense of independent self and in her reluctance to marry, the artist later shows herself to be. This is particularly evident in her exchanges with Henry Tamworth Wells, who wished to marry her.[62]

Her sense of herself as a *woman* artist is evidenced by other notes in her sketchbooks at this time, when she was in her early twenties. In 1852 her own recommended reading includes *Women of France, Women of Christianity, Memoirs of Margaret Fuller Ossoli,*[63] while she transcribes a piece from a life of Charlotte Corday thus:

> Fidelity to its own impulses is the test of a noble nature – She seemed to feel instinctively that great thoughts are always better nursed in the heart's solitude, that they can only lose their native depth and intensity by being revealed too freely before the indifferent gaze of the world.

An unattributed note, probably written in 1852, reads: 'He saw for *woman* as for *man*, no other limits than those which the *intellectual powers* of the individual prescribed.'

She was bringing a similar intensity to her technical studies at this period, too: she attended Leigh's from 2 February 1852 at least three times a week, and was toying with Henry Wells' idea that she should go to Paris to study (as he had done). Her sketchbooks, again, give evidence of the thoroughness of her approach:

> Seldom or never paint highlights on to transparent colour . . . in painting a portrait, make a careful drawing or outline on the canvas by this means you learn the faces and become familiar with form and expression . . . In first sketch of chalk drawing [?] put in light and shade in white and stump freely and decidedly [?] put frills round throats a little lower than in nature. A man's head is generally 9" long. Measure your sitter from the inner corner of the eye to chin.

> The best way I have tried as yet of painting the hands and indeed all flesh is to model them in venetian red and white only – when dry glaze gently with rose madder and raw sienna and work into it and get the shadows as true as possible not bright in colour and when dry work in where wanted delicate opaque grey when dry finish with touches of opaque and transparent colour as required . . .

The sources of some of these strictures are given, some are personal experiences – she included many detailed notes from a lecture series she attended on the human form by John Marshall, probably in 1852. Her art education took a particular step forward, however, when she went to Paris in April 1852 with her father, staying from early April until mid-May. Wells 'advised me where to go in Paris', and she records an admiration for Scheffer and Delaroche. Though to a modern observer, such preferences seem somewhat conservative, Scheffer's influence was to come through in 'Elgiva' (1855) [pl. III] to no harmful effect, and Delaroche's impact was to give way to that of Couture (in 'La Veneziana', 1860 [fig. 7]) and to the influence of older established examples such as the Venetian masters. It must be noted, though, that to admire Delaroche and Scheffer was not out of the way, in 1852: Mrs Grote's biography of Scheffer, published three years after the artist's death (1860), is symptomatic of the esteem in which he was held by some quarters of modern opinion.[64] Boyce, however, did not choose to study under either Delaroche or Scheffer when she later went to study in Paris (though she apparently kept her good opinion of them at least until 1855, when she described them as 'two names in the highest walk of French art').[65] At home, at this time, she certainly admired Millais, a respect which can perhaps be seen reflected in the artist's first eventual Academy exhibit, 'Elgiva', since this uncommon subject was one which Millais treated in 1847.[66]

Joanna Boyce's father died in September 1853, an event that checked her industrious and enthusiastic progress for a while. Although she was taken out of town (to Torquay) to distract her from the sorrow she felt at the loss of such an encouraging parent and supporter to her ambition, in November her diary records: 'I began painting my sketch – unsatisfactory – idle – Have a sense of something wanting to give me energy – the dear encouraging eyes of my darling father, to whom alone I was sure of giving pleasure.' Still, she produced work, though on a small scale: there are some tiny children's heads in oil from this period, including the 'Little Red-haired Boy' otherwise known as the 'Babbacombe Boy' still in the possession of the artist's family. At the beginning of 1854 she commenced what was to be her first success, a head of Lizzie Ridley, sister of Joanna's brother Matthias's fiancée, in the guise of 'Elgiva'. She began with a chalk drawing on 1 February, and by March recorded that both George and Wells were pressing her to send the work when finished to the Academy exhibition, though she was reluctant to do so so soon after her father's death. At this time the tendency to earnest application and self-discipline that has been noted already as a feature of her memoranda to herself, came in useful and shows itself again in her notebooks:

> A passionate desire and an unwearied will can perform impossibilities or what seem such to the cold and feeble. If we do but go on some unseen path will open among the hills. We must not allow ourselves to be discouraged by the apparent disproportion between the result of simple efforts and the magnitude of the obstacles to be encountered. Nothing good and great is to be obtained without courage and industry.

This passage from Sharpe's essays is to be found in a notebook dating from 1854. In line with such sentiments, she enlisted at the School of Design in April 1854 and made fitful weekly attendances, working in her own painting room at home, though her mother's opposition to her painting was a great worry to her. (On what this opposition was based is uncertain.)

Perhaps through her attendance at the School as well as through the artistic connections of George with the Pre-Raphaelite circle, the artist was at this time in contact with several other young women aspiring to be artists. Her notebooks mention Bertha Farwell and Jane Todhunter:[67] there is a pencil sketch of a woman at an easel inscribed 'Miss Todhunter, spring 54', while in the summer of 1854 she went sketching with Farwell. She was reading Anna Mary Howitt's *An Art Student in Munich*, though she thought little of this artist's work at the Portland Gallery that spring, describing it in her diary as 'not at all marvellous'.[68] Even so, in October and November of that year, Boyce records visits to the Howitts', with and without the Farwells, while there is talk of her going to Dusseldorf or Munich (presumably to study), which must have been an idea derived from Howitt's experience. Also, a notebook from this period contains a sketch of the frontispiece to Henry Vizetelly's *Evangeline* of 1850, by Jane Benham, who was a great friend of Howitt, having been with her in Munich.

Boyce's artistic efforts of 1854 came to fruition when her 'Elgiva' was accepted at the Academy in 1855, and was greeted very favourably. Ruskin noticed the painting in the supplement to his *Academy Notes*. This indicates that someone (an interested party, perhaps) had pointed the work out to him as worthy of note. He especially eulogised its expression and handling, saying:

If this artist, looking always to Nature and her own thoughts for the thing to be expressed, will strive to express them, with some memory of the great Venetians in her treatment of each separate hue, it seems to me that she might entertain the hope of taking place in the very first rank of painters.[69]

The *Illustrated London News*, in response, noted that Ruskin 'has discovered a promising genius in Miss Joanna Mary Boyce'.[70] Ford Madox Brown referred to the work as 'the best head in the rooms',[71] and the *Athenaeum*, recalling it six years later, declared ' "Elgiva", a head, is remembered by every artist who saw it'.[72] Despite the encomiums, however, the picture was still in the family long after the artist's death, appearing in the sale of George's possessions in 1897.[73]

As well as this success, 1855 marked the beginning of an issue which was to continue unresolved for some time: this was the question of marriage to Henry Wells, who had been pressing her to commit herself to him for some time. She was very reluctant, using words like 'slavery' and 'dependence' and 'degraded' in her letters of demur to him. She agreed, however, to become engaged, on the understanding that this state should last two or three years. Obviously of much greater excitement was the change in her fortunes brought about in the latter part of the year when, in September, she went to Paris with her mother and brother Bob. In October, Mrs Boyce returned home, and Joanna was left to study. She contemplated asking Rosa Bonheur to take her on as a pupil, but finally enrolled at Thomas Couture's *atelier*, where the most striking aspect of her studies was the life class.[74] She writes home (*not* to her mother, from whom she was anxious to keep knowledge of the precise nature of the studies she was pursuing) that although she had felt anxious and reluctant about it at first, she was now sure that any girl could study from the nude model as though it were a bunch of flowers or a landscape, and come to no harm! The sketches from the nude in the notebooks which survive include male and female models, but some are studies very evidently from the statue or cast, rather than from life.

From the evidence of the notebooks, she worked a lot in chalk and charcoal, but she also painted, for while in Paris she completed a portrait head of Mme Hereau, the landlady at the pension where she stayed, and she began a large oil of 'Rowena offering the Wassail cup to Voltigern'. This was, in George's words, 'painted from a handsome Polish girl at Paris',[75] and was rejected at the

Academy in 1856, though its confident handling and daring composition gave it much character. This work seems to have either disappeared or been destroyed, and is known only from a photograph which is dated August 1857. To what extent the stay in Paris influenced her art – other than simply bringing it to a higher level of accomplishment – is a tantalising question. The general impression she relates in her letters of the modern French school was that she thought its pictures were better than their English counterparts.[76] She especially noted Delacroix as a fine colourist, although she regretted his extravagant treatment of subject. But her opinions are more precisely conveyed by the pieces which she wrote for the *Saturday Review*, solicited by the establishing editor of that journal, Jones, who was a friend of the Boyces. Her two columns, 'Remarks on some of the French Pictures at the late Paris Exposition', appeared in December 1855, followed by a review of the Academy show in five instalments in May 1856.[77] She picks out on the French scene Cogniet, Rousseau, H. Vernet, Meissonier, Delacroix, Ricard and a few others. Her enthusiasm for the French painters, however, is somewhat modified in her Academy criticism, where she makes a case for what amounts to the Englishness of English art, praising especially the Pre-Raphaelite painters:

> The Pre-Raphaelite movement has done some good, and will do more; and the extravagances that its leaders fell into in some of their first pictures, such as Millais's 'Carpenter's Shop', were but the necessary results of a great change . . . they have taught us by their pictures, aided by Ruskin's words, that an artist's strength lies in a child-like sincerity, and in the shunning of pride, which is always allied to servility. If Frost and Pickersgill, and two or three other young men who were talked of as 'rising artists' some years ago, had learnt the lesson, we should not find them sinking deeper and deeper into the slough into which indolence and pride have led them . . . The ridicule and the narrow-minded criticisms that have abounded in the press against the Pre-Raphaelites and their champion have fallen harmless – so far, at least, as the principles for which they have fought are concerned. The great men in the group have walked calmly onward, heedless of the strife of trivial tongues, and the walls of the Academy during these last few years have been but the theatre of their triumph.

The Ruskinian alliance which she makes between artistic and moral excellence characterises the whole article – she had opened her review thus:

> Six picture exhibitions are now open in London, containing all that our artists have been able to accomplish for 1856. Have they worked that we may be mentally and morally the better for their labours, or merely that our purses may be lighter, and our rooms furnished with pleasing pictures? Money, we know, with artists as with other men [sic], is unavoidably, and not always pre-judicially, a main incentive to sustained exertion; but let us hope that a simple love of nature and art, an earnest striving after excellence, and, with some at least, impatience to give forcible utterance to the multitude of thoughts within, have had their place too.

Her espousal of Pre-Raphaelite values – of industrious seeking after the visual truth, of authentic though it might be unusual colour, of a certain favoured physical type thought to express spiritual as well as physical beauty – comes through in most of her works, more and less combined with an awareness of the Renaissance inheritance which she derived equally from Ruskin and from her time in Paris. The precision of 'Elgiva' [pl. III], the earthy but vivid colouring of 'The Heathergatherer' (1859) [pl. IV], the minute handling of 'Sidney' (1859) [pl. V] and the red-haired boys (1850s),[78] testify as much as the angularity of a nativity drawing in her sketchbook with its Siddal-like madonna, and the vivid colouring of 'Do I like Butter?' (1861) and the 'Bird of God' (1861), to a Pre-Raphaelite sensibility which yet retains an individual appearance. This might explain why critics did not specifically ally her to the movement. Her preference for one or two models of distinctive appearance, red-haired and in some treatments not unlike Elizabeth Siddal facially, is another Pre-Raphaelitism: she used Charlotte and Lizzie Ridley, and Lizzie Turnbull, over and over. Even her little boys from the Welsh trip have red hair! At the same time, it is significant that the female figures in her work always appear strongly individual if they are adult: the heathergatherer, the Venetian woman, the mother in 'The Child's Crusade' (1860) [pl. VI], Rowena, the unfinished 'Sybil' and 'Elgiva' establish the dominant psychological note of the work by their faces and forms. In thus far, Pre-Raphaelitism could not wholly capture her, with its male-defined females, iconic or decorative, woven into the overall visual pattern of the picture. The artist planned a number of works which were unexecuted at her death, which do recall the world of Pre-Raphaelitism: it is tantalising to speculate on what she would have made of 'Autumn, from Keats', 'King Cophetua and the Beggar-Maid', 'Lady of the Castle', Charlotte Ridley as 'Catherine Sforza', which were listed by her as works to do in the near future.[79] Indeed, the unfinished 'Sybil', 'Gretchen' [fig. 29] and 'Undine' suggest that Boyce's style would have continued to take strength from Pre-Raphaelite tenets while remaining different from it, somewhat more robust – in a French-derived way – than its works habitually were. It is not insignificant that of the Pre-Raphaelite Brothers, it was Rossetti and Madox Brown who specifically praised her work.

Critics picked out her industry, vividness and force without attributing it, in fact, to Pre-Raphaelitism or to any other modern trend: some made parallels with Venetian old masters. 'No joy the blowing season brings' (1858) was described by the *Times* critic as 'a picture which, for power and gloomy impressiveness, seems to us to excel everything else here . . . It is, indeed, almost the only work in the room which rouses the mind to questioning'. 'The Heathergatherer' (1859) was, to the *Critic* reviewer, 'earnestly and vigorously painted'. 'Peep-bo!' (1861), wrote the *Illustrated London News* reviewer, is 'a work full of nature and feeling'.[80] She did not exhibit those works which might most nearly have been seen as Pre-Raphaelite ('Sidney', 'Shanklin', or the Babbacombe or red-haired boys) and critics would not know the industry which went into each work – there are countless preparatory sketches and studies for 'Peep-bo!', and for the central figure in 'Gretchen' – or the detailed landscape studies she made or the cloud-scapes which still remain in the artist's family. Thus her resounding talent was, singularly for a female artist, unrelated to any Svengali or *éminence grise*, and allowed to claim its very own credit.[81]

In May 1857, after spending a period in Brighton nursing the ever failing George, she started out for Italy with friends, including Henry Wells, and one result of this tour was her marriage to him in Rome in the last month of that year. She learnt Italian for the trip, and seems to have spent all hours of the day and night sketching and studying and painting, for her notebooks are full of studies of peasants working in characteristic costume, and of fellow travellers (e.g. a nun on the train from Nîmes to Arles on 4 June), of sketches inscribed Blois, Bordeaux, Pau, Biarritz, Lourdes (in May), which gave way to Spanish locations in June, which in turn become Italian locations in July, August and September. Also there are numerous portrait sketches, both anonymous and identified, from along the way. The stay in Italy included visits to Florence, Rome and Naples. While in Rome, she began 'The Child's Crusade' [pl. VI], which was not finished until 1860, but the most outstanding result of her Italian trip was 'La Veneziana' [fig. 7], which appeared in the RA show of 1861 (along with 'Peep-bo!' and 'The Heathergatherer' [pl. IV]).

Although the *Athenaeum*'s obituary referred to 'The Child's Crusade' as 'her most important work known to the public', [82] it was 'La Veneziana' which attracted more attention than any other of her works. The *Saturday Review* wrote:

> Mrs H.T. Wells vindicates her claim to be one of our best female painters by her striking 'Veneziana'. Here we have a marked female profile, sharply projected, like a Bellini, against a green background. The Venetian beauty has golden, not to say yellow, hair, and a vengeful expression which it is not pleasant to contemplate. But there is unusual force in the execution. [83]

It was this force, and the expression, which gave rise to much comment. The *Athenaeum*'s critic wrote as follows about the picture:

> Mrs H.T. Wells has a fine and characteristically sinister-looking study of a head, styled 'The Veneziana', a profile of a lady with small reptile-like eyes and tawny-coloured hair, rank and harsh; a cruel, square jaw and heavy, pitiless face. [84]

The obituary notice which came only a few months later in the same journal, declared: 'As a young and consequently incompletely practised artist, Mrs Wells' works erred rather in excess of strength than the common fault of feminine tameness. Her "La Veneziana", also now at the Academy, is an example of this.' [85] This says much, of course, about the common expectations of what women's art might be. The *Critic*'s obituarist trod the same ground, saying: 'To unbounded enthusiasm for art, to masculine and vigorous powers of mind were united in Mrs Wells an unmistakably feminine character.' [86] Her work strongly yet simply reflects the strong-minded woman evidenced by her own writings and by the opinions of her associates; Elizabeth Siddal wrote to D.G. Rossetti, on hearing of Joanna Boyce's death:

> It is indeed a dreadful thing about poor Mrs Wells. All people who are at all happy or useful seem to be taken away. It will be a

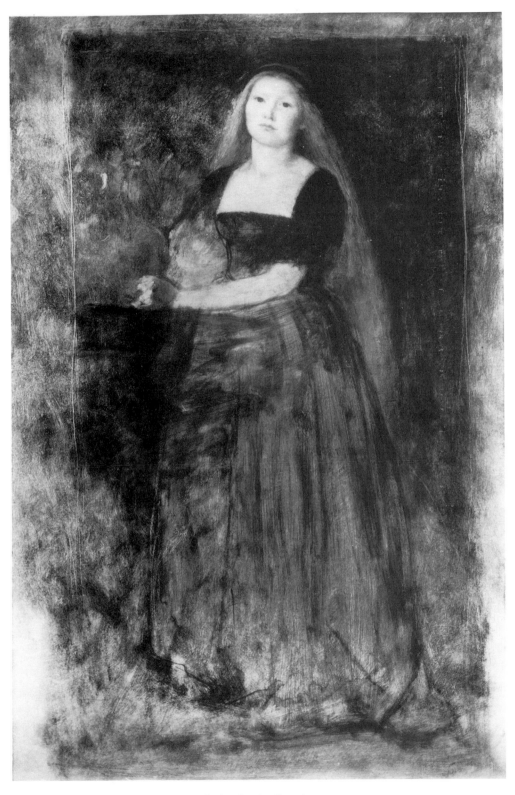

29. Joanna Boyce Wells, 'Gretchen', 1861 (unfinished). Oil on canvas.
Reproduced by permission of the Tate Gallery, London.

fearful blow to her husband for she must have been the head of the firm and most useful to him.[87]

Although the excess of emotion to which premature and unexpected death gives rise must be treated with some reservation as a guide to real assessment of character and achievement, it is obvious from Boyce's work that she was already, at 30, a confident and gifted artist with enough facility and strength of purpose to take her much further than she had thus far gone. She was referred to as the, or one of the, most gifted female painters of her time in Britain, not only at the time of her death but afterwards too:

> Miss Boyce was, in fact, much more of a 'painter' than most of the Pre-Raphaelites, her work being remarkable for warm, deep colouring and a true feeling for pigment . . . [These are] paintings which excite interest in a talent in many respects ahead of its own time.[88]

What struck contemporary judges most was her power, but to a later eye her variety is also impressive: she achieves a British *juste milieu*. Although most valedictories put her high in the ranks of the *women* painters of the time, it is interesting to note that the *Critic's* obituarist had the temerity and conviction to write, quite simply, without any sense at all of special gender-related pleading: 'Her untimely death is a real loss to the English school.'[89]

Emma Brownlow (King)

It was from Boyce's and Ward's generation that most of the women who became recognised as artists of note during the mid-century came. Those women, born around 1830, came into their twenties at the opening of the period and gained reputations on the shoulders of which the next generation could rise to equal standing. Osborn, Blunden, Solomon, for instance, were all born between 1829 and 1834. Equally, from this generation came the women who, though they did not become stars, swelled the tide of female artists which, as I have described, changed the ebb and flow of mid-Victorian art. One such, Emma Brownlow, was born in 1832, the youngest of three daughters. Her father, John Brownlow, was secretary to the Foundling Hospital in Coram Fields, St Pancras, and this institution dominated the family's life, although Emma's career eventually led her as far afield as Europe and Australia. Despite this unusual experience, she is a type of the preponderance of female artists in her time: consistent and ambitious over and above her genre, producing work by which she meant to earn money over a long period, while functioning also as a wife, mother and daughter, in a middle-class urban household.

She drew and painted from a very early age, though there is no evidence that art was in the family. There is no evidence of her receiving any training in art, and her juvenile sketches show a late maturing technically. Even so, the themes which occupied her, while being clearly drawn from contemporary trends in painting, illustration and satirical graphic art such as the middle-class family might know from magazines, for a teenage pencil are interestingly adult. A pencil drawing of 1848 depicts 'A "Special" taking leave of his Family', the separate expressions of distress in each member of the family well-observed though childishly rendered. A scene dated 1849, titled 'The Lecture', shows a skeletal speaker boring his apparently proletarian audience to sleep and flirtation, again with well-observed distinctions between the different characters but in crude and caricatural depictions. Brownlow's taste for social comment, strongly evident from these early pieces, regrettably did not persist until the time when her technical powers had developed to do such subjects pictorial justice. Another drawing, from May 1849, inscribed 'The Drawing-room and the Street' [fig. 30], used the popular two-part comparison between the haves and the have-nots, making its point through the contrast between the hedonistic upper classes and the oppressed poor. Very effectively – though whether by accident or design, at such a young age, is debatable – the upper-class scene pushes the destitutes' space to the right, compressing the paupers' picture-space into a strip narrower than it is high, while the space occupied by high society is broader than it is high, giving an effect of constriction on the one hand and of unrestricted expansion on the other. The use of shade on the side of the oppressed and light on the oppressors' side is also very telling, as is the fact that exchange is limited on the right-hand side to the landlord and the pauper group, while among the left-hand side crowd there is a multiplicity of exchanges taking place. Another drawing, 'The Fashion of the Day' (1850) [fig. 31], echoes this latter scene, showing the upper bourgeoisie at leisure, and tending to make fools of themselves, though their foolishness is silly rather than wicked. A more mature sketch is 'Vaccination by the Parish', dated May 1853 [fig. 32], which, with its informal and naturalistic composition and potential for expressive variety, could

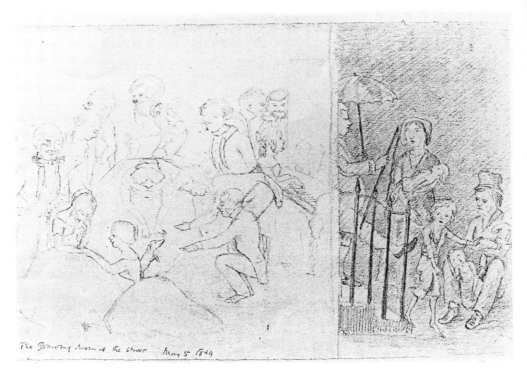

The Drawing room & the street   May 5 1849

30. Emma Brownlow, 'The Drawing-room and the Street', 1849. Charcoal on paper. Private collection. (Photo: Julie Phipps)

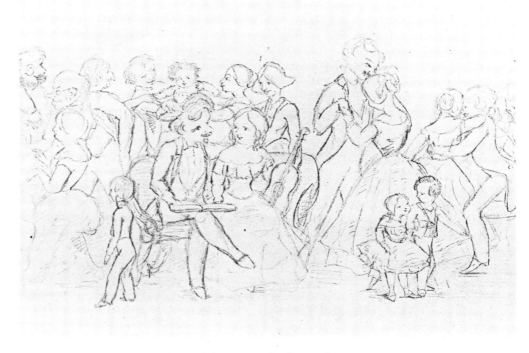

31. Emma Brownlow, 'The Fashion of the Day', 1850. Charcoal on paper. Private collection. (Photo: Julie Phipps)

have made a satisfying oil painting, though it seems not to have
been worked up.

Doubtless the Hospital environment encouraged a social con-
science in the young woman. To judge from the variety of gesture
and expression in these early drawings, many were observed from
actual experience, but they were still fanciful as pictures.
Brownlow's first exhibited picture, however, was based firmly on
her lived experience: 'The Foundling Girl' appeared at the
Academy in 1852, and was the first of a number of works which
arose from the artist's relation with the Hospital. It is only in these
works that her interest in socially critical subjects endures: in 1853,
a work called 'The Orphan' at the British Institution may have been
a Hospital-based picture; in 1858, 'The Foundling restored to its
Mother' [pl. VIII] at the Academy was a Hospital subject; while the
1860s saw 'The Christening' [pl. IX], 'The Sick-Room' [pl. X] and
'Taking Leave' [Pl. XI], as well as a more anecdotal piece, 'The
Orphan Friends', which was followed in 1877 by 'A Foundling girl
at Christmas Dinner'.⁹⁰

Brownlow's exhibiting career continued steadily over three
decades (she appears to have last exhibited in 1877, at the Society
of Lady Artists), including in its scope not only the main London
shows but also provincial exhibitions. From showing two or three
pictures a year in the 1850s, she graduated to a period in the
mid-1860s when she might exhibit a dozen pieces at various shows
in one season in London, the Midlands and the North of England.⁹¹
However, her production remained unevenly received critically
throughout her career, and, indeed, the materials in the possession
of her descendants show that, while the ideas she had for pictures
were many and varied, it was not always the most arresting or
stimulating that she chose to work up into exhibition paintings. She
exhibited almost exclusively in oil, but her preparatory work was
carried out in pencil and watercolour, and she continued to sketch
in pencil and charcoal for her own purposes. How many of her
sketches and plans for paintings were never worked up is
uncertain, since many of her exhibited titles remain unidentified.
Some works were lost between Britain and Australia, leaving no
record of what they were, while some paintings are still in various
hands in New Zealand, and are as yet unidentified. Some drawings
from the 1850s, though, were certainly made into exhibited works,
and contain ideas which surfaced again and again over the years in
her paintings. These include an interior with a poor, fatherless
family, dated September 1853, related to 'Cottage Interior' of 1853

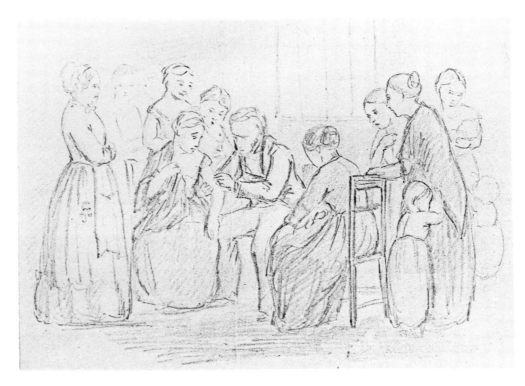

32. Emma Brownlow, 'The Vaccination', 1853. Charcoal on paper. Private collection. (Photo: Julie Phipps)

a drawing in what would nowadays be described as 'scraperboard' of a young woman in a kerchief with a basket under her arm, dated July 1856, which is related to many of the artist's later continental women workers and peasants; a slight drawing of a Breton-looking young woman in prayer, inscribed 'Evangeline', and dated October 1857; a cottage interior with an old woman sitting in the inglenook, dated 1859, and a similar scene with a young mother and child, dated April 1859. These drawings accurately suggest what the range of her exhibited subject-matter was to be: that is to say, what can be called domestic genre and continental genre, verging on the fancy picture on occasions.

Domestic scenes such as she exhibited during the 1850s ('Hush don't wake the Baby' (1853), 'Granny's Lesson' (1856), 'Helping Granny' (1857), 'Our little Brother' (1858), 'A Peep at the new Baby' (1859)) were common enough subjects for a female painter, but Brownlow did not have the domestic experience of such scenes (neither she nor her sisters were married at this point) and she was as doggedly middle-class as such subjects are plebeian. Brownlow managed gratifyingly often, however, to steer clear both of the voyeurism that such subjects often betrayed in the hands of the middle-class painter and the sentimentalism that made them attractive to the middle-class audience.

Her attempts to expand the genre, however, were not necessarily critically satisfactory: 'The Conscript's Departure' (1865), for instance, was described in the *Art Journal* as 'a subject beyond the artist's reach', while 'Between the Acts' (1866) was criticised as defective in its narration.[92]

The strand of continental genre winds its way through Brownlow's work almost from the start ('La Fille du Poissonnier', 1854, 'Left in Charge', 1860 [fig. 33]) and its long duration can be explained not simply by fashion but also by the fact that the artist travelled abroad both in the 1850s and 1860s, certainly in the latter case expressly for artistic purposes. There is no documentation on a journey in the 1850s, but the artist's descendants possess water-colour landscapes dated April and June 1850, and inscribed 'Switzerland', which have the look of first-hand observation, rather than of copying. The dominance of the continental note in her exhibited pictures of the 1850s makes a European trip in this decade almost incontrovertible, and given that, later on, the artist included Swiss locations in her exhibited work ('Lobgesang at Berne' (1861), 'The Fountain, Berne' (1862)), it seems wise to conclude that she did make an early trip to the Continent, which took her as far as Switzerland, via France and perhaps Belgium. It is quite certain that she made a trip in 1863 to Brittany, to which can be ascribed the inspiration for many later works, as we shall see.

By the early 1860s, she had attracted some regular critical attention, though its tenor was uneven. The *Art Journal*'s critic had picked out 'Helping Granny' and 'Village School near Boulogne' in the SFA's first year, as works which 'will attract attention from their truthfulness of character, manifested in subjects of an opposite nature to each other.[93] One of her Academy exhibits, 'Granny's Lesson', of 1856, was greeted by one critic as 'equal to some of the best genre works in the exhibition'; the *Builder*'s critic called her, in 1858, 'a young artist of promise'.[94] By 1869, though, a cautionary note sounded in the notices she received: 'Let the artist beware of reproducing the colour and manner of another painter: she is quite strong enough to work on independently'[95] (tantalisingly, the *Art Journal* critic did not vouchsafe who this 'other painter' might be). The work in question was 'Sunday Morning', shown at Manchester. (From the latter 1850s, she sent works to Liverpool (from 1857), Birmingham (from 1858) and Manchester, while during the 1860s she sent work to at least those three as well as Sheffield, Worcester and Glasgow.) In 1861, a handful of critical comments illustrate both the negative and positive aspects of her technical develop-ment: 'A Prayer for the absent one' at Suffolk Street was, according to the *Art Journal*, 'so firmly painted as to be even masculine in manner'; while the *Athenaeum* thought 'Lobgesang at Berne' at the Winter Exhibition, 'heavy and coarse in handling, and vulgar in one or two points of design', although it 'has real merits of a high class, in portrayal of character, grouping and expression'.[96]

The 'Lobgesang at Berne' is a good example of how the artist had progressed from her early sketches: it is characteristic of the artist that she tries for the maximum, rather than making the most of the optimum. Given the lack of ambition that female artists were often accused of, this cannot be seen as entirely regrettable, and in 1866, in response to another of her more substantial works, 'Between the Acts', the *Illustrated London News* critic wrote: 'It is impossible not to commend the intelligence Miss Emma Brownlow has shown on several occasions in her conceptions, notwithstanding that her powers of expression lag too far behind her ambition.'

Such was Brownlow's standing as an exhibitor in the London galleries when, in 1863, she set out on what she herself called a 'courageous search for the picturesque'.[97] The authenticity of costume and setting which such works as hers demanded could

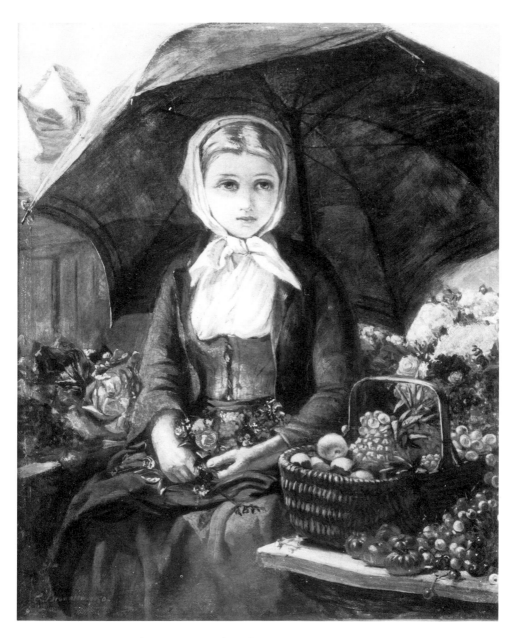

33. Emma Brownlow, 'Left in Charge', 1860. Oil on canvas. Private collection. (Photo: Sotheby's)

become stale when taken from books and dolls and other paintings, and it was not unusual for British artists to journey abroad for sights, sounds and souvenirs which would animate their pictures. Brownlow's need was for correct costume, gesture and facial type, rather than for the right location, since she rarely set her figures outdoors and tended to restrict her picture space to closed interiors. Her works from the 1850s and early 1860s were not regularly challenged on their authenticity, but she evidently felt she must go to her source. Since there are no extant figure drawings from her presumed first trip abroad, it seems reasonable that she would by now feel the need for that sort of material. (She does not mention, in her account of this journey in 1863, any previous trip, nor does she compare any experiences on this journey to previous similar ones, but she has people in Paris to meet and chaperone her who might well be previous acquaintances.)

Brownlow and her sister Elizabeth left London on 6 June and returned two months later (4 August). Nothing is known of the circumstances which permitted the trip (that is, whence came the money, and whether it was conditionally acquired), but it is evident from the artist's diary of the journey that their finances were very nicely calculated. Brownlow's diary, in fact, records minute aspects of the time away, and it will be quoted from copiously here since it provides an insight, not only into her character and her ways of working, but into a British artist 'doing' Brittany. A couple called Perret were the sisters' hosts in Paris, where they did the sights before venturing into the provinces. The Exposition, as Brownlow calls the Salon, featured that year the Salon des Refusés as well as the regular show: Brownlow was no less conservative than some others of her contemporaries in her appraisal of the state of French art at the time:

> Saw an immense number of pictures, good, bad, and indifferent, also a great number of those which had been rejected by the jury, almost without exception to my mind with justice, including one (the only one that I saw by an English artist) by Whistler – it was more like a piece of bad whitewashing than anything else.[98]

They left the capital for Rennes, safeguarded as ladies had to be: 'Mrs Perret went with us to the railway and put us in charge of a very agreeable English lady – also going to Rennes'; thence to the port of L'Orient, 'where we were met by the waiter of the Hôtel de France with a letter from Mrs Maubert giving us full directions for our

further journey'. Their destination was Le Launay, a small comm-
unity where they were to stay and from which they ventured out to
additional locations. Even *en route* (the journey lasted six days)
Brownlow began the job she had come to do:

> On arriving at Plouay we stopped to water the horse and refresh
> ourselves at a picturesque little inn – in a most quaint village. I sat
> down outside the inn to make a little sketch of passing figures
> and was very soon perfectly surrounded by all the boys and girls
> and many of the adults of the village, who crowded round me too
> closely to be pleasant to my olfactory nerves – notwithstanding
> the energetic efforts of an old man to keep them at a respectful
> distance, and who tried to fix one or two in a regular soldier
> position for me to draw them more easily.

In this day's expenses she lists, for the first time, outlay on
'wardrobe': 2 fr. 50 c. for a local costume cap. Such items recurred in
plenty in the following weeks: on 17 June she paid 103 fr. for a
Langonnet dress and cap; on 1 July, 1 fr. 80 c. for a cap at Gourin; on
8 July, 15 fr. and 13 fr. respectively for a man's and a woman's dress,
the former Gourin, the latter Langonnet; on 15 July she bought a
'costume of Quimper' for 12 fr. 50 c.; she bought belts, collars,
aprons, caps and dresses. The evident use she made of these
purchases is that after her return, her works include much more
particularised costume than before. The sources of her purchases
were varied:

> Mme Phillipe took us to the house of a very rich farmer, whose
> daughter, a girl of sixteen with clear olive complexion and large
> soft ox eyes, showed us all her grand fête dresses and even
> dressed herself completely in the most gorgeous and walked out
> in the sun that we might the better see the beauty of her attire. I
> then purchased one of her old dresses complete, for which I gave
> 100 fr. – just £4. I also bought one of her everyday caps for 3 fr.
> (25 June)

> After dinner we went in search of a Quimper costume. A child
> whom we got a man to ask refused to sell hers so the man sent his
> servant with us to show us where they are made after some
> trouble we secured two jacket affairs and one second-hand, for
> which I had to give 12 fr. and also half a franc to the servant who
> took us there. Could not hear of any place where the cap and

collar are to be had. Must try and buy one of the Bonnes, and make up my mind, as I always do, to be fleeced. (15 July)

It is very evident that the 'search for the picturesque' was a demanding affair: the two women attended popular events wherever they went, visiting the prosaic and the extraordinary, Brownlow always reporting most diligently what the people did and did not wear, and whether or not they were 'quaint' or 'picturesque' (her terms of approbation). Thus:

> Drove to Gourin to see the fair – lots of cattle and people but a decided want of colour in the dresses – the Gourin people wearing sort of brown holland coloured coats and those from other villages wearing blue . . . (15 June)

> Sunday. Cloudy but fine. Drove in dog-cart to Gourin and were just a few minutes too late to see the people come out of church, but saw a very great number of them in their Sunday dresses, standing about outside the church and in the streets, shops, etc. Some of the dresses were pretty, the Langonette, in particular. (21 June)

> Sunday. Up at about five and off in dog-cart before eight to the Pardon at St Barbe, one of the grandest Pardons in Brittany. The road in parts perfectly horrible and very trying to the springs. We reached St Barbe at eleven and passed many peasants on the road, all in holiday attire. On arriving at our destination M. Maubert left us and took the horse back to Faouet and we having camp-stools took up our position and watched the people . . .' (28 June)

The work resulting from these endeavours was considerable and Brownlow seems to have been endlessly industrious, using material over and over, working on more than one piece at once and utilising good and bad weather alike.

As was to be expected, she was not immune to exploiting the sentimental possibilities of her subject-matter for a British audience: 'Had a girl in Gourin costume to stand in the garden for a little love scene' (20 June); 'Mrs Maubert called me into the kitchen to look at the old charwoman's daughter, whom I detained and made a little sketch of her feeding chickens' (19 June). And indeed, the touristic interest she took in her subject, akin to collecting rare specimens for an album, was sometimes exposed to her as the objectionable attitude it was:

After lunch Marianne's son Louis came in full Gourin dress to stand for scene in garden as I was unable to get my man during the week, all being engaged on the farm except on Sundays. It appears that there is a prejudice against sitting for me, the idea being that some evil will befall those connected with Protestants. (5 July)

In our walk we saw an uncommonly pretty girl in the Rosporden costume and we asked her to come to the Hotel the following morning, but she seemed frightened and would not come. (13 July)

On 10 July, the two sisters moved on to Quimper, the schedule for their activities being much the same as before, and their attitudes no more enlightened:

Quite disappointed with the appearance both of the people and streets, both of which we had been led to expect to find picturesque. The men are very plain and common looking, with ordinary costume, nothing at all peculiar, and the women's dress is absolutely ugly. (19 July)

Sketching in Quimper market, the artist found again that her attentions were not necessarily wholly welcome to her subjects:

I made some slight and very rapid sketches but the people seemed either frightened or offended when they discovered that they were the objects of my attention, and either turned their backs or got out of sight as fast as they could, and if they did not at first perceive that I was looking at them, somebody was sure to tell them, so that I was surely sketching under difficulties. (18 July)

They travelled on to Dinan and to Avranches, exchanging Breton for Norman landscape, but 'After dinner we explored the town and came to the conclusion that it is most uninteresting. There was not a single sketchable person or object of any kind' (25 July); 'Not a picturesque figure to be seen' (26 July), and went on, via Vire and Caen, to Paris, which they reached by train on 28 July. Here, a few more sightseeing trips furnished more opportunity for Brownlow to comment on her contemporaries, this time her compatriots:

> We were just preparing to set off for the Louvre, when Mrs Perret came to our room to ask us if we would like to join a party and go to the Ste Chapelle as they had an order so of course we went . . . The Ste Chapelle is 800 years old and the medallions are of course very Pre-Raphaelesque. They are however restoring them and reproducing them after the original designs, and I am sure that Millais and his PRB would jump for joy to see the awkward and ungainly objects that now adorn the walls. (30 July)

They went through the ritual of obeisance at the feet of the old masters, as any English visitor to Paris, artist or no, went through. Due to the paucity of information about the artist's early life, it is not known whether she went to the National Gallery or the British Institution in London to study and copy when she was younger,[99] but she notes the students in the Louvre:

> Abt. 12 we got to the Louvre where I was much pleased by inspecting the sketches and designs of the old masters, Michael Angelo, Raphael, etc. Then into the sculpture galleries . . . Then into the Salle d'Apollo [sic] and the long Gallery, in which there were many artists copying, some of them very badly. (31 July)

Brownlow's estimate of the modern French school was typical of her period:

> Went to the Luxembourg and was much pleased with the paintings. There is a very nice Bonheur 'Loading a haycart' which pleased me much. There is a large painting by Vinon [?], of a female martyr, a very young girl tied in a chair, having her feet roasted. It is beautifully painted, but the subject like too many of the French school, very painful. In the passage leading from the larger gallery to the smaller, were some chalk drawings, portraits and small, of which I did not think much . . . (1 August)[100]

The sisters left Paris for home on 4 August, having been away for two months and having spent, the artist's diary records, £48 17s 4½d. They almost left behind them the fruits of the adventure:

> On arriving at the station I found that my box of paintings etc. which had been in the care of Joseph, was left behind. Of course we were extremely vexed and obliged to send Mr Perret back in a cab for it and we had to wait for an hour and pay 12 francs extra, to

go by Calais instead of by Boulogne, as the trains were an hour later. Mr Perret and the box arrived only just in time for the Calais train and we had to run, which was no joke on a hot day with two very heavy bags in one's hands.

She made no conclusion in her diary about the usefulness or satisfaction of the journey, but its effects were to be seen in her work from then on. A number of her exhibited paintings from the remainder of the decade can be directly related to her trip abroad: 'Waiting for a customer, Quimper Market' (1864), 'Cabin Door in Brittany' (1864), 'A Wedding Dance, Brittany' (1866), 'Cottage Interior, Brittany' (1866), 'Une Chaumière, Brittany' (1866), 'The Beggar's Story' (1867), 'The Riverside, Quimper' (1870).

The latter part of the 1860s was, in fact, a particularly fruitful time, with the Foundling Hospital commissioning a series from her. The commissioners were benefactors of the Hospital, one of whom commissioned his portrait from the artist as well: Lt. Col. Hyde.[101] These paintings are uneven in their achievement, with the most satisfactory being perhaps the earliest, 'The Foundling restored to its Mother' (1858) [pl. VIII], where the figures are easily related to the space in which they exist, their relationships are well organised, and the colouring is not too heavy – elements which work less well in 'Taking Leave' (1868), and 'The Sick Room' (1864). In all the scenes, however, the grouping of the figures – each of the pictures features at least five figures – is interesting and convincing and pleasantly casual; the most strained grouping being that in 'Taking Leave' (1868). These paintings cannot be conceived as being public commissions, although the Hospital is a public institution, because they were and have remained the private property of the Hospital, rarely being lent elsewhere. Additionally, they are private in the sense that they refer intensely to the inner life of the Hospital – in 'The Foundling restored', the composition and to some extent the meaning of the picture is based on the Hospital's art collection, with its inclusion of the Hospital's Hogarth painting rendering it especially significant to its commissioners and owners. This painting was, however, reproduced in the *Penny* magazine in 1866.[102] One factor which lessens the impact of the set of works is their small scale, whether determined by resources or lack of confidence: this characterises them firmly as domestic scenes, not heroic pictures.

Emma Brownlow's life changed somewhat in 1867, when she married. Her husband, Donald King, was a singer in the theatrical world, whom she had met through the Hospital choir. Henceforth she called herself Mrs Brownlow King for professional purposes, and although she gave birth to four children (born 1869, 1870, 1870, 1872) and her husband proved to be unreliable in financial matters, and died in 1886, she seems to have continued a steady output of work until the early 1870s. By the later 1860s, she had had five paintings bought by Art Union prizewinners,[103] had added the Crystal Palace to the list of galleries where she exhibited and had sold other praised works (e.g. 'On Thoughts of Charity Intent' to the Duchess of Cambridge in 1865). A lack of detailed information about her patrons and sales makes it impossible to know to what extent she was able to live by her paintings: papers relating to the Brownlow family in the County Hall, London, fail to mention expenditure on painting materials or income from artistic endeavour, but it is evident that King's unreliability (and a hint of dishonesty) made her financial situation less than easy in the 1860s and 1870s.

Quite a number of her pictures from this time can be presumed sold, however, since so many titles from this period are not to be found in public collections nor do they remain in the family. These invite discussion of her treatment of modern issues. 'News from the War' may well be nothing but a contrivedly titled sentimental fancy – the subtitle is 'to whom a victory speaks of *his* return, and a defeat means only *he* is lost' – but 'Between the Acts' seems, from critical descriptions, to return to the contemporary mood of social concern with which her early drawings were preoccupied; the *Illustrated London News* reviewer described it thus in 1866:

> A poor woman – a widow, as we learn by portions of her garments lying about among the dingy tawdry finery of the green room – has just left a stage where she has been enacting the part of some tragedy queen, and now impatiently taking the tinselled diadem from her brow, stoops to kiss her poor delicate-looking child, her widowed heart cruelly wrung, perhaps by some passages in her part of terrible application to her own case.

The *Ladies' Companion* review expands, that 'the squalid room exhibits all the bareness of poverty, and the wretched habiliments and worn-out boots littering the floor and table are eloquent of sad realities'. As has been shown to be the case with so many female painters of the period, Brownlow treated the world of women by preference, but her apparent conservatism and her evident technical limitations could have been enough to dissuade her from more contentious or topical excursions within that world: and she wanted to sell. Had she kept to the more challenging path which her early sketches suggest, and which these few paintings of the late 1860s recall, she might well have emerged critically from the crowd of domestic painters with whom she was identified, but not found many buyers.[104]

Her exhibitions waned in the 1870s and ceased altogether after 1877, though a letter of mid-1874 from Brownlow's mother to the family advisor, Wintle, suggests that the artist's four children 'will be entirely dependant [sic] on her for education etc.' Also in 1874, the artist's sister died (John Brownlow having expired the previous year) and although Donald King lived until 1886, he himself expresses anxiety in papers of 1876 about the possibility that he might die suddenly, leaving his dependants indigent. An address of 1872 in Herne Bay, Kent (doubtless for health reasons) suggests another factor for the artist's increasing withdrawal from the London exhibition scene at this time. In short, what seems to happen in the latter three decades of the artist's life is that she gives up her art for her family: the invidious choice between being a woman and being an artist has to be made, and the woman (or, rather, conventional notions thereof) wins out over the artist.

The 1880s and 1890s saw a series of moves (back to London, to the Isle of Wight) and family deaths (King in 1886, her daughter Marian the same year, her mother some time between 1881 and 1886), culminating in a staggered emigration to Australasia, for reasons of health. The artist's son John, was sent to Sydney in 1887; the artist herself and her two daughters went to New Zealand in 1888, returning in 1889, to take up an unsettled residence in the south of England (moving from the Isle of Wight to Bradford-on-Avon to Bournemouth, the location always determined by its healthiness and its expense). Throughout this time there is no mention in the artist's correspondence with her advisors of any earning activity on her part as a painter,[105] and this, combined with the lack of evidence of work dated this late in her career, must lead to the conclusion that she did, in fact, give up painting. She was by now, of course, in her fifties, and undertook yet another voyage to Australasia at the end of the 1880s for the sake of her children's health, sailing for Auckland in 1896, and thence to Ceylon in 1901. Later that year, she returned home and took up residence in Croydon from whence she moved to a healthier place (she had written to Wintle in February 1900, 'For myself, I have been in very failing health for some time past'), eventually living in Kent, where she died on New Year's day 1905. Photographs of this period show that Brownlow's eventful life had told on her: in 1883 she already looks weary, resigned and unhealthily plump; while in 1904 her seventy-odd years show very clearly through her smile. Although she had produced a substantial body of work, and had been moderately successful over the years, the irresistible impression remains that she never quite pushed herself far enough to become more than an uneven painter who had potential. Probable lack of art education and certain conflicts of commitment – characteristic of so many women painters of her generation – undoubtedly feature in this to an enormous extent. She is typical of the woman of her time in that she ultimately gave her family commitments – that is to say, not only childcare but breadwinning too – priority over her commitment to a single-minded and self-justifying art. Yet she is quite untypical in the energy and persistence which she injected into her art, and it is to be regretted that more of her work does not remain to allow a critical assessment of just how much potential went unrealised in the long run. Brownlow is also sadly typical of many female artists of her generation, in that even the modest reputation which she justly enjoyed in her own lifetime, no longer exists.

Louisa Stuart, Lady Waterford

Louisa Stuart, Lady Waterford, born in 1818, was one of the most celebrated amateurs of the mid-century and, thereby, somewhat a-typical of the non-professional female painter, who flourished rather in the shadows than in the limelight. She fully represents the type in other respects, however: she had a marked but idiosyncratic talent, and she used it for pleasure not for financial reward. Additionally, the time and the interest she had for art were derived from a lifestyle which allowed a large amount of leisure and an appreciation of the arts for their own sake, and she retained a self-deprecation which kept her from true artistic fame and serious success. She was aristocratic, and to some extent this was a necessary condition for the amateur, for this meant not only leisure but also funds and opportunity for the practice of art, and a background and milieu in which taste was a quality most diligently pursued and cultivated.[106]

Lady Waterford was cited, just after her death in 1891, as an example of the female artist by Florence Fenwick-Miller in her

'Ladies' Column' in the *Illustrated London News*.[107] It is notable that, even at this late date, debate about the ends of women's artistic endeavours and about the use of their creative energies was still worthwhile and even necessary, engaging the young generation and the older together. Fenwick-Miller wrote, in part:

> Mrs Jopling has been writing about the reason why women do not more frequently attain the first rank in art.[108] She attributes it mainly to the fact that most girls who have the means to study art at all do so merely for their own pleasure, and lack the urgent goal of necessity . . . One feels how true this is when one sees that even amidst the distractions of society some ladies snatch time to do just enough excellent work to show that they might do better. In the present exhibition of the New Gallery there is an admirable portrait of Mr Paderewski by Princess Louise Marchioness of Lorne; and the genuine ability of the Marchioness of Granby as a portrait-painter is well-known. Even more remarkable as an instance of this, however, is the collection of the works of the late Louisa, Marchioness of Waterford, which Princess Christian opened to the public the other day at Countess Brownlow's house in Carlton House Terrace. Striking and original as these works are, they ought to have been better . . . [It is] sad that such original talent as Lady Waterford displayed on the works now shown was so much overlaid and smothered by her social position. Lady Waterford was not married till she was thirty years old, and she had not any children – facts which have some bearing on her work in art.

Though few other critics discussed, even by implication, the relevance of marriage and motherhood to the amateur's achievement, Fenwick-Miller's overall assessment of Waterford as an artist is typical of the verdict that was generally reached. A closer look at the artist's life, however, both emphasises and qualifies the judgement of her as a 'might-have-been', over whom one shakes one's head sadly but understandingly.

Louisa Stuart was born in Paris in 1818, her father being at that time the British Ambassador to France. The family returned to England in 1824, to reside at Highcliffe Castle, Hampshire and to take its part in British high society. Louisa was presented at Court in 1835, and she and her sister Charlotte were apparently celebrated for their charm and beauty. Charlotte was a year older than Louisa, and a very important person in her younger sister's life: in Virginia

Surtees' words, 'the two sisters were bound to each other by the closest ties of affection, strengthened by sharing the same inner spiritual life, and united by the same artistic endeavour'.[109] A contemporary makes a somewhat different point, but does not contradict the notion of their mutual importance:

> In their devotion to each other, Charlotte and Louisa were one, though as opposite as possible – Charlotte gentle, retiring, clever, and goodness itself, never saying or doing what she ought not; Louisa, in the highest spirits, always getting into trouble by hearing or seeing what was not intended for her . . . and perfectly devoted to her paintboxes at ten years old.[110]

Charlotte was to marry in 1835, and twenty years later was obliged to go to live in India with her husband as Vicereine of India, where she died in 1861, but in their younger lives the sisters were very close, and developed an interest in art together. Their parents took them to Naples and Rome in their youth, and Louisa accompanied Charlotte and her husband to Italy in 1836, the two women particularly spending time in Rome. An account of Louisa's artistic education is found in Clayton:

> Lady Waterford, as a child, was taught to copy large chalk heads after French pictures. These studies, with a few lessons in landscape from Mr Page, formed an unsatisfactory groundwork. Later, copying a portrait in oils from Sir Joshua with an artist named Shepherdson completed all she ever learnt from masters. Lady Waterford's real teaching was gained from the art treasures of the galleries at Rome . . .[111]

Clayton's romanticism should perhaps be tempered by the recollections of someone who remained a close observer of Waterford's progress, her first cousin, Charles Stuart, who, in his *Short Sketch of the Life of Louisa Marchioness of Waterford*, published in 1892, recalled:

> The children were in their earliest years admirably educated by their wise and excellent mother, herself no mean artist; and Louisa, almost from her infancy, evinced a strong taste and talent for drawing. This talent was always encouraged, and I have no doubt she had many drawing masters, but I do not remember the name of any instructor of note.

The influence most admitted by the artist and of most significance in determining her aesthetic position, was that of John Ruskin, whom she met in the early 1850s. Even before this encounter, however, her own tendencies in art can be seen to have inclined towards a Ruskinian combination of love and observation of nature with moralising themes carried out in an awareness of Italianate ideals. She had married in 1842 Henry Lord Waterford, whose estates were in southern Ireland, at Curraghmore. Hare further recounts a truly Ruskinian industry on the artist's part at this period:

> She had already also begun the series of 'little books' which were her lifelong companions, and which her friends grew to look upon as part of herself. These many volumes, one of which was always within reach, were mere little 'betting books' in which she sketched passing people, scenes, or events; or, still more, fleeting ideas and inspirations in pencil, pen or colour, usually finishing them by candlelight.
>
> Whenever Lady Waterford was left alone, she would send for Miss Palliser, and they spent whole days in a little painting-room, where they had models, and worked hard as long as daylight lasted, only going out to walk at dusk.[112]

A letter to her mother of November 1849 suggests the sort of subject-matter which was to remain her preference throughout her life:

> I am scratching ideas for my 'Virtues and Contrasts'. For the contrast to 'Thirsty, and ye gave me to drink', I am thinking of making a field of battle and a stripped (I could not stand a uniform) and dying soldier calling to some women passing by with pitchers of water on their heads, which they are making signs to refuse, their backs half turned – as if he was a dying man on the enemy's side and they would not help him. Do you think I can make all this understood? I was so glad to think of a subject without the eternal ragged people as a type of poverty and misery, which is in general, so far from the truth in reality.[113]

This indicates Waterford's awareness of trends in popular art as well as her wish to set against them forms of more grandeur and boldness,[114] embodying always a Christian moral rather than a worldly one. This classical ambition led her to look for the universal application even of the specific which she observed, in

Ruskinian fashion, around her and in her own fancy. A letter of late 1851 describes well this position, and conveys the enthusiasm for art itself which was supposed to bespeak the amateur in its best sense:

> I do *love* my art (dare I call it mine?) far more than ever, and long to do a great work. Meantime I labour at the merest correctness, which leads me to discover more and more in every work of Nature; a dead leaf in all its curves and forms seems to disclose so much more than one sees at first . . .[115]

The Pre-Raphaelite sympathy which speaks here, and which brought Waterford and Ruskin together, is first named as such in an undated letter to Mrs Bernal Osborne, written probably in 1852 or 1853:

> I hope to be in London in June, and have especial curiosity to see what the Pre-Raphaelites have done this year, whether they are beginning to allow themselves a little beauty in moderate quantities. I respect them for abstaining from the *pretty*, and am sure theirs is the only school which will come at real beauty at last, so we must be content to let them pass through all their phases of ugliness first.[116]

In June 1853, the artist was enabled by Ruskin to visit Millais's studio while she was in London for the art season. She also called on Hunt during this stay in town, and sufficiently impressed the whole circle to be included in the names for the Brotherhood's projected sketching club in early 1854. In his turn, Rossetti recalled a visit by the admiring amateur in June 1855, again arranged by Ruskin: 'He sent here the other day a stunner called Marchioness of Waterford, who had expressed a wish to see me paint in watercolours, it seems, she herself being really first-rate as a designer in that medium',[117] he wrote to William Allingham at the end of the month. Early in July he wrote to his mother:

> An astounding event is coming off tomorrow. The Marchioness of Waterford has expressed a wish to Ruskin to see me paint in watercolour, as she says my method is inscrutable to her. She is herself an excellent artist, and would have been really great, I believe, if not born such a swell and such a stunner . . .[118]

In his own prejudiced way, Rossetti makes the same point that both Jopling and Fenwick-Miller were making so much later. Waterford's ultimate non-consummation of her talents, however, was as much hampered by her residence in Ireland as by her gender and by her class with its attendant duties, for she was thus out of the mainstream of art events and discussion and could engage with other artists or art enthusiasts only by letter or at long and irregular intervals. She maintained an interest in the Pre-Raphaelite movement (mostly through Ruskin) that extended eventually to a concern with the ideas and personalities of the second generation of the movement, particularly Burne-Jones.

What Ruskin did for the artist's work is arguable, depending on one's position on Ruskin himself. Clayton, writing in 1876 and presumably paraphrasing Waterford herself, put forward a moderate assessment of his influence: 'She has never had a master for figure drawing, or subject painting, or composition of any kind, but always remembers gratefully the friendly interest shown in her works by Mr Ruskin.'[119] Waterford herself, in her letters and diary, supports that interpretation of Ruskin's significance for her: 'Ruskin is the reverse of the man I like, and yet his intellectual part is quite my ideal . . . There is a charm in Ruskin's writing that I find in no other, though he often provokes me, and I sometimes disagree with it.'[120] Some judgements made after the artist's death, however, from people who could have known very well what they were talking about, differed due to their own opposition to Ruskin. Mrs Steuart Erskine, in the *Studio* in 1910, wrote:

> Lady Waterford at one time had lessons from Ruskin, the only lessons which she is ever known to have taken since her childhood. These lessons did more harm than good. Ruskin worried her and insisted on her painting minutely in the Pre-Raphaelite style, in a manner totally foreign to her nature . . . Still, she had a great admiration for Ruskin, and read every one of his books with eager interest; while he had enthusiastic admiration for her as a colourist.

Ruskin's 'lessons' took the form of seemingly endless advice and criticism transmitted personally and by letter, seldom complimentary and often recriminatory. His and Waterford's own letters indicate the line which Ruskin's interest in her art tended to take. In 1855, he declared to her that 'in drawing, as in music, the greatest *power* can only be attained by those who have capacity of greatest tenderness: – that with *refinement* you gain at once grasp and decision'.[121] He was soon commending to her his own favourite models: 'By the bye – do go into the National Gallery and look at the *leaves* round the head of Bacchus in Titian's 'Bacchus and Ariadne' – and at the vine leaves – and at everything.' Such recommendations recurred often over the years.

What Ruskin's strictures also convey, is the urging towards harder work and more methodical industry that women in general were pressed by critics to undertake to improve their work. If this is forcing her towards Pre-Raphaelitism, then it was in the constructive sense which recognised women's enforced amateurism as one of their greatest hindrances to real achievement in fine art. Ruskin, however, was only erratically understanding of the reasons why a woman – not just Lady Waterford – suffered from a lack of application and a paralysing self-deprecation. He seemed to have seen his role as schoolmaster rather than companion which, though it might in the end be useful to a woman, exploited her low self-esteem and habitual position of disciple of male wisdom. Waterford, though a thinking woman, shows herself to have accepted this intellectually conventional position, even though she might emotionally rail against it periodically. She recalled in 1863: 'Ruskin's visit was only a moving one, as the cottage was quite full. He condemned (very justly) my frescoes, and has certainly spirited me up to do better.'[122]

Though her preferred subjects and stylistic features reflect Ruskin's enthusiasm for Titian, Veronese and earlier Italianate examples, it need not be thought that such preferences were not the artist's own. Venetian colouring and Renaissance uses of the allegorical and monumental figure occur often over the years: 'Sweetest Eyes' [pl. XII], 'The Stairs of Life', 'Autumn with a Sieve', 'Looking out to Sea' [fig. 34] and the frescoes [figs. 35, 36] which she mentions above, commenced in 1861 and seen by the artist as her major work (though not her best), all show these features. At the same time, however, her classicism was not meant by her to be a simple reproduction of the old masters, and, indeed, for all the familiarity of the devices or types she uses, her work has a freshness and animation which has no stale imitation about it. In 1863, she wrote to a friend:

I want to do a *modern* representation of the Holy Family, represented by a real poor cottage mother and child, who have taken refuge in a snowy barn, and are found and comforted by

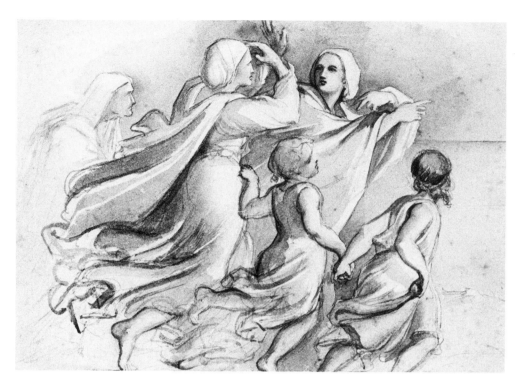

34. Louisa, Lady Waterford, 'Looking out to Sea', undated. Watercolour.
Reproduced by courtesy of the Board of Trustees of the Victoria and Albert
Museum.

the love of poor neighbours, who bring their offerings, as the shepherds and kings of old – taking the composition of the old masters exactly as a model, and trying to treat modern dress and rags as picturesquely as I can.[123]

In similar vein, classicism becomes modern in such pieces as 'Supper after Hunting', with its saint-like silhouettes; 'Family Group at Curraghmore', like a *sacra conversazione*; 'The Child's Secret', resembling a Madonna and child; 'The Reapers', redolent of a Ruth and Boaz scene (all illustrated in Hare).

In 1859, Louisa retired to the Northumbrian village of Ford. The series of frescoes on the walls of the schoolroom at Ford (murals, strictly speaking, rather than frescoes, since the painting is in watercolour on paper and board which was then mounted on the walls) depict children in Biblical scenes or narratives, with an endpiece of 'Suffer the little children to come unto me' at one end, and 'Christ among the Doctors' at the other.[124] They betray Ruskinian interest in natural detail, with an Italianate use of roundels and draped figures. The variety in composition and figural grouping is effective, but the success of those figures is very uneven and their placing within their contexts runs from the ambitiously successful ('Samuel and Miriam', [fig. 36]), to the awkward and frankly unfortunate ('Cain and Abel'). The colouring is impossible to assess fairly now, but was, to judge from material now in the possession of the current occupier of Ford Castle, of lesser importance to the artist than was the composition. The unsatisfactory elements of these pictures – the faulty anatomy, the flaws in perspective, the idiosyncratic compositional devices – contrast strongly with the good drawing and the broadly flowing line, and make one wish that Ruskin's reproaches on accuracy and method had enjoined her to a more solid form of Pre-Raphaelitism than she, in fact, ultimately manifested. In the few pieces still remaining which show tighter line and closer study, like the Victoria and Albert Museum's 'Mentone Fisherman' [pl. VII], none of the charm is lost with accuracy, but its discipline adds to the rigour that supports charm.

Nearly all Waterford's drawings and paintings are undated, indicating both her prolific activity and the fact that her work did not have for her the status of complete art objects.[125] These are surely characteristics of the female amateur, and make for work which is pleasing to the spectator but unsatisfying to the artist's peers, it seems. Hare's response to this does not reflect very

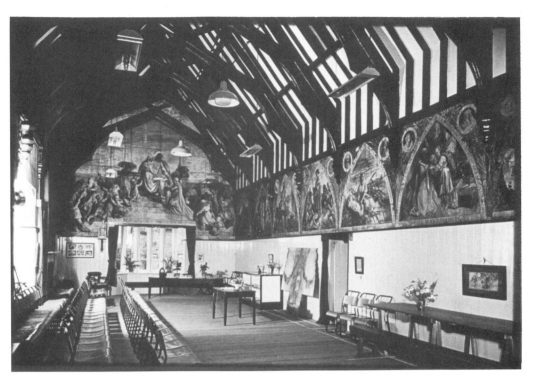

35. Louisa, Lady Waterford, Ford School Frescoes, 1862–83. Mixed media on heavy paper. Reproduced by permission of Lord Michael Joicey. (Photo: J. Arthur Dixon for Waterford Hall)

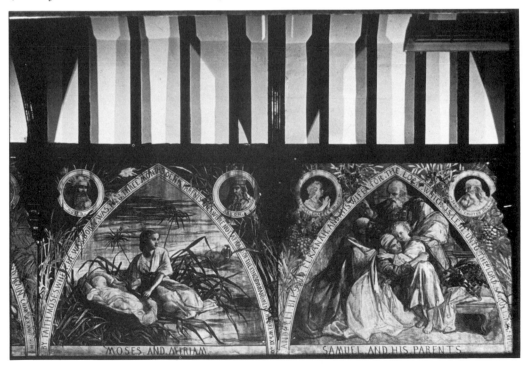

36. Louisa, Lady Waterford, 'Samuel and Miriam' from the Ford School Frescoes, 1862–83. Mixed media on heavy paper. Reproduced by permission of Lord Michael Joicey. (Photo: J. Arthur Dixon for Waterford Hall)

creditably on the artist as an intelligent adult:

> People have often blamed Lady Waterford's pictures because they were not finished more highly. It was not in her to finish them. She painted as the birds sing, because she could not help it. The thought, the impression, the inspiration, it may be, came to her, and she felt impelled to transfer it to paper. Beyond that she could not go. What was said was said, and what was thought was thought. Her pictures were her words and her thoughts.

This does not do justice to the industry with which she practised her art, which is testified in her own writing and by the observation of others, but it does suggest the art for art's sake approach which had great romantic appeal. A letter from the artist herself, however, to her cousin and fellow artist, Eleanor Vere Boyle, in response to Clayton's request for information on Waterford for *English Female Artists*,[126] shows a greater amount of insight into her own situation as an extraordinary amateur than her biographer displays:

> The honest truth is, I had far rather Miss Clayton should say nothing about me. How can I say this *civilly?* The school pictures are not good enough to deserve mention, and the idea of an account of them in print is quite odious to me . . . It goes against the grain to an extent I cannot describe to have it in any way spoken of as a thing that is worth it. So, dear Ella, do say 'I know my cousin Lady Waterford had rather not have anything said about her works. She is not satisfied with them herself, and would take it as a kindness that, if named, it should be in the most cursory way as *attempt* in the right direction'. I wish you could see me inside out, and that mock modesty is not the reason of my saying this, but a feeling (which I believe a right one) that these things, or anything I have ever done, cannot be classed as real good things, only as the work of one who would have been an artist if it had been her fate to earn her bread and to go through a greater amount of study.[127]

This letter was written in 1875, and as she got older, Waterford seemed to perceive the mixed blessings of her situation more and more, the conflicting demands which her position and her ambition made on her having an increasingly frustrating effect. To EVB again, she wrote in 1878:

Oh, I have not a minute to draw. I feel often so discouraged when I have to think of bills and affairs, and servants and people to look after. Art only comes in with the dregs, and then I am tired out in body and mind, and a book is the only rest. No, a poor woman who is a proprietress has *no power* to make anything of Art, and I saw my own great shortcomings very clearly at the Grosvenor Gallery. I feel the tortoises have all won the race, and endless women can do better than me now.[128]

And the following year:

I am greatly discouraged about my artwork. Not a creature cares, or knows, or observes if I do a thing or not, and if it is done, it is passed over unseen. Not that praise signifies, but poor humanity needs encouragement, or one becomes too listless.

She was aware that the situation of women in art had changed, as the letter above indicates. In the 1860s she had met Annie Dixon who, as a woman who practised professionally, was an invigorating contrast to herself; she thought her 'a character resembling those in Currer Bell's novels', and recognised her as 'honest and independent' (Dixon was a portraitist). Her awareness of Clayton's book doubtless brought her notice of many other women artists, too, both professional and amateur; and in writing to EVB she was corresponding with a woman who, though like herself an amateur, had achieved the recognition that only completed and whole works could command.[129] It was in a letter to this artist, in 1880, that Waterford referred to the most telling change that women in the arts had experienced during Waterford's career: 'I get rather dispirited at my failures, and the want of that knowledge and *finish* I see in all women's work at exhibitions when they have had good training: there was none in my day'.

The new step, of exhibiting her drawings, which Waterford took with the opening of the Grosvenor, not only brought her to wider attention than before but gave her an opportunity to see herself in a new perspective. It was evidently a new impetus to work:

I am so afraid I shall have little done for the Grosvenor but I am working, and am doing the married pairs for it. Shall I call it 'Three Phases of Life', or 'Youth, Middle Age and Old Age?' I fear it won't be understood.

I have done two poor little drawings for the Grosvenor Gallery from a child's rhyme called 'The Shower' – the fine young ladies caught in the rain, and the poor girls not minding it.[130]

The self-deprecation which never ceases should perhaps be attributed to the artist's Christianity, which would be enough in itself to explain her humility towards her talents and her refusal to glorify her pictures as objects in themselves. This ideology would also conspire to curtail her ambition for fame and her discontent with her lot. Virginia Surtees supports the idea that it was the Christian motive which was Waterford's moving spirit, but sees it in a positive light:

> The direction of her life was ordered by deeply held religious convictions . . . and although later her High Church views resolved themselves into the more moderate doctrines of the Church of England, she never departed from her belief that life should be founded on prayer, and . . . it will be found that Lady Waterford's search was directed towards humility in a life of service.[131]

In the end, Waterford's achievements were by no means ignored: at her death in 1891, a large exhibition of her drawings and paintings was held privately in London, to which critics responded with enthusiasm and reservation, whether they were art-lovers or observers of the activities of the upper classes.

Already in 1863, critics had described her as 'one of our best amateur artists', but the adjectives undermine each other's effectiveness: the received notion that she *was* an amateur to some extent conditioned the reception that her work could have. For instance, it was her allegorical, fanciful and infantine pieces which were mostly recalled by commentators after her death, not her modern or even her Shakespearean subjects; while it was her modesty, not the ambition which so confused her, which was recalled as characteristic of her on her exhibitions in 1892 and 1910. The opening remark from the catalogue to this latter exhibition of over 300 pieces of work sums up as well as any observer did what Waterford's position was: 'The pictures that are exhibited here today are the work of a lady whose life was not especially devoted to art, but whose whole being was imbued with the sense of it.'[132] The claims that were made for her work, both before and after her death – made from the safety of her accepted amateur status – seem now over-ambitious. For Ruskin to mention

Veronese in the same breath as her name, for Watts and Burne-Jones to suggest she could be 'an artist as great as Venice knew', to say that her sense of composition had rarely been surpassed,[133] diminishes her art rather than elevates it in retrospect, so exaggerated do such parallels seem. Had she been a professional artist, she must have been an artist like Watts himself, or Leighton, though a woman would not have been accorded their status. Louisa Waterford, surely because she was female and aristocratic and a remarkable, instinctive artist, stood in her own day as a contradiction in terms.

Her example bade fair to break down those mutually exclusive categories 'woman' and 'genius' as well as those jointly oppressive categories 'woman' and 'amateur'. That such a breaking down did not, in the end, take place in her case, was mostly attributed to her equivocal stance on the question; this demonstrates quite resoundingly how persistently women themselves are held responsible for their own failures, by the very forces that govern women's behaviour and inhibit women's choices.

Rosa Brett

A very different sort of amateur was Rosa Brett, whose position as a woman – located within a middle-class family, overshadowed by a successful brother, expected to be a second mother to her siblings, and equivocal about fame though not about her love for art – is much more typical of the period than was Waterford's. Very much the type of 'the ones that got away', Brett's representative value is much the same as Brownlow's, though her aesthetic position, firmly within Pre-Raphaelitism, is very different.

Rosa Brett was born in 1829, the daughter of a soldier, Charles Curtis Brett, and his wife Anne Philbeam (the *Dictionary of National Biography* has her name as Philbrick), the only girl of five children. The family was resident in Dublin because of the father's army posting in the early years of Rosa's life, but later took up residence in north Kent (where they were to stay for the length of Rosa's career). This became the region of her inspiration, providing the locales for most of her landscapes and the themes for her rare figural work (there are sketches in her notebooks and studies of hop-pickers and hopping equipment).[134] Information about her early life has not come to light, even with the help of the artist's family's papers: she first emerges as a recognisable individual in her diary of 1851 (actually started 7 December 1850).

At the end of 1850, Rosa had evidently been learning painting and drawing for a while with her brother John, for both are working for local patrons. The first entry in her diary reads:

> John went again today to Lushington's for his portfolio, they bought none of his drawings but chose one of mine, a view of York copied from one of Mr Booty's [?] done in pencil on coloured card, with Chinese white on the highlights, they of course thought it was John's it having no name to it. They gave a guinea for it. I was very much surprised to hear they had chosen one of mine this being the first I ever sold – gave John 5/- Arthur 1/- and 6d between Theodore and Edwin out of it – painted out the picture of the blight for Dr Plumbley and gave Arthur a music lesson did not go out today not being well enough.

In spite of her faulty punctuation, one senses a sensible and straightforward, not falsely modest but by no means confident young woman, with no idea of asserting her art herself: it reaches the world via her brother, as it was to do again later when she had become more of an artist. Already indicated here is the ill-health which was to set her back in later years, and which was a hindrance to her independence as it was with so many women of her time. This, combined with her being the only girl in a family where self-sacrifice on the part of some members was needed if others in the circle were to achieve their ambitions, anticipates the checks which her career suffered.

Entries in her diary for a few days in the middle of winter 1850, give an idea of the daily round that was typical for her at this period:

> 11th. December. Painted at the 'blight' gave Arthur a lesson went out, and in the evening mounted some more drawings.

> 13th. December. This morning housework as usual, painted at the 'blight' and finished it, afterwards went to see Grandma, returned at about 5 o'clock. I then set some more drawings helped John to rearrange the painting room. After tea I dressed and went with Arthur and Theodore to hear a lecture on the works of Charles Dickens.

The routine she followed was an arduous one – she writes of working until dark; of going to bed at 1 o'clock in the morning; and on one occasion of rising at 2 in the morning to work before breakfast – and it often included whole days spent on other people, usually the male members of the family. Thus her diary entry for Tuesday, 7 January 1851: 'After breakfast Arthur began to practise, he practised all day till bed-time . . . I sat by during all Arthur's practice'; 8 January 1851: 'Spent the whole of the day until 6 in the evening in directing John's circulars and inclosing them.' In the conventional spirit of womanly self-sacrifice to more important people, it was her brother John in particular who was the recipient of much of this willing self-sacrifice. She writes in mid-February, when a 'Fungus' has replaced the now finished 'Blight' as the work in progress, of how far this might go:

> Mr N. King and his brother called they came into the Painting room I had to make my escape not wishing anyone to see me working at the Fungus as the work passes for John's.
> Mr Dobney called to see John's picture he brought with him a Mr. Batter soon after Plomley came and they were all in the Painting room together, and I was listening outside the door.

From her evidence, Rosa and John worked in collaboration at this time, but it was John who took the pupils and John who was promoted, and seeking promotion, as an artist.[135] Both the troublesome 'Blight' set (of at least seven drawings) and the 'Fungus', she records as being joint creations, and John conceived plans which involved the two of them going out together on sketching expeditions to produce saleable work. The products of such excursions into the surrounding Kentish countryside are of a very variable quality, and Rosa's and John's are, but for their signatures, much of a kind in motif and touch. As John became more experienced (during the 1850s), of course, his work shows a confidence which his sister's work does not necessarily reveal. The extent to which the two collaborated comes out so strongly in the 1851 diary that it is disappointing to find commentators of John Brett's work completely failing to consider the role his sister played in his early career and giving neither consideration to the therefore questionable authenticity of his early work nor credit to Rosa's own early work.[136]

The two were certainly very productive at this time, though many of the pieces mentioned by name in Rosa's diary are no longer definitely extant: during the spring of 1851, for instance, she mentions an 'Aylesford', a 'Thurnham', a 'Red Cow on Penenden

Heath', and reports sketching trips to Ightham, Boxley and Detling (all in August) and other locales. Her industry already prefigures a Pre-Raphaelite conscientiousness, which her thorough sketch-books from the 1870s confirm as an enduring approach. Passages from her notes of 1851 recall the earnestness of Ford Madox Brown, bespeaking a seriousness in her art which was undermined by her reluctance to assert herself publicly, now or later. The endeavour for excellence which can result in never achieving satisfaction in the work produced, familiar from Waterford's letters, is obvious from her diary:

> 21st. August . . . washed out the sky – the Ult. Marine sky I put in yesterday – washed or rather sponged it out clean and put it in again, darker, but not quite so flat. Dined and went to sketch at same place as yesterday . . . returned home after sunset very tired indeed, the distance being rather long, the weather hot and roads hilly, got 2 sketches.

> 22nd. August . . . went out in the field and began to sketch it, but having a bad headache found the light too much for my eyes, so obliged to come in, set to work at my little picture in our garden with the Ult. Marine sky, painted till dinner, after dinner painted again, part of the time in the garden, I can paint much better out of doors from nature than in the house.

> 25th. August . . . began with the garden scene I finished yesterday it is as I thought it would be horrid . . .

She displays a modern acceptance that *plein-air* painting is the thing to do, which is, it seems, undeterred by the inconveniences of weather or of subservience to the etiquette of not being out alone. Brett's industry, however, at the same time as it bespeaks her earnestness and her Pre-Raphaelite approach to the subject, can be read less positively, as reflective of the profligate expenditure of energy which such women were expected and encouraged to make on pastimes of very varying fruitfulness. Even so it is plain to see that, once it becomes apparent that both Rosa's and John's art could contribute to the family (financially) rather than take away from it (in consumption of time and energy), this early industry bears fruit. Nevertheless, it must always do battle with the artist's domestic ties, ill-health, and self-denial.

Her brother John – who seems, from his own letters and diaries, to have suffered no lack of assertiveness – gave his view of Rosa's character in his diary in February 1853 (by which time the once constant companions were separated; John having gone to London to seek success as an artist):

> I respect her talent and admire her depth of character and love her real 'heart' though the stream flows so silently and deep beneath the surface as only to be noticed occasionally and when called forth in circumstances when other powers of the soul avail not . . .

Without a certain knowledge of whether Rosa ever had any formal instruction in art, the techniques and knowledge of art-world processes which she got from John are extremely important to take into account. Once he went to London, Rosa became a more independent worker, but she continued to take advice from her brother and their letters are full of painters' talk. He seems to have become more and more self-absorbed as his career took shape. In his diary for March 1852 however, he wrote: 'in books and art I have spiritual companions and in my sister a material one'. However, Rosa relied on him for assistance and advice throughout the 1850s. A letter from John to Rosa in 1858 (when he was abroad) gives not only detailed technical and practical advice but also praise of her assiduity:

> I am rather astonished at your painting proceedings I must say. I thought I was doing rather a feat to get up at 5 and to work by $\frac{1}{2}$ past 7 am! I am glad you can manage to carry out your scheme . . . About the sky, I have just got my sky in. The blue I put on with a sharp tool, bouncing it down on its point perpendicularly, driving the paint into the grain, using no medium (you hardly ever want medium if you finish at once;) and laying the paint scantily. You can get it beautifully flat this way. (Afterwards you can with your finest sable fill up any little holes), but after bouncing it in, I pat it very delicately with the broadside of the brush held between thumb and finger, to make it lie down. The clouds I put in pretty much at once as I mean them to be – you may depend all very good painting is done at once.

How closely she followed his advice, or how completely she relied on his assistance, is difficult to say, when his works from that period have survived but hers have not (or cannot be identified). However, John mentions some pieces by his sister in 1852: her portrait of Edwin, which she is working on in April of that year – 'the resemblance is good', he notes; and 'Rosa has lately made a few first-rate sketches on Preraffaelite principles' he observes on 30 September that year. In November, John notes that she is working on a portrait of their father. John notes a plan afoot in December for Rosa, too, to come to live in London: not as an artist, however, but as housekeeper to John and another brother, Arthur, who was to go to London to study music. This plan seems to have come to nothing though, due no doubt in large part to the fact that from the beginning of 1853 Rosa became increasingly unwell, though she continued to work and to travel for work. In January she and John went to Reigate, at the end of June she was in London, and there are three fine pieces of landscape dated Farnhurst, July 1853. However, John's diary records that in February, 'she seems more enthusiastic than ever notwithstanding suffering physically', at the end of May she is again 'unwell', at the end of July 'Rosa has been very unwell' and is receiving homoeopathic treatment. By the end of November, whatever her illness was, it had become most serious:

> . . . to crown all Rosa's health improves not at all under the various means that have lately been tried with so much hope and have failed with so much cold hopelessness . . . Her life is still dwindling away in which though she bears it with astonishing heroism prevents her doing much or enjoying anything.

In the spring of the next year, John noted that the family would like to send her to Germany for treatment, but the money was not available. What the nature of her complaint was is not clear, but certainly she was very ill for a long time, for in October the next year (1855), her father recorded in his diary that she was attending the Spinal Institution, despite having made a trip abroad earlier in the year (attested to by some fine and delicate drawings of a topographical bent, signed and dated April and July 1855). Rosa Brett's interest in art seems not to have waned throughout her illness. In March 1854, John had written to encourage her: 'For you I have carved out a membership in the old watercolour society, and that *once got*, your fortune is made and I have *no* doubt of your ability to get it, when you shall have got *health.*'

It was three years later that Brett made her first foray into the public arena, with an Academy exhibit. (It is not possible to tell from family papers whether or not she had submitted a work before, which had been rejected.) 'The Hayloft' [fig. 37], now lost,

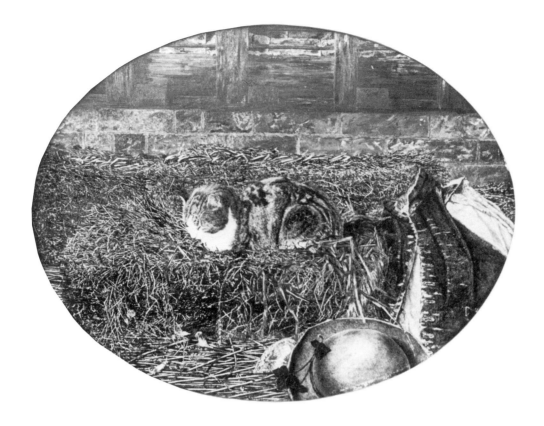

37. Rosa Brett, 'The Hayloft', 1858. Oil on canvas. Whereabouts unknown.
(Photo: Courtauld Institute of Art)

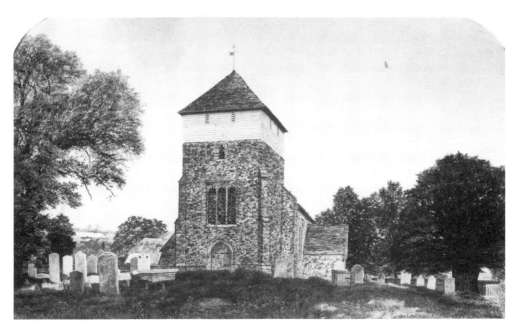

38. Rosa Brett, 'Detling Church', 1858. Oil on canvas. Private collection.
(Photo: Sotheby's)

was a small oil in an oval frame. The artist sent it to John, who responded:

> Dear R, I have not time and have not sufficiently gotten over the excitement to write a criticism on your picture but just write this to say it came safe and to tell you I feel quite snuffed out by it – I am considerably taken by surprise and have not yet recovered my equanimity. It has faults – not important ones, but has also some of the finest passages of painting I have seen by any painter, and the great advantage of the certainty of your doing still better – I think that will do for one dose. A young model who was present soon after I opened it this morning no doubt thought my squeals and high leaps indicated a decided case of deranged mind – she looked on in mute astonishment. You must reconsider your determination about secrecy . . . I already find it impossible . . . Woolner to whom I spoke of a wonderful picture by an unknown PRB was agonising in his enquiries – as to how old you were – and whether you were a swell – no suspicion that you were a she. – The thing is infinitely laughable in the intensity of its PR-ism. Write soon and tell me if I may tell indeed, I have told lies enough today over it I won't go on further. Your JB

The mystery over the artist's identity, or, more particularly, gender, continued effectively until 1862: the *Art Journal* critic reviewed her 'Thistles' in the 1861 Academy as being by 'Rosarius, whoever he may be'. When she reappeared at the Academy in 1867, it was under her real name. John's comment on her mystification being 'laughable in the intensity of its PR-ism' presumably refers to the early reputation of the Brotherhood for secrecy and the arcane. The reasons for the artist adopting the masculine pseudomyn of 'Rosarius' can be imagined.

There is no doubt that both John and Rosa were keen Pre-Raphaelites, their enthusiasm derived from Ruskin to a large degree, as was the case with so many aspiring artists of their generation. John must, also like others of their time, have tried to interest Ruskin in their work, for in 1860 he wrote to Rosa: 'I will tell old White to come and see your Pic, also every one else of consequence – I shall hardly have the face to ask JR to come again – I don't think he would . . .'.[137] Ruskin certainly failed to mention Rosa's début in his *Academy Notes* of 1858, neither did he review her work in any of the subsequent *Notes*, but, as is well known, her brother John did secure the critic's interest to some effect. Indeed,

Ruskin's championship of John Brett, even though it waned later, made Rosa's brother a much-debated artist throughout the 1860s and 1870s, and it is surprising that she did not receive critical attention simply as his sister, as was female artists' usual fate. Throughout her exhibiting career, however, she attracted little more than half a dozen notices.

At some point in its travels through the galleries, 'The Hayloft' got a buyer: in July 1859, John recorded in his diary that 'Prince will not pay Rosa for her cat'. She seems to enter a new lease of artistic life with this venturing out into the art world, and at the end of 1858, her brother recorded 'Rosa tolerably well as ardent impulsive and unbendable as usual', and noted that she was painting. ('Detling Church' [fig. 38], a fine and confident painting, dates from then.)

During the next year or eighteen months Rosa Brett continued to produce drawings and paintings, not necessarily for exhibition. From 1859 date a large study of horse-chestnut blossoms and a small oil of a mouse in undergrowth, among other things. This latter piece could be her 1867 Academy piece 'The field-mouse at Home', which elicited generous criticism from the *Athenaeum* reviewer: 'a perfect gem in its way, and although comprising nothing more pretending than the little creatures and grass, has plenty of subject'.[138] Her next work of scale, however, was the oil which was eventually her next Academy exhibit, 'Thistles', which she commenced in June 1860 and finished before the year was out. Essentially a still-life picture, 'Thistles' sets a living group against a bright Kentish landscape, the background more generalised to set off the Pre-Raphaelite detail of the observation of the main subject. The *Athenaeum* critic remarked upon it as being 'remarkable for fidelity of imitation and solidity', although the *Art Journal* reviewer chose to make an example of it, saying, 'It might be difficult to get more interesting thistles . . . but they are only thistles after all . . .' To devote such attention to a 'low' subject, was in itself a very Pre-Raphaelite statement, though this critic does not use the term in his criticism. The curved frame emphasises its Pre-Raphaelite style, and the bright, light hues the artist employs amplify that influence.

Her next work followed this pattern: 'Foxgloves' was shown at the Academy in 1862. Also dating from this year is the magnificent painting, 'The Old House at Fairleigh' [pl. XIII] which she started in July 1862 and finished in the autumn. Given her increasing rate of production and evident confidence in her work at this time, it seems unlikely that this pleasant and well-observed work, with its happy colours and rich though not obtrusive detail, would not have been shown in some show or other. Two other pieces which survive could also date from this productive period: a small square oil study of a blossoming chestnut tree in a garden, unfinished and inscribed by a later hand 'Garden of their house at Detling'; and a vivid study of two female figures who have not yet been identified [fig. 39].

Another small oil which survives undated, which the Tate Gallery calls 'Study of a turnip field . . .' and dates to after 1863,[139] is probably from the later 1860s, since its colouring is more mature and more subtly true to nature than her surviving early 1860s work. Towards the end of the decade she turned towards landscape and generally more open space in her paintings than had been the case in the earlier part of the decade. ('Thistles', though it has an open background, is essentially a close-up, while the 1860 picture of the artist's mother in a garden has a closed exterior for its background.) A watercolour landscape of 1869, entitled 'Barming, Kent' shows a similar subtlety of colouring, though the palette is a very different one; while sketchbook studies of 1870, 1871 and 1872 display a similar intensity.

All of Rosa's recorded subjects in the next two or three years are drawn from nature. Her father's diary for 1863 records her activity: in March she is ordering a frame for her picture, a week later ordering more watercolours, the next month she has work rejected by the RA, but in July 'Rosa employed Painting in the back Orchard'. The next year his diary tells the same story of indefatigable industry and zeal. From the later part of the decade portrait drawings and flower studies survive, and she evidently kept up some production of finished oil pictures, since one was accepted for the 1867 Academy ('The field-mice at home') and one for the 1869 exhibition ('Morning in the marshes'). Little information is available from family records at this period about Rosa's progress, for presumably the main interest would have been John's development under the aegis of Ruskin, but a portrait drawing by John of his sister, dated December 1867, shows a more confident woman than his earlier drawings portrayed. Certainly the work she had been producing entitled her to look thus self-assured.

Notebooks and sketchbooks in the possession of the artist's family record that in late 1868 she was studying skies particularly, and this interest continued into the next year, with special attention being given to sunrise and sunset. Also many sketches of birds, sheep, trees, landscapes, often unidentified and not always finished. Rosa Brett's meticulous, Pre-Raphaelite approach to nature has

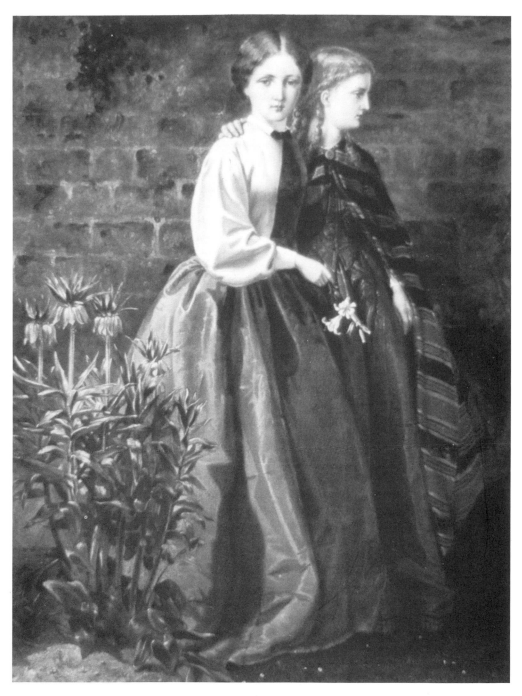

39. Rosa Brett, 'Two Ladies', 1864. Oil on canvas. Private collection.
(Photo: Sotheby's)

already been remarked upon, but it is in the sketchbooks of the
1870s that it is most evident [fig. 40]. The preparatory material
(which, it must be concluded, was not all worked up into oil
paintings, although colour and texture are meticulously prepared
for in her sketchbooks) dating from this decade shows her mostly
interested in wooded landscapes and skies, the locations of such
subject-matter mostly local to her home and including Bexley
(1877), Broadstairs (1879) and typically Kentish scenes characterised by hop-growing paraphernalia (1870). The location of a scene
is often not noted, but the direction of the sunlight and time of day
often are, in neat tiny notes. Diverse and characterful sketchbooks
from both the 1870s and the early 1880s – when some drawings of
Bettwys Coed, Snowdon, and other North Wales locations are
mixed up in with the Kentish (e.g. Sevenoaks, 1881) settings[140] –
make it regrettable that the finished pictures she exhibited during
this period have disappeared.

She showed at the Academy in 1871, 1873, 1875, 1876 and 1881,
and, though the latter two years' pictures were presumably more or
less still-lifes ('Starling and Bluetit', 1876; and 'Iris', 1881), the other
titles indicate that the works might have drawn on her sketchbook
material ('A Spring Afternoon', 1871; 'A Winter Afternoon in Kent',
1873; 'A Doubtful Greeting', 1875). The fact that in 1871, 1873 and
1875 her Academy exhibits drew critical attention (albeit brief)
would suggest that the pictures in question were quite accomplished. In all cases, the criticism was from the *Art Journal's*
reviewer, and indirectly suggests Pre-Raphaelite character. The
most finished piece that remains from this decade, is not a painting
but a drawing of chicks: three separate drawings, framed together,
signed and dated 1870 (June) and done in Margate, from the
inscription. They are quite charming drawings, showing a fine
sensitivity of touch to texture and young animal form, relating to
another smaller pencil drawing, dated 18 May 1873, of a cat lying in
straw and inscribed 'Portrait of Bunny'. These sensitive pieces
contrast curiously with a much larger and less delicate drawing of
two rabbits under foliage (undated). The intense observation
which produced these drawings evidently went to other natural
subjects too: a pencil sketch of flowers, dated 25 May 1873, bears
the note:

Ragged Robins Stamens very short and light. Then the petals.
Petals darker on the underside. Then on the upper Calix a rich
medder [sic] which varies very much and rather fluffy. Stem

198

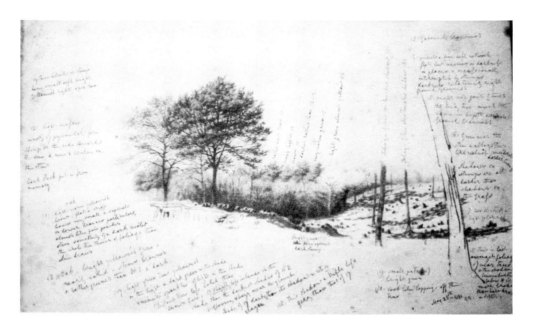

40. Rosa Brett, Sketchbook, 1870/71. Pencil on paper. Private collection.
(Photo: author)

rather fluffy and purplish towards the flower. Leaves near the flower purplish on the underside.

Rosa Brett's last exhibit at the Royal Academy was her 'Iris' in 1881. She was then 52 years old. Since 1867 she had exhibited under her own name, but had received little of the notice that her brother was now used to.[141] Though there is no evidence that she actually sought fame any greater than, say, being an Academy exhibitor or, indeed, than being the sister of a famous artist, it is regrettable that her art was not more regarded in her own time if only because a measure of fame might well have served to develop her work.

She died in 1882; her brother's diary for 27 July 1882 reads:

The next family event of importance is of the saddest kind: the loss of my only sister Rosa. She died five days before Gwendolen was born ... This is a very great loss to our children who were her greatest pets. Edwin and Alice took care of her during the latter weeks of her life which ended in their little farmstead at Caterham, and the grass grows over her in Caterham churchyard.

She had spent all her life, as many mid-Victorian women did, as a 'relative creature', yet in her work she attained an independence that is impressive, even if it was not recognised publicly in her own day. Modesty, allegedly becoming to a lady, served the 'lady-artist' badly.

Notes

1.   Clayton gives only one page to her (*op. cit.,* vol.2, p.129), and most mentions of her are only as an appendage to her painter brothers Abraham and Simeon. See, most recently, Susan P. Casteras, *The Substance and the Shadow* (Yale Center for British Art, 1982), p.95; and *The Solomon Family of Painters* (Geffrye Museum London, 1985).
2.   See the *Manchester Guardian,* 11 October 1893, for obituary of Annie Mutrie; Clayton actually writes, in her brief account of the two artists, 'These ladies have invariably declined, from feelings of delicacy, to make any particulars of their life public' (*op. cit.,* vol.2, p.289). The DNB, however, has an entry on Martha (vol.13, p.4333) to which is added a note on Annie.
3.   Though not in her own words Thornycroft's life and work are described in Elfrida Manning, *Bronze and Steel* (1930); the author is the artist's grand-daughter.

4.   William Frith, *My Autobiography* (1887/88) ch. 52, 'Lady Artists'.

5.   Henry Ottley, ed. G. Stanley, *Biographical Dictionary of Painters*, etc. (1866) (with supplement); Sarah Tytler (Henrietta Keddie), *Modern Painters and their Paintings* (1874), ch. 8; Samuel Redgrave's *Dictionary*, published in 1874, had an entry on Boyce/Wells, but omitted Ward and the two Mutries, as well as such candidates for inclusion as Thornycroft, Solomon and Osborn; the Preface, however, included the comment that 'it cannot be assumed . . . that all who ought to find a place have been included'.

6.   Ernest Chesneau, *The English School of Painting*, trans. Lucy Etherington (1891); shortly afterwards, Walter Shaw Sparrow's massive *Women Painters of the World* (1905), obviously intended to rectify the situation of partial recognition seemingly by noting any female who had ever put brush or pencil to canvas or paper.

7.   In addition to Chapter 1 above, see Parker and Pollock, *op. cit.*, for a more universal and complex investigation of the assumptions and prejudices which put female artists in the position they customarily hold in art history. Brief accounts of these artists can be found as follows: Howitt, P.G. Nunn, *Canvassing* (1986); Thornycroft, Nunn and Garrity, 'Women, Sculpture and Heroism in the Nineteenth Century', *Feminist Art News*, vol.2, no.2 (1985), pp. 14–18; Bodichon, John Crabbe, 'An Artist Divided', *Apollo*, vol. 113, May 1981; Osborn, L. Nochlin and A.S. Harris, *Women Artists, 1550–1950* (Los Angeles, 1977).

8.   *Connoisseur*, September 1824, p.57 and *Who Was Who* (1916/1928), p.1092.

9.   Tytler, *op. cit.*, p.300.

10.   The connection also extended to make contact with the Williams family, of which Caroline F. Williams was the only prominent female member.

11.   Henrietta Ward, *Memories of Ninety Years* (1924), ch.2, p.22. This, along with the artist's other autobiographical publication, *Reminiscences* (1911), is the main source for this account. The artist's descendants have been very helpful in making works available which were previously unknown.

12.   James Dafforne, 'British Artists, their style and character', *Art Journal*, no.77, 1 December 1864, p.357.

13.   Ward, *Memories*, ch.1, p.2.

14.   Ibid., ch.2, p.28.

15.   It cannot be exaggerated how frequent this situation seems to have been in the early years of female artists. It can, of course, be easily explained by the nature of a girl's education at this time, encouraging the arts of music and drawing or painting as suitable outlets for female creativity. Earlier examples of this circumstance can be seen in Angelika Kauffman's sympathetic 'The artist hesitating between the arts of painting

and music' (1794, Nostell Priory, Yorkshire), or Anguiscola's self-portrait of 1561 (Althorp, Northampton).

16. There is no record of her having made it into a painting at any later stage.

17. According to the artist's *Memories*, the work was two still-lifes, but her *Reminiscences* would have them as two heads. Graves lists them as 'Study of heads'. Incidentally, he does not list her alleged 1846 entry.

18. Ward, *Memories*, ch.3, p.33.

19. Their general style of figure painting was similar, but their choice of settings and their groupings not; Henrietta was more various than Edward, in her production of simple, small-scale domestic scenes as well as complex historical dramas. Without the benefit of seeing more of Henrietta's early, middle and late works, one could only hazard a guess that she would have become less similar to her husband as she went on. However, as the *Times* critic noted in 1863, 'If Mrs Ward indicates her master in her method, this is only natural. But her picture requires no gallantry or indulgence from the critic on the score of the painter's sex' (7 May 1863, p.7). The artist does not herself meet the challenge of such criticism in her autobiography, either by refutation or by agreement and explanation.

20. Germaine Greer, *The Obstacle Race* (1979), ch.2 'Love'. Ward is mentioned in ch. 3, 'The Illusion of Success'.

21. Ward, *Memories.*, ch.1 p.1. Similarly, 'It was owing to Edward's advice that I concentrated on Art, which I never regretted doing' (ch.3, p.34).

22. 'The plan was confided to Wilkie, to whose sense of adventure it made an immediate, if vicarious, appeal. He became a fellow-conspirator and willingly undertook all the arrangements' (K. Robinson, *Wilkie Collins* (1951), p.50).

23. Ward, *Memories*, ch.3, p.41.

24. Clayton, *op. cit.*, vol.2, p.108.

25. In sum, Alice, Leslie, Eva, Flora, Wriothesley, Beatrice, Enid, Stanhope.

26. Ward, *Memories*, ch.9, p.124.

27. These works are all untraced.

28. *Art Journal*, 1 June 1851, p.155.

29. Whereabouts now unknown.

30. Respectively, *Athenaeum*, 17 May 1856, p.622; *Art Journal*, 1 June 1855, p.176; ibid., 1 June 1854, p.170.

31. *Athenaeum*, 20 May 1854, p.626.

32. 'I determined to go regularly, in spite of very determined opposition from Mr Jones RA, who was Keeper of the Schools. With an utter absence of chivalry, he actually convened a special meeting to exclude women . . .' (Ward, *Memories*, ch.4, p.58).

33. Dafforne, *op. cit.:* 'In order to perfect herself in drawing the human figure, Mrs Ward, about this time, went through a course of anatomical

studies at Mr Cary's academy in Bloomsbury Street, from which she derived advantages that were impossible to be obtained in any private studio.' Criticism of Ward's work almost never concerned her command of figures or anatomy.

34. *Athenaeum*, 27 March 1858, p.407; the work is presently untraced, but the *Athenaeum*'s review of it gives an idea of its subject-matter: 'The philanthropist is parting with his cottage-tenants at Cardington; he is seated at a cottage-door; his cane hangs at his chair. It is a father parting with his children. The frank kindliness of his face is well painted, and so is the awe and respect of the child and the buxom mother. The groom with the saddled horses at the inn-door tells the story of departure . . .' (8 May 1858, p.598).

35. *Art Journal*, 1 June 1858, p.167.

36. Ibid., 1 December 1862, p.236.

37. Dafforne, *op. cit.*, p.359.

38. S.C. Hall, *Memories* (1871), p.487.

39. The artist herself evidently shared prevailing opinion, that her domestic works were pleasant rather than powerful, and therefore less consequential than the historical drama or moral picture: 'I always enjoyed painting tiny children, and generally managed to spare time from more serious work to paint either a group, or single figure in miniature, for Edward's birthday' (Ward, *Memories*, ch.23, p.248).

40. This last painting and 'Queen Mary . . .' are untraced; while 'Sion House' was sold at Christie's, 14 July 1972.

41. 'Elizabeth Fry' is in a private collection in the USA, although a later replica is in the Friends' House, London; 'God save the Queen' remains untraced.

42. *Athenaeum*, 19 May 1855, p.591.

43. Ibid., 17 May 1862, p.668.

44. *Saturday Review*, 24 May 1862, p.593.

45. *Art Journal*, 1 January 1863, p.97 and *Athenaeum*, 5 January 1861, p.23 (the painting was engraved in this year).

46. Respectively, *Athenaeum*, 8 November 1862, p.597; ibid., 19 May, 1866, p.675; *Art Journal*, 1 June 1868, p.102; *Spectator*, 2 June 1855, p.575; *The Times*, 2 May 1868, p.11.

47. Ward, *Memories*, ch.5, p.71.

48. Ibid., ch.4, p.59.

49. Witness the *Times* critic, typical of many such instances, when he wrote in reviewing the Academy show of 1863: 'Mrs Ward – grand-daughter, daughter, and wife of artists – if not a member of the Academy has an Academician for a husband, and should write RA after her name, with the Miss Mutries, Mrs Carpenter, Mrs C. Newton, and some other of our paintresses, if the Academy were as catholic now as it was in the last century, when it opened its ranks to Angelika Kauffmann and Mary Moser' (7 May 1863, p.7).

50. It is difficult to be sure how well bought she was, since her autobiography makes only passing references to sales and patrons, and press accounts of sales tend to select the most famous artists or works to report, leaving one ignorant of the fate of less prominent pictures. However, of her celebrated works, at least 'The Princes in the Tower', 'Palissy the Potter' and 'Howard's Farewell' were bought immediately or shortly after their appearance, while 'The Queen's Lodge, Windsor' was acquired by the Walker Art Gallery in 1925 from a private individual, as was the case with 'Chatterton' presented to the Bristol Art Gallery in 1909. Records of a sale of works at the artist's death have not come to light.

51. Ward, *Memories*, ch.17, p.196.

52. Tessa McKenzie, *The Art Schools of London* (1895), p.80.

53. *Art Journal*, 1 June 1879, p.119.

54. *The Lady*, December 1887, vol.6, p.427.

55. Ibid., July 1888, vol.8, p.28.

56. She exhibited one work in 1889, one in 1890, one in 1893, one each year from 1903 to 1907; one in 1918 and one in 1921, but no exhibit is recorded later than these, despite the artist's claim to have been represented at the Academy in the year of her death.

57. *Connoisseur*, September 1924, p.57.

58. *Saturday Review*, 23 May 1863, p.662.

59. *The Critic*, 27 July 1861, p.109; the *Athenaeum* responded similarly *Athenaeum*, 20 July 1861, p.89.

60. For more detailed information on George Price Boyce, see the recent revision of his diaries, published as *The Diaries of George Price Boyce*, ed. Virginia Surtees (Norwich, 1980).

61. I am indebted for precise information about the artist's life to numerous members of her family, chief among whom Mr John Street and his son Mr Jonathan Street, made available copies of letters by the artist and her family as yet unpublished; and Mrs Anne Christopherson, in whose keeping the artist's sketchbooks remain. Other descendants of the artist allowed me generous access to those works which remain in the family's possession. References here to opinions, actions or events involving Boyce within her family, unsupported by other references, are taken from letters and diaries which I have been allowed to read in the possession of the artist's family (though see unpublished BA thesis by Julia Ford, Loughborough College of Art, 1979 on the artist's and her husband's work).

62. H.T. Wells (1828–1903) miniaturist and later portraitist and subject painter.

63. Margaret Fuller, (later Margaret Fuller Ossoli), an American feminist, author of *Woman in the 19th Century* (1845), who died in 1850 aged 40. See *Dictionary of American Biography*, vol.7, p.63.

64. Harriet Grote, *Memoir of the Life of Ary Scheffer* (1860).

65. In her account of the French pictures at the 1855 Paris Exhibition

written for the *Saturday Review* (1 December 1855, p.80). Jones (the *Review*'s founder) was a friend of the Boyces, and Bevington. (The *Saturday Review*, 1941) claims that the artist probably wrote other pieces for the paper in its first five years (p.294). There is a letter with the artist's sketchbooks dated May 1856 to Jones, requesting payment for 'her contributions'.

66. A sketch for Millais's oil painting is in the City Art Gallery, Birmingham; the painting itself, which was exhibited at the Academy in 1847, is still in the artist's family. It is much different from Boyce's treatment of the subject, but no other Elgiva was shown at the Academy between its exhibition and Boyce's.

67. The former exhibited subject paintings at the RA (1856–61), BI (1856) and National Institution (Portland Gallery) (1856), which were slightly, though favourably, reviewed; the latter exhibited watercolour portraits at the SFA (1857/58) and is no doubt a member of the Todhunter family which Mary Howitt records visiting on 23 August 1853 with Anna Mary (Howitt, *op. cit.*, vol.2, p.104).

68. Boyce was certainly in a minority, for the work in question is the much-discussed 'Margaret returning from the Fountain', which other members of the Pre-Raphaelite circle found very impressive, and which generally received a good press; her comment does indicate that she had been led to expect the work to *be* 'marvellous'. See above p.94, 105.

69. *Academy Notes* (supplement); Cook and Wedderburn, *op. cit.*, vol.14, p.31.

70. *Illustrated London News*, 7 July 1855, p.23.

71. Ford Madox Brown, *Diary*, 22 May 1855.

72. *Athenaeum*, 20 July 1861, p.89.

73. The painting is currently in the possession of a descendant of the artist.

74. For detailed information on Couture's teaching at this period, see the excellent *Thomas Couture and the eclectic vision*, A. Boime (Yale, 1980) (which, however, does not mention Boyce).

75. Photograph in the possession of the artist's family, inscribed in reverse in George's handwriting. The model is interestingly similar to Charlotte Ridley, the model for 'La Veneziana'; 'Mme Hereau' is lost.

76. It is not clear whether or not the Couture painting was in his studio at the time when Boyce was there (it is now in the National Gallery of Scotland), but she might have known it anyway.

77. *Saturday Review*, 1 December 1855, p.79; and 29 December 1855, p.153; and 10 May 1856, p.31 to 7 June 1856, p.125.

78. The reference for most of the artist's works is the catalogue to the memorial exhibition at the Tate Gallery in 1935, in which 31 of the artist's works were exhibited, but of which visual records do not necessarily exist, and of which a large proportion was destroyed during the Second World War, from the collection of Mrs Arthur Street, in Bath, Avon.

79.   This list appears among the artist's papers, and I am grateful to Julia Ford for drawing my attention to it; in testament to the artist's industry, it runs to some thirty projects, and was drawn out in 1861, the year of her death.

80.   *The Times,* 24 November 1859, p.9. This was a review of the Winter Exhibition; *Critic,* 27 July 1861, p.109; *Illustrated London News,* 27 July 1861, p.87.

81.   She escaped disadvantageous comparison with her husband through being patently a far superior artist; perhaps, had she continued her career, some attribution of her talent would eventually have been made to Couture, even though he was not especially esteemed in Britain at the time. The *Critic*'s elaborate obituary notice, however, managed to haul in the family connection, with reference to Wells and G.P. Boyce, saying 'Mrs Wells was not only wedded to an artist . . . but came of an artistic stock' (*Critic,* 27 July 1861, p.109); it was, of course, the case that George's becoming an artist was largely due to his sister's encouragement, anyway (see Arthur Street on GPB, *Architectural Review,* vol.5, 1899, p.152).

82.   *Athenaeum,* 27 July 1861, p.121.

83.   *Saturday Review,* 25 May 1861, p.121.

84.   *Athenaeum,* 11 May 1861, p.635.

85.   Ibid., 20 July 1861, p.89.

86.   *Critic,* 27 July 1861, p.109. Since femininity in handling would have connoted a tentativeness which cannot be seen in the artist's work, and femininity in conception would have connoted a domestic or sentimental strain which is rarely seen in her work ('Peep-bo' is a domestic work; 'Do I like Butter?' could be construed as sentimental), the femininity of which the critic speaks can best be located in the artist's choice of female protagonists: although her *dramatis personae* include males ('The Child's Crusade', the several red-haired boys, the Italian boy either 'Poverino' or 'Carminello') the female characters (the Sybil, Elgiva, La Veneziana, Gretchen, Undine) predominate markedly.

87.   Letter of June 1861, quoted in Stanley Weintraub, *Three Rossettis* (1978), p.8.

88.   *The Times,* 19 June 1935, p.12. The occasion was the exhibition at the Tate Gallery already mentioned; it included most of the finished works mentioned here. Her work has also been shown posthumously in Birmingham, 'Victorian Pictures', 1937 and the Tate 'Pre-Raphaelite Exhibition', 1923.

89.   *Critic,* 27 July 1861, p.110; this point had been more deliberately made earlier in the passage, where the writer had declared: 'As an artist Mrs Wells was among the most vigorous and interesting of those [of either sex] who were rising into public notice.' However, the final verdict did relate to 'women in the domain of art': 'In behalf of that deserving and as yet drooping Cause, how much would such an example as she (with life) could have set have done; how much would it have sustained and fortified

weaker fellow-labourers of her own sex.'

90.   'The Orphan' and 'The Orphan Friends' are lost, although the former may be in New Zealand, though as yet unidentified. Another, possibly Hospital-related work, is 'Les Orphelins', shown at the sfa in 1873, now untraced. I am very grateful to the artist's grandson and his daughters for giving me access to visual evidence of the artist's early work and those pieces still in the family.

91.   In 1864, she showed at least ten pictures; in 1865, at least twelve, and very possibly fourteen; in 1866, eleven; records of her provincial exhibits, however, are incomplete.

92.   *Art Journal*, 1 March 1867, p.88; *Evening Star*, 15 January 1866.

93.   *Art Journal*, 1 July 1857, p.215; both works not now known.

94.   Unidentified newspaper cutting in album compiled by the artist's grandson; work now unknown. *Builder*, 10 April 1858, p.243; the work in question was 'Our Little Brother', the whereabouts of which are now unknown.

95.   *Art Journal*, 1 October 1860, p.306.

96.   Respectively, ibid., 1 May 1861, p.140; *Athenaeum*, 23 November 1861, p.693; ibid., 9 February 1861, p.200.

97.   Entry for 11 June in the artist's diary of the trip. All the following quotations regarding the trip are taken from this as yet unpublished source, which was generously made available by the artist's grandson.

98.   Diary, 9 June. The picture referred to is, of course, Whistler's first 'White Girl'. In the words of a much more avant-garde compatriot, D.G. Rossetti, one finds an interestingly similar failure to appreciate the innovative character of painting in Paris at that time: the Pre Raphaelite wrote in a letter of 1864: 'The new French school is simple putrescence and decomposition . . .' (quoted in Hilary Taylor, *James McNeill Whistler*, 1978, p.25).

99.   In the possession of the artist's family there is an oil sketch which is signed 1853 and inscribed 'copied from an unfinished sketch by Heaphy Emma Brownlow 1853'. Thomas Heaphy Junior did live in Henrietta Street, where the Brownlows lived from 1843 onwards, so it may be that the young Brownlow was in some measure his pupil. No other copied material survives among her juvenilia.

100.   Compare the verdict of Boyce: 'Now a Frenchman's notion of "high art" consists, first, in an enormous canvas, life (or larger than life) sized figures, and an historical incident – if horrible, so much the better' (*Saturday Review*, 10 May 1856, p.31); in her notes for this passage, in her sketchbook, she uses the same word, 'painful', as Brownlow: 'A Frenchman's idea of high art consists primarily in a large canvas and life-sized figures and generally some painful or repelling historical [?] for a subject.'

101.   See Benedict Nicholson, *The Treasures of the Foundling Hospital* (Oxford, 1972) and Nichols and Wray, *The History of the Foundling Hospital* (1935).

102.   There are two versions of the picture, between which the main difference is John Brownlow's age.

103.   See Table page 114.

104.   The *Spectator* mentioned her among painters who 'exhibit domestic figures or groups of merit' at the BI in 1857 (14 February 1867, p.183), while the *Times* review of that exhibition in 1858 mentioned her in the company of G. Smith, Bromley, Hemsley, Barnes, Henderson and Nicol, and 'others much too tedious to mention' (8 February 1858, p.9); this was the continuing note of status she was accorded critically – worthy of mention but not outstanding.

105.   On the contrary, most of her letters are concerned with her indigence, and reveal her financial dependence on the pension derived from Donald King's investment in the Drury Lane Theatre trust fund.

106.   For some account of Waterford's life, see Virginia Surtees, *Sublime and Instructive* (1972), and the same author's *Charlotte Canning* (1975). Also Augustus Hare, *Two Noble Lives* (1893).

107.   *Illustrated London News*, 11 June 1892, p.134; Fenwick-Miller was a feminist writer and journalist active in the latter two decades of the century. Dr Rosemary van Arsdel is currently researching her work.

108.   The reference is to Jopling's *Hints to Amateurs*, (1891). For a less favourable reference to this volume, see the *Magazine of Art*, March 1891, p.xxiii.

109.   Surtees, *Sublime and Instructive*, p.1.

110.   The speaker is Sophia Thellusson, later Lady Rose, who was a friend to Waterford in young and adult years; quoted in Hare, *op. cit.*, vol.1, p.153.

111.   Clayton, *op. cit.*, vol.2, p.338.

112.   Hare, *op. cit.*, vol.1, p.243; probably relevant here are pieces listed by Hare as 'Boy minding Crows', 'Woman gathering Sticks', 'The Ox-Plough', 'The Gleaners', 'Girl with a Milk-Pan', 'An Irish Peasant', 'Irish School-girl', 'The Cottage-door, a scene in Ireland', and others (Hare, vol.3, p.193 ff.).

113.   Letter dated 21 November 1849, quoted in Hare, *op. cit.*, vol.1, p.334; this series of drawings is now in the possession of the current occupant of Ford Castle, Lord Joicey; in sepia on A4 sheets, the set consists of 'Hungry, and ye fed me', 'Sick, and ye visited me', as well as 'Thirsty, and ye gave me to drink', with their negatives (contrasts, in the artist's words). I am grateful to the owner for allowing me access to these drawings.

114.   The topical theme of gleaners and reapers was treated by her a number of times, and often given a Biblical slant, as in 'A Time to Sow', 'The Joyful Harvest', 'They that sow in tears shall reap in joy', 'And the Reapers are the Angels', 'Ruth and Naomi' (all listed by Hare, as above, note 106). The ever-popular source of Shakespeare also claimed her, in 'Ophelia', 'Othello', 'As you Like it', 'Hamlet', and her numerous Romeo and Juliet pieces (these latter are discussed by the artist in letters to Mrs Bernal Osborne, 19 February 1863, Hare, vol.3, p.239 and 15 December

1867, Hare, vol.3, p.291 and to EVB, 1 December 1875, Hare, vol.3, p.364).

115. Letter to Janet Ellice, dated 14 November 1851, quoted in Hare, *op. cit.*, vol.1, p.347.

116. Undated letter to Mrs Bernal Osborne, quoted in Hare, *op. cit.*, vol.1, p.247.

117. Letter to William Allingham, 26 June 1855, quoted in Doughty and Wahl, *op. cit.*, vol.1, p.257.

118. Letter to the artist's mother, 1 July 1855, ibid., p.260.

119. Clayton, *op. cit.*, vol.2, p.339.

120. Quoted in Surtees, *Sublime and Instructive*, pp.4, 6.

121. Letter to Lady Waterford, probably 1 July 1855, quoted in Surtees, *Sublime and Instructive*, p.8; see also Pamela G. Nunn, 'Ruskin's Patronage of Women Artists', *Woman's Art Journal*, vol.2, no.2 (Fall/Winter 1981), for more on Ruskin's artistic significance to Waterford.

122. The artist's diary, quoted in Hare, *op. cit.*, vol.3, p.254.

123. Letter to Mrs John Leslie, 10 January 1863, quoted in Hare, vol.3, p.236; a Holy Family couched in classical language, appeared at the Grosvenor Gallery in 1878 (no.168), while in 1873 she sent another drawing of the same subject to the Grosvenor (see letter to EVB, quoted in Hare, vol.3, p.317).

124. I am grateful to the current incumbent of Ford, Lord Joicey, for allowing me access to the preparatory material for the frescoes which is in his possession. Ford and its inhabitants provided much material for the artist during the 1860s and 1870s.

125. Hare's list of subjects attempted shows how many themes were tried time and time again, while her surviving drawings show how incompletely she could leave an idea. She evidently, however, had so many ideas for images that some must have remained unworked or incomplete through an embarrassment of riches. Hare wrote to his mother while staying with the artist in 1861, 'Painting is her great employment, and all evening she makes studies for the larger drawings which she works upon in the mornings' (Letter dated 17 October 1861, quoted Hare, vol.3, p.141).

126. Waterford heads the Amateur section (vol.2, pp.338–340).

127. Letter to EVB, 31 October 1875, quoted in Hare, vol.3, p.361; Charles Stuart comments on the relationship between the two amateurs thus: 'Mrs. Richard Boyle (EVB), a cousin of Lady Waterford's, was too congenial in artistic taste and talent, as well as in feeling, not to be a most welcome addition to her society' (Stuart, *op. cit.*, p.20).

128. Letter to EVB, 23 May 1878, quoted in Hare, vol.3, p.388; Mrs Steuart Erskine quotes a letter from the artist of 1879 which says, 'I can only say these exhibitions are the best levellers I know; one has no more illusions about oneself and no flatterers are of avail' (Erskine, *Studio*, 1910 p.283).

129. Boyle's published sets of drawings included 'A Children's Summer' (1853) and her illustrations 'Fairy Tales' by Hans Christian Andersen

(1872) and 'Beauty and the Beast' (1875).

130.   Letter to Honoria Thompson, 10 March 1881, quoted in Hare, vol.3, p.409, and to the same, 28 November 1881, quoted in Hare, vol.3 p.415.

131.   Surtees, *Sublime and Instructive*, p.3.

132.   Catalogue, Loan Exhibition of Watercolour Paintings by Louisa Marchioness of Waterford, Carlton House Terrace, April 1910, p.9.

133.   Surtees, *Sublime and Instructive*, p.5; the *Magazine of Art*'s review of her work in the Old Masters Exhibition at Burlington House in 1893 claimed her composition to be supreme (p.114). This exhibition contained 75 drawings, along with work by Blake, Calvert and Palmer.

134.   Various branches of the artist's family have generously made available to me the visual and written material which they possess relating not only particularly to Rosa Brett but to the whole family. Any sketches or drawings, sketchbooks and finished works whose whereabouts are known, which are mentioned here, are in the possession of the family unless otherwise stated.

135.   He is already recorded by Rosa as having paying pupils in her diary, while the remarks about buyers and commissions indicate that John has been promoting himself locally for some while.

136.   See, for instance, Allen Staley's *Preraphaelite Landscape* (Oxford, 1973), which devotes a chapter to the work of John Brett and which has evidently been written with the benefit of materials relating to both artists in the possession of their family, yet makes scant mention of Rosa, and not as an accessory to John's early work.

137.   Letter dated 22 March 1860. There is no evidence to support the idea that Ruskin ever saw or encouraged Rosa's work.

138.   *Athenaeum*, 1 June 1867, p.732. The artist's critical notices were very scant; it was the *Athenaeum*'s critic who had noticed her 1861 exhibit 'Thistles', and when she showed at Old Bond Street in 1869, the *Illustrated London News* critic made mention of her, though briefly.

139.   The painting was included in the exhibition 'Landscape in Britain', 1973, as no.316.

140.   Much of her travelling in this period seems to have been done in the company of her brother's ever-increasing family, and his interests are reflected in the quayside and boating studies in some of her sketchbooks.

141.   It seems probable that in these later years, the artist drew and studied but did not make many pieces up to finished paintings, since if she had, some such works would surely have survived within the family as her early work has done. There is the distinct possibility of her illness having left her susceptible to premature ageing or a recurrence of weakness or debility. It should be noted though, that her rate of exhibition was no slower than it had been even in her earlier, more productive years. She must have produced, in finished work, at least twice the number of works she exhibited, if watercolours and oils are taken into account.

5
The End of the Century

In the second edition of *An Art Student in Munich,* published in 1880, Anna Mary Howitt looked back to the time when the book first appeared   the mid point of the century:

> The difficulties which the habits of society of that day placed in the way of a young woman seeking an independent career in Art, or, indeed, in any other direction, have now almost wholly passed away, and thus, one of the objects to which the book was designed in its modest way to contribute has been largely attained.[1]

The female artist had undoubtedly become visible, between 1853 and 1880 [figs. 3, 12, 13, 16, 17, 19], but although she had been encouraged, had been acknowledged to be in a unique position, and had been championed against unfair treatment hitherto sanctioned by tradition and men's self-interest, though her numbers had increased and her self-confidence matured, still:

Women's place in contemporary art is a strong contrast to women's place in literature. It is yet confined, yet unconquered as a broad acknowledged ground, in spite of the personal fame achieved by such masters [sic] as Rosa Bonheur, Nelly Jacquemard, Mrs Ward, Madame Escalier, and others at home and abroad. Celebrity comes quickly to the clever pen, but the pen must help the painter to find his [sic] fame, for his brush will not conquer it alone. And the women artists of modern days have been, somehow or other, neglected and ignored by most authorised dispensors of fame.[2]

Indeed, in the last twenty years of the century, it became apparent – or becomes so now if we look back at the evidence – that battles had been won, but not the war. Howitt's was an optimistic comment: certain ideas had been reformed, but there had been no revolution, and there was even, to a marked extent, a regression in the 1880s and 1890s. Symptomatic of the rearguard action that surfaced after the gains of the 1850–79 period, was the *Athenaeum*'s obituary notice of Thomas Thornycroft, the sculptor husband of sculptor Mary Thornycroft, in 1885: it described him as 'the well-known sculptor, and father of Mr Hamo Thornycroft'. Also the publication *Academy Pictures*, published by the *Magazine of Art* as a pictorial souvenir of the annual Academy exhibition in 1891 listed only one woman in the rising stars, Marianne (Preindslburger) Stokes, who was not only referred to as Mrs Adrian Stokes, but was included under the rubric 'the younger men who, to judge by their present exhibits, are destined to carry on the traditions now sustained by the members of the Royal Academy' (membership was still closed to women).[3] The forces of reaction had had enough of women's challenge, and dug in their heels. William Frith, with his narrow view of what constituted the art world, stated firmly in his autobiography of 1888: 'Whether we shall have female Academicians or not depends upon the ladies themselves . . . A female President is not impossible.'[4] (Earlier, in 1871, *Punch* had run a feature titled 'Coming Events' on women's rights which had included the satirical prediction that 'Mrs Angela Raphael Reynolds RA has been elected President of the Royal Academy'.)[5]

No doubt, from a reformist point of view, the matter *was* closed – but only if women were still supposed to be second-rate artists, to be content with being the also-rans or the exceptions to prove the rule. Those who grasped the potential challenge of the radicalism of the 1850s and had a more urgent interest in ensuring its fulfilment could see there was still work to be done. Feminist energy generally was still vehemently at work in party politics, in the issue of prostitution, the vote, medicine, and marriage.[6] It must surely be a reflection of the unrelenting challenge which the women's movement was making globally, that the opposition to women's continued progress within the art world had such a reactionary character; lines of attack from the 1850s debates were, in the 1880s and 1890s, given a second wind.

The attribution of female talent to a male relative was still in the armoury of weapons used to resist female achievement: Flora Reid was compared with her brother John; Marianne Preindlsburger was pushed under her husband Adrian Stokes' umbrella, as was Elizabeth Armstrong under her husband Stanhope Forbes'; several late Pre-Raphaelite women were lumped together as D.G. Rossetti followers or Burne-Jones imitators.[7] Another familiar line was the designation of certain qualities deemed 'good' as masculine or belonging to men; and, tirelessly revived from the early years of the debate, the suggestion that fine art was, after all, not women's proper sphere but design was: 'women are doing most excellent work in the art crafts; so excellent, indeed, that it occurs to me it would be wiser if many who are now trying to win positions as painters and sculptors were to direct their energies and abilities into the less ambitious groove of applied art; success of a quite satisfactory kind might be theirs.' Thus Fred Miller in 1896 in the *Art Journal*.[8] Even the old chestnut of history proving that women were not destined nor able to be great artists was resuscitated to wave its banner once more,[9] showing that certain quarters of opinion had been holding fast, from the 1850s, through the 1870s, to beliefs whose false logic and biased rationales had apparently been exposed as specious years before.

The press, though it found less space for women artists or women and art as a subject than it had previously, is the site of much of this reactionary debate. The *Art Journal* and the *Magazine of Art* expressed the rearguard defence, while the *Illustrated London News'* columnist, Florence Fenwick-Miller, put the progressive view, and magazines like Oscar Wilde's *Woman's World* (begun 1888), the continuing *Englishwoman's Review*, women's movement papers which sprang up as the suffrage struggle surged, and even a conservative periodical such as *The Lady*, gave voice in their different tones to a woman-oriented opinion. An *Art Journal* article of June 1879 heralding 'An Exhibition of Women's Work', shows how explicit was the reaction against the previous decades:

If the position of the needle as the sole or the chief implement of the graceful industry of woman has been somewhat impaired by the attention which the ladies of our own day have given to the pencil, the chisel, and the brush; to music, to literature, or to a wide range of occupations once considered proper to the ruder sex; none the less does the needle continue to be par excellence, the woman's implement[10]

And in the *Magazine of Art* of 1884 under the title 'Women at work: their functions in Art' it was suggested that 'Art' should be left to those who are man enough for it:

The home in fact has endless uses for art . . . Let genius stand alone as the teacher and apostle of art, and leave to talent and dexterity the handicrafts. Our picture exhibitions would then be temples of art, and our homes the idealisation of utility.[11]

Yet women continued to flock into the Academy, the Slade and sundry private art schools that flourished in the 1880s in response to the Slade's successful policy of equal opportunity for men and women. In Tessa Mackenzie's 1895 booklet *The Art Schools of London,* of 56 separate institutions or facilities listed, by far the majority catered explicitly for (what they imagined to be) respective male and female students' needs, while ten establishments are explicitly or almost certainly for women only. (Though in many cases, a school or class charged female students at a higher rate than male).[12] Also in the last decade of the century, the Academy Schools finally extended their female students' education to include study from the nude model (1893),[13] and the female portion of the Slade's student body came resoundingly into its own, with a generation of women that included Gwen John, Edna Waugh, Ethel Walker and Ursula Tyrwhitt.[14]

Also in that other telling field, exhibition, the 1880s and 1890s show clearly the increasing numbers and progressive confidence and ambition of female artists, though critical coverage of their exhibition regrettably still shows that it was male work that defined the standard of 'Art', and which was looked to for gratification and achievement.

Numbers of exhibition galleries continued to rise, with short-lived venues or societies springing up and dying out. The arrival of the Grosvenor Gallery in 1877 had set the trend for taking a definite 'position' within the field of modern art. The New English Art Club, established as an annually exhibiting body in 1886, is the most conspicuous reflection of this, while the Fine Art Society (established 1876) represented another strand of taste, incidentally much more open to women than the misogynistic NEAC. The Grosvenor became the New in 1888, and other commercial venues for art were the Nineteenth-Century Art Society and John McLean's gallery.[15] Some women were conspicuous beneficiaries of these enterprises, such as Elizabeth Thompson (Lady Butler), the overnight success of 1874, and Helen (Paterson) Allingham, who was frequently given one-woman shows by the Fine Art Society in the 1880s and 1890s. Generally, however, the one-artist show was an opportunity only rarely enjoyed by female artists in this period.

The SFA continued, as the Society of Lady Artists, changing its name yet again in 1899 to the Society of Women Artists – a sign of change of style, as well. Its number of exhibitors fluctuated in the last twenty years of the century, from 363 in 1880 to 393 in the last SLA year (1898), the low point being 225 contributors in 1895.[16] Its exposure of female artists was thus still much higher than the Academy's, whose shows, though including an increasing amount of women's work between 1880 and 1900, still presented a predominantly man-made exhibition, female artists numbering under 300 at the end of the century (1899, 293; 1900, 282) in any one Academy show.

A certain quarter of the criticism of SLA shows echoed almost completely critical comments from some twenty years earlier. Thus the *Magazine of Art*'s critic in 1889:

> It is difficult to see why there should be a Society of Lady Artists at all. Ladies have always received impartial treatment from the hanging committees of the older artistic societies, and it seems unnecessary that they should hold exhibitions which represent no school, no creed, and only differ from their neighbours in the fact that all the pictures they contain are painted by 'lady artists'.

Still, there were as many women as before who found the SLA more appropriate to their art, their aims and their ambitions than other galleries. It was, however, at the RA and the Grosvenor (and later the New) that the most successful female artists of the *fin-de-siècle* came to light. Henrietta Rae made her debut at the Academy in 1881, Elizabeth Armstrong Forbes in 1883, Marianne Stokes in 1884, Anna Alma-Tadema in 1885 (her mother Laura Epps had exhibited since 1873), and Lucy Kemp-Welch in 1895. Elizabeth

Thompson Butler's star gradually waned, with the century. The New featured Annie Swynnerton, the late Pre-Raphaelite school, Susan Dacre and sundry others who made a short-lived name for themselves. Women who had already become a regular feature of certain exhibitions, such as Starr, Osborn, Jopling, Anderson and Anna Lea Merritt, were still seen among the London shows every year, though many of these artists were in their sixties or seventies by the end of the century. Anderson's last recorded exhibit was in 1899 at the age of 76; Ward's last showing was in 1921 at the age 89; Osborn's in 1905 at the age of 71; Starr's in 1909 at the age of 64.

An innovation related to exhibition which occurred in the 1880 to 1900 period was the incursion of women as critics of art exhibitions. Though Boyce/Wells had written occasionally for the *Saturday Review*, criticism had been, as far as can be told, an exclusively male preserve. During the 1880s and 1890s, several women took up exhibition reviewing as well as the writing of art journalism and art history. An *Art Journal* article of 1892 on art critics mentioned Jameson, Margaret Oliphant, Julia Cartwright and Helen Zimmern as writers on art and Alice Meynell and Lady Colin Campbell as critics.[17] A study of the work of these women would show that their voices were, however, telling largely the same story as that put forward by the male mainstream which tolerated them.

Patronage and employment were fields, again, in which women were evidently doing better overall than they had, but in which, equally clearly, the fundamentals had remained unchanged. The rise in design-based art practice which the end of the century saw, thanks in part to the Arts and Crafts movement, to the instituting of design work exhibition as formal as that of fine art work, and to the individual examples of William Morris, Henry Cole, E.W. Godwin and Whistler, benefited women in the short term. The old idea of fine art being out of bounds to the female heart and hand, but craft being appropriate to them, allowed women a place in embroidery, silver-smithing, fabric design, the making of jewellery and ceramics, and illustration. Anthea Callen has documented these areas well in recent times,[18] and the *Studio* magazine's pages reflect very clearly from its inception (1893) onwards, that women were finding work in the applied arts to critical and public approval. (The *Studio* itself seems to have patronised female illustrators to a considerable extent.)

As fine artists, however, women working between 1880 and 1900 seem to have fared only cosmetically better than earlier generations examined here. True, 1890 saw the purchase of an oil painting by a woman for the Tate Gallery – Lea Merritt's 'Love locked Out' [fig. 22] – and there are works in many provincial museums in Britain by artists active in the 1880 to 1900 period (DeMorgan, Kate Bunce, Swynnerton, Stokes, Alice Havers, Elizabeth Armstrong Forbes, Thompson, both mother and daughter Alma-Tadema, Allingham)[19] which were bought before the end of the century. But this increase in attention was no more than should have been expected, with the numbers of women producing painting and sculpture so much greater than before.

It is worth noting that all the above-mentioned were painters: female sculptors seem to have fared comparatively worse, with 'artist' still largely connoting only painters. We see from the comments made on the purchase of the Lea Merritt by the President of the Royal Society of British Artists, the limits of progress:

> One of the loveliest of the Landmarks in the realms of Art has been discovered within the lifetime of most of us. I mean the formal, authoritative recognition of the fact that women can paint pictures.[20]

Apart from the obvious fatuousness of the remark and its embarrassing attempt to flatter, such public expression on the woman and art question at this late date quite obscures the development in women's *sculptural* attempts that the end of the century saw. As Susan Beattie has pointed out, shifts in sculptural practice and patronage during the last three decades of the century, especially the fashion for small, domestically scaled pieces such as statuettes, made women's sculpture more feasible.[21] Even though, in practice, a large or monumental work was often not the literal achievement of the artist (whose concept would have been embodied in a model, usually of wax or plaster) but of technicians who enlarged the concept and rendered it in bronze, marble, or other stone, the received image of the sculptor as a Michelangelo-type figure wielding a heavy tool on some elemental block was strong enough to have made the idea of women attempting sculpture seem, to the conservative mind, rather like a flea attacking an elephant. Such images as the photograph taken of Harriet Hosmer perched on a ladder alongside the huge statue of Thomas Hart Benton for which she had been commissioned in the 1860s had exploited rather than exposed that heroic image of the sculptor [fig. 3].

Somewhat bizarre, or at least unexpected, in this light, is the promotion of aristocratic women as amateur sculptors towards the end of the century. Princess Louise (one of Queen Victoria's daughters), the Duchess of Colonna, and Sarah Bernhardt were among those who fell into this category. That the Michelangelo model was still credible to reactionaries even so, is shown by comments made in the *Studio* in 1896 in the face of a noticeable increase in the number of women producing sculptural work:

> No matter how poetic the idea, how ethereal the finished bas-relief or statue, its fashioning implies much hard work, and no little severe manual labour. Not that one need run away with an idea based on the more or less apocryphal story of Michael Angelo hewing his statue of David straight away from the huge, rough block of marble . . . Still . . . the art of the sculptor in its noblest form demands strenuous labour, so that you may regard it as being tolerably secure from invasion by the new woman, or the mere dilettante; for it is a most perfect instance of fine art inextricably allied with fine craft.[22]

Sculpture depends, even more than other creative media, on patronage for its prosperity, and as long as the terms 'woman' and 'sculptor' seemed impossible or ridiculous companions, patronage would not be forthcoming to enable women's three-dimensional work to get beyond either the plaster stage or, at most, the statuette stage. This makes any discussion of female sculptors' choice of materials or scale meaningless in general terms, but there were some individual examples of fulfilled intention during this end-of-the-century period (e.g. Mary Grant's memorial fountain to Henry Fawcett of 1886, still to be seen in Victoria Embankment Gardens, London [fig. 41]). These show that a woman might enter the field of sculpture as it stood on quite credible terms. A conspicuous factor affecting the way in which a woman might engage in sculpture in the 1880s and 1890s was, however, the marked resurgence of the female nude, the appropriation of the female figure to represent abstract (and often reactionary) concepts, and the adoption by supposedly avant-garde male sculptors of the current favourite female image of symbolist painters, the *femme fatale*. What was a female sculptor supposed to do with such imagery? To judge from the evidence, the answer seems to have been either avoid it (thus being relegated to portraiture, domestic anecdote borrowed from painting, and the decorative) or copy it (thereby producing surely an inauthentic art which, thus weakened, could all too easily be dismissed as second-rate).

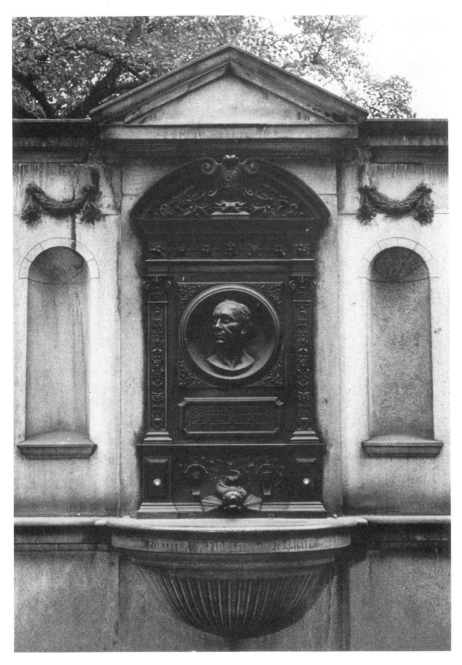

41. Mary Grant, Henry Fawcett memorial fountain, 1886. Bronze and stone. Victoria Embankment Gardens, London. (Photo: Julie Phipps)

Three female artists were conspicuously successful in the late part of the century, and their success can be considered to encapsulate the state of the 'woman (and art) question' at the end of the Victorian era. These three women are Helen (Paterson) Allingham, Elizabeth (Thompson) Lady Butler and Kate Greenaway. The first had begun as a graphic artist working for such papers as the *Graphic*, then specialising in watercolour; Butler was well known for her oil paintings; Greenaway was a commercial success with her coloured illustrations for children's books, though she too had started as a black-and-white artist for the press. Their success indicates the sort of female artist that the end of the century was willing to accept: put simply, sculpture was still out of the question, design work was not important enough to merit fame, and in two dimensions femininity was required and rewarded. That Allingham and Greenaway became more and more popular while Butler's reputation petrified, shows us that a traditionally feminine art – small in scale; watercolour; addressing itself uncritically to domestic experience and incident, the appearance and behaviour of children, the quaint and the picturesque; pleasing by its aesthetic charm but not arresting by its creative genius – was still (or again) the acceptable mode of women's creativity as far as the art world was concerned. Stylistic fashions play a part in this too, of course. Butler's bourgeois realism and the *'grande machine'* were going out of favour along with the Academy that promoted them, while a design-based fine art whose practitioners looked to a wide range of creative forms (even though they might ultimately wish only to revivify their established icon, the oil painting) came more into vogue. (Similarly, it is as indicative of British aesthetic conservatism as of Victorian sexual politics that the French-inspired painting of Elizabeth Armstrong Forbes and other Newlyn or late Realist artists was not more approved than it was.) If women *would* be artists – as, by 1880, it was undeniably evident that they would – the opposition would all the more doggedly approve a certain model and discourage or ridicule or ignore any other.

The situation for women artists in Britain at the end of the nineteenth century can perhaps be symbolised by *Ladies at Work* which appeared in 1893. A collection of essays, it was prefaced by Mary Jeune, Lady Belcher, herself an amateur artist. She introduced the book thus:

Of all the changes which mark the social revolutions of the nineteenth century none are more remarkable and more far-reaching in their effects than those affecting the position of women. Perhaps we may call them complete as far as they have gone, though in the future we cannot doubt that their results will be still wider and more revolutionary. As regards the position and influence of women, there is not much left to desire . . .[23]

Her comments relating specifically to art were equally blithe: 'Medicine, science, teaching, literature, and art are all open to her, in all of which she has won laurels . . . given capacity and physical strength, a woman's chance of distinction is very little behind that of her masculine opponents. Such sanguinity, encouraging as it might seem, is quite inadequate to a real equality for women being achieved, when compared with the contemporaneous expressions on women's position from Eleanor Marx (Aveling), for instance, or any part of the suffrage movement. The essay on art, by Florence Reason, emphasises education and personal resolution as keys to success, scorning the romantic notion of chance and genius being the most likely paths to achievement in the arts. She pays little heed to the negative elements that still inhered in women's situation (even those of the middle classes, whom she is most obviously addressing), concentrating on the positive, as in her reference to the RA Schools:

> The men-students have more advantages, both in the way of study and of substantial prizes, than the women-students, but the ladies have frequently carried off some of the more important medals and other awards in spite of their disadvantages.[24]

Using a masculine generic, she talks of 'artists' in general, but recommends portrait painting in particular as perhaps the most lucrative genre, saying that in this way 'some women earn several hundreds in the course of a year'. She makes no mention of husbands, children, the power of the critic, the prejudice of the dealer, the resentment of the fellow artist, the tradition of history, the divisive categorisations of creative fields, never mind a factor which feminist scholarship in our own time has revealed as so influential in determining a woman's executive relation to art, those images of women presented as Art.[25]

The Victorian period witnessed the emergence of women as artists: by its end, it seems as if the stultification of the female artist was on the horizon. In the present day, we see the relationship between women and art being readdressed, the debate is on again. If we take heed of what happened between 1850 and 1900, the fate of the modern woman artist will, it is to be hoped, resolve itself more satisfactorily than that of her Victorian sisters.

Notes

1.   Howitt, *An Art Student in Munich*, second edn (1880), Preface; by this time, the author was herself no longer active in the arts in any obvious way: she made 'spirit drawings' derived from her interest in clairvoyance.
2.   'Women's Pictures at the Academy', *Woman*, 18 May 1872, p.334; the writer is explaining why s/he has chosen to review women's work separately, as a positive discrimination. The review was in two parts, the second appearing on 1 June, p.364.
3.   *Athenaeum*, 5 September 1885, p.310, and *Academy Pictures*, 1891, p.117. The representation of female artists in this publication ranged from 4 women (out of a total of 128 artists) in 1890 to 5 women (out of a total of 193 artists) in 1899; the highest number of female artists shown was in 1895(17) but the total of artists that year was 252.
4.   William Frith, *My Autobiography* (7th edn, 1889), p.472.
5.   *Punch*, 30 September 1871, p.133.
6.   See R. Strachey, *The Cause* (1928); Hollis, *op. cit.*; and Bauer and Ritt, *op. cit.*
7.   See for instance *Illustrated London News*, 5 May 1888, p.495 (a review of the Grosvenor Gallery); *Athenaeum*, 28 April 1900, p.534; *Magazine of Art*, March 1881, p.179; *Athenaeum*, 25 May 1889, p.669; *Saturday Review*, 6 June 1885, p.756.
8.   Fred Miller, 'Women Workers in the Arts and Crafts', *Art Journal*, April 1896, p.116.
9.   See Florence Fenwick-Miller, 'The Ladies' Column', *Illustrated London News*, 7 January 1888, p.6 for a spirited rejoinder to this old argument. This writer frequently addressed herself to the subject of women and art: see also *Illustrated London News*, 26 March 1887, p.343, and ibid., 31 January 1891, p.160; and 16 February 1895, p.214, on the death of Mary Thornycroft.
10.   *Art Journal*, 1 June 1879, p.107; the writer, one FRC, writes as if the question of women's fit occupation were a new one, and not an issue at least twenty years old: 'A contention is now hot, we will not say between the two sexes, but between two schools which take opposite views as to the position of the line that should be drawn between the habits and the occupations of the sexes.' Note that a line '*should* be drawn' – it is just a question of where, for this writer.
11.   Leader Scott, 'Women at work: their functions in Art', *Magazine of Art*, March 1884, p.98.
12.   One of the most interesting in latter times, Hubert von Herkomer's

school in Bushey, Herts, where (among others) Lucy Kemp-Welch was trained, is still extant, as is that relic from even former times, Heatherly's.

13.   'Woman, and her chance as an Artist', *Magazine of Art*, April 1888, p.xxv. See also in the same periodical, 'Women at the Royal Academy Schools', February 1889; and 'Reform of the Royal Academy Schools', March 1890.

14.   See Germaine Greer, *op. cit.*, and for the previous generations, see Charlotte Weeks, 'The Slade Girls', *Magazine of Art*, July 1883, p.329: the artists specified are DeMorgan (Pickering at that stage), Greenaway, Hilda Montalba, Jessie McGregor and Edith Martineau.

15.   The Nineteenth Century Art Society started in 1884. Other exhibition spaces to open up in this period were Tooth's, Dowdeswell's, Boussod and Valadon, and Goupil's.

16.   The number topped 400 in 1885 (412), the same year in which the number of women included at the RA took a steep rise (224 from 162 the previous year). There seems to be no particular reason for this.

17.   'Art Critics of Today', *Art Journal*, July 1892, p.193. The author was 'Aliquis'.

18.   Callen, *op. cit.* See also Rozsika Parker, *The Subversive Stitch* (1985).

19.   See *Women's Art Show,* exh. cat., (Nottingham Castle Museum, 1882).

20.   Wyke Bailliss, quoted in *Great Victorian Pictures*, exh. cat., (Arts Council Great Britain, 1978), p.59.

21.   Susan Beattie, *The New Sculpture* (1983), ch.7, pp.194-9; some sculptors mentioned by Beattie from this period are Margaret Giles, Ruby Levick, Ellen Mary Rope, Gwendoline Williams, Esther Moore, Florence Steele, Lilian Simpson.

22.   'Afternoons in Studios: a Chat with Mr George Frampton, A.R.A.', *Studio*, January 1896, p.205; the writer is EBS. I am indebted to Andrea Garrihy and Sheila Hourahane for helping me to clarify these questions relating to sculpture; see also the useful chs.3 and 4 in Benedict Read, *Victorian Sculpture* (1982).

23.   *Ladies at Work* (1893), p.1.

24.   Ibid., p.49.

25.   See *The Substance or the Shadow: Images of Victorian Womanhood*, exh. cat. (Yale Center for British Art, 1982).

Appendix:
The Contemporary Literature

From about 1850 onwards, the topic of women and art made frequent appearances in written forms as various as the newspapers, novels, stories published serially in magazines, and essays. A female artist appears as a fictional figure as early as 1848 (Anne Brontë's *The Tenant of Wildfell Hall*) and again, more thoroughly, in 1850 with Mrs Dinah Craik's *Olive*, while Anna Mary Howitt's autobiograpical account, *An Art Student in Munich*, was published in 1853. The *Illustrated Exhibitor* serialised a story called 'Sisters in Art' in 1852 which may have been written by someone close to Howitt, though it was published anonymously. The 1860s saw numerous articles, such as F.T. Palgrave's 'Women in the Fine Arts' (*Macmillan's Magazine, 1865*) in the bourgeois press. However, the first non-fiction full-length book to pose the 'woman (artist) question' as worthy of detailed discussion, in this country, was the American Elizabeth Ellet's *Women Artists in all Ages and Countries*, appearing here in 1859. In this brief résumé, this will be considered as a forerunner of all the later discussion of the topic, followed by two interesting articles – not in major periodicals, but very rich in their debate of the question – from 1864 and 1870, and the invaluable Ellen Clayton's *English Female Artists*, of 1876. George Moore's essay 'Sex in Art', from the end of the century, will hint at the state of discussion at the end of the Victorian era.

The following review of Ellet's book suggests that she has been one of the first to jump on a new bandwagon (the somewhat tart tone is that of an *Athenaeum* reviewer):

> Let a subject seem popular, and immediately we have the universal book about it. A dagger-stroke is aimed at a king; forthwith, assassins of all ages and countries are recorded in a facile epitome. The Big Ship goes down to the sea; at once our compiler is at the Ark on Ararat. A youthful prodigy appears; in a twinkling every marvellous boy and girl, from the earliest period to the present time, is cited to figure in a timely volume. Nothing is easier, or, in general, more unsatisfactory than this summarising, significant of a few visits to the public library, the ransacking of one or more bibliographies, with a vague account of raw reading and discursive transcript. Mrs Ellet, in floating down the current which has set in from the intellect-of-women point of view, and in joining those who appear readier to talk than to act, is purely and simply a collector and assorter of rough materials.[1]

The stated aims of the author should be considered in assessing the significance, as well as the achievement, of the book, however:

> It is manifestly impossible, in a work of this kind, to include even the names of all the women artists who are worthy of remembrance. Among those of the present day are many, who have not yet had sufficient experience to do justice to their own powers, and any criticism of their productions would be premature and unfair . . . No attempt has been made to give elaborate critiques, or a connected history of art. The aim has been simply to show what woman has done, with the general conditions favourable or unfavourable to her efforts, and to give such impressions of the character of each distinguished artist as may be derived from a faithful record of her personal experiences.

The book's index listed 565 names, and presented the reader with one chapter on eras previous to the fifteenth century, two on the sixteenth century, five on the seventeenth century, six on the eighteenth century, and five on the nineteenth century. The nineteenth century claimed the most space of all the periods treated and the longest discussion of a single artist was devoted to the author's contemporary and compatriot, Harriet Hosmer. (Angelika Kauffmann ran a close second.)

The British contemporary artists whom Ellet mentioned were: Fanny Corbaux, Elizabeth Murray (neé Heaphy), Mrs Monckton Milnes, Louisa (sic) Rayner, Florence Caxton (sic), Jane Benham Hay, Barbara Leigh Smith (later Bodichon), Miss Mutrie (which sister is not clear), Anna Mary Howitt and Margaret Carpenter: not a methodical list corresponding to the fame or success enjoyed by individual artists at the time of writing, and biased towards painting without acknowledging that this was so.

The *Athenaeum*'s critic thought the book partial (as opposed to complete): 'The book is irregular, and often tedious: it is written in the style of flaccid facility inveterate among compilers; still, it may have its hour of welcome.' It obviously did, for Bentley brought out a second edition the next year. It was the subject of the book which was popular, evidently, because Ellet's other compilations were not republished here. The information which the book offered was more in tune with the increasing interest in women artists in this country at the time, than some of the sentiments in which she clothed the same, yet her very equivocation as regards her political position on her subject is typical of the uncertainty engendered in many minds at this time by the increasing topicality of women artists. Thus:

> Should the perusal of my book inspire with courage and resolution any woman who aspires to overcome difficulties in the achievement of honourable independence, or should it lead to a higher general respect for the powers of women and their destined position in the realm of Art, my object will be accomplished.

Yet:

> Woman is the type of the ornamental part of our life, and lends to existence the charm which inspires the artist, and furnishes him [sic] with an object for his genius.

And, discussing the position of women in the middle of the 1800s:

> At the present time, the prospect is fair of a reward for study and

unfaltering application in woman as in man; her freedom (without regarding as such the so-called 'emancipation' which would urge her into a course against nature, and contrary to the gentleness and modesty of her sex) is greater, and the sphere of her activity is wider and more effective than it has ever been.

Perhaps the seriousness and usefulness of the book can, ultimately, be judged by the fact that it contained *no* illustration of the works of the subjects. (The second edition carried a frontispiece of a portrait of Anne Damer.) In this way, it contributed very little to breaking down that barrier of invisibility which women's work has been hidden behind, although it gave women artists a substantial push forward out of the shadows.

Five years later, however, the public and the art world had more hard evidence to go on. The Society of Art Quibblers took as the theme for one of their weekly meetings in July 1864 (9 July) a paper by a Mr Freezor of their membership, entitled 'On Female Artists'.[2] Much more radical sentiments were expressed therein:

> Men who limit a woman's mission to the strict fulfillment of her duties as a wife and mother, appear to think she was merely formed to be the nurse, consoler, and submissive wife, ministering only to their own individual necessities and pleasures. Surely this is a very mean and selfish theory. The fulfillment of duties incidental to her sex ought not to shut out a woman from the exercise of her intellectual powers, or prove the grave in which to bury talents calculated to benefit and advance the race.

He thought that traditional notions of women's innate mental inferiority to men failed to satisfy the claim that women could be great artists: 'Woman is generally allowed to be more imaginative than man, and imagination combined with refined feelings and delicate sentiments form the chief essentials of an artist's success.' Citing Henrietta (sic) Browne, Elisabeth Jerichau, Henrietta Ward, Emily Osborn, Miss Mutrie (presumably the elder, Martha) and Rebecca Solomon, he asserted that 'Eminent female painters are peculiar to our own times':

> That a woman may fulfil her domestic and maternal duties and yet contrive to excel as an artist, has been fully demonstrated of late by the many ladies who, while most exemplary as wives and

mothers, have yet attained the highest excellence as painters, musicians, and authors.

He went on to address himself to the hard facts behind the appearances, saying:

The success these ladies have achieved is the more surprising when we consider the many difficulties they must have encountered while pursuing their studies, not least of which is their exclusion from the schools of the Royal Academy.

And:

The statistical returns show us that the female population is in excess of the male about half a million, and, therefore, also show us how many females must of necessity be debarred from matrimony, and consequently, how many must be dependent on their own efforts for the means of living.

He concluded with an appeal to his *confrères* to support and to assist women artists:

When, therefore, they seek art as a profession, let us not withold our encouragement and help, but rather let them find their brothers in art, anxious to give their talents a fair field, and hold out good strong helping hands to aid their toilsome ascent over the rugged path to fame.

There followed, however, an interestingly varied response on the part of the collected Art Quibblers, the range of which reflected the 'state of play' on the 'woman (artist) question' in 1864. Mr Potter inveighed against the Royal Academy's exclusive policies, and was followed by Mr F.G. Oakes in similar vein, who advanced that: 'If tested by real merit ladies would frequently win their way into the Academy to the exclusion of male students having less talent.'

The *arrière-garde* now showed itself, first in the person of the chairman, who asserted: 'If the ladies had real artistic power, the mere fact of their exclusion from the Academy would not retard its development, and we should yet see it fully displayed.' Mr Benny, then, prompted no doubt by this breath of *retardataire* hot air, rose to say that, 'although full of respect for the character of woman and warmly appreciative of her power and influence, he could not regard the sex as intellectually equal to the male sex'. His justification: 'History would not permit him to do so.' He went further, to assert that 'If women now excelled in art, and were the equals of our great men-painters, he thought this fact due rather to the degradation of art down to the reach of female excellence than the advancement of female excellence to the highest powers of art.' Mr Wall countered him thus:

> Suppose the man at home entrusted with its humble duties, shut up in its peaceful circle, and in a purely dependent position, and the woman free and independent, but with the spur of necessity in her side, battling with might and main to attain that excellence in her trade, profession, or calling which was essential to the preservation of home and the pleasures and comforts of those she loved. Did not Mr Benny think it exceedingly probable that under these circumstances men would be what women are now and women what men are now?

There followed enthusiastic debate on the nature and effects of male and female education. Mr Potter pointed out that, in history, 'Learning was the peculiar privilege of men only', but Mr Holyoke opined that 'It was not desirable to give women the education we gave men, because such an education was neither fitted for their social position, nor for their intellectual powers.' Mr Evans concluded that, 'although women might succeed in the humbler walks of art, they could not excel in its higher sphere', but the hitherto silent Mr Foot suggested that, 'It was not fair to give the verdict before a trial had come on, and condemn women for not excelling in arts they had not yet been afforded a fair opportunity of studying.'

The discussion moved on, inevitably, to the 'mission of women', and Messrs Wall and Buckman held forth on the power, influence and importance of mothers – chiefly, it seems, of great men – and Wall concluded, rather negatively for women determined to be artists, that:

> A practical knowledge of art, even if it leads to no great works by female hands, gives posterity no grand pictures or glorious statues, will give us an improved race of Englishmen . . .

In the following issue of the paper (1 September 1864), a letter appeared signed by 'A Female Artist', commenting on the report of the meeting. She was at pains to bring the men's attention to 'a crowd of female artists who lived and flourished in the past', whom, she felt, had been overlooked in the discussion. She named Sabina von Steinbach, Charlotte, Arch-duchess of Austria, Margaret van Eyck, Irene de Spilimberg, Properzia Rossi, Sofonisba Anguiscola, Elisabetta Sirani, Lavinia Fontana – all of whom had figured in Ellet's book of five years earlier. There had (of course!) been no women present at the Quibblers' meeting to advance this or any other modifying observations.

In 1870, *Art Pictorial and Industrial* published a three-part article on 'Female Artists and Art-Schools of England', which attempted an almost encyclopaedic coverage of its theme.[3] The writer was J. Cordy Jeaffreson, not a specialist either in art or in women, but someone who shows therefore how widely the subject of women artists now appealed as a serious and involved topic. He started his discussion by considering Kauffmann and Moser, the two original female Academicians, who were by this time generally spoken of in discussion as the harbingers of the race of female artists in Britain. Jeaffreson called Moser 'the Miss Mutrie of a century since', and, claiming that there were 'few persons who now-a-days give any thought to female artists of the last century', he considered at some length the circumstances in which such people had worked:

> Ever again amongst women who made themselves famous in the European capitals after the revival of the decorative arts, the reader encounters a lady whose noble lineage indicates that her skill with the brush was no ancestral inheritance or result of paternal instruction, and as often forms the acquaintance of a matron whose meagre history refers her artistic culture to the influence of the religious house in which she spent the years of her girlhood; but of the comparatively few women-painters who contributed to the celebrity of the Flemish, Italian, or Spanish schools, the majority were children of the studio . . .

He amplifies this familiar point:

> Domestic restraints, stronger always upon girls than boys, have withheld from artistic enterprise many hundreds of women, who, had they been of the hardier and more adventurous sex, would have broken away from their rural home, and found in the studios of the capitals congenial occupations for their recognised

faculties . . . The boy, who had learnt to love pictures and conceive an ambition to be a great producer of them, was in most cases so far master of his own movements that he could walk the round of the studios in the capital of his own native state, and seek employment in them.

Jeaffreson's discussion, in the first part of the article, was based primarily on the Royal Academy's history: he gives a table which records women's work appearing at the Academy from 1770 to 1793, but cautions that it should not

. . . be imagined that the works of female artists thus exposed to public criticism were always of considerable merit . . . not a few of the works which swell the sums of the foregoing statement of women's artistic industry were produced by gentlewomen of quality or fashion, dabbling in the arts under the supervision of obsequious drawing-masters, or by children incapable of pro-ducing a sketch that would now-a-days win critical approval from anyone outside the artist's domestic circle.

By contrast, Martha Mutrie and Henrietta Ward provide 'conclusive evidence that, instead of having retrograded, female art has greatly advanced'. He considers the argument (which the Quibblers tackled) that women's artistic inferiority is proved by their absence from art history, arguing reasonably that:

Women's exclusion from the higher schools of learning, and the obvious inferiority of the education generally accorded to girls by social usage, may, it is conceived, be held in some degree accountable for the subordinate position, and humble merit of the fair sex in science and literature . . . it will probably never be fair to the gentler sex to place their intellectual achievements in severe contrast against those of men, and to estimate woman's mental value by the result of such a comparison, since in every probable state of society, marriage, and the maternal cares arising from marriage, will always be the chief business of the best of womankind, whose powers will consequently be withdrawn to a considerable degree from the highest fields of intellectual endeavour, on which the strongest and noblest of the male sex in future times, no less than now or in the past, will labour with undivided attention and all their forces.

The rest of the article was devoted to an examination of female
art education, the author declaring:

> I have courage and indiscreetness enough to suggest that
> women's position in art may have been less favourable than
> some of her less generous censors imagine. Is it clear that the
> studios and best art teachers have been no less accessible to her
> than her masculine competitors? that she has prosecuted artistic
> labour on terms of equality with workers of the sterner sex? . . .
> when the most has been made of the liberality of the old masters
> towards female students, it cannot be maintained that the girls of
> past generations had the same facilities as young men for
> procuring artistic instruction.

He suggests that Ellert (sic) was inclined in her book to exaggerate
the support which past women received from contemporary
masters. He is particularly enthusiastic about the Female School of
Art and the South Kensington School, contrasting the happy and
industrious picture they represent with the continuing reluctance
of the Academy to further the artistic chance of women. He
mentions by name Fanny Corbaux, Sarah Setchel, Margaret Carpenter and Margaret Gillies, and makes a vague reference to Louisa
Starr, the first female winner of the Academy Schools' gold medal.
This is a selection of names which, in 1870, does not indicate an
up-to-the-minute knowledge of what women are achieving in the
arts, although all of these names are worthy of mention within the
overall theme of the subject.

Many more names were offered to the public's eye in Ellen
Clayton's two volume book of six years later, *English Female Artists*.
The author – billed as 'the author of *Queens of Song*, etc.'[4] –
accounts for over 200 artists, ranging in time from Lavinia Teerlinck
and Anne Carlisle operative in the 1600s to a host of living artists
including herself. (She explains this disarming vanity thus: 'There
is always a certain personal interest attaching to the writer of a
book; therefore a slight account of this otherwise insignificant
designer may be acceptable to some readers.')

Volume I runs to 427 pages and Volume II to 431, and they deal,
respectively, with pre-1800 and the nineteenth century. The book
as a whole is dedicated to Elizabeth Thompson, 'in testimony of
admiration for her genius', and other accredited inspirations
included Ellet's work, and such chestnuts as Bryan's *Dictionary of
Painters*, Chamber's *Biographical Dictionary*, the writings of

Waagen, Jameson, Farington, Ottley and the Redgrave brothers. Of the history of her subject Clayton writes, in characteristically romantic language:

> Our native paintresses, as the old-fashioned art critics and compilers of biographical dictionaries quaintly term them, have left but faintly impressed footprints on the sands of time. They do not glitter in the splendour of renown, like their sisters of the pen or of the buskin. It is a difficult task to obtain a sparse list of their original works, or glean any scattered remarks on their most valued copies of great masters. Even the most romantic or admired of these fair dreamers on canvas or ivory have scarce an incident beyond the commonplace in the brief record of their public or private career.

Modern scholars would agree with her, yet her living subjects are not, in general, better presented than those whom death had deprived her of access to: all her subjects are clothed in sentiment. The *Art Journal*'s reviewer remarked on this point:

> Strange as it certainly is, we learn from these volumes far more, as a rule, of the lives of those who died half a century, and even more ago, than of those who are yet with us . . . there are many ladies whose names she gives of whom much more might well have been said, and some of whom more is said than seems necessary.

Indeed, the length of the entry Clayton makes for any artist seems to depend less on merit than on availability of material. Thus, Anna Blunden has 30 pages dedicated to her in the second volume, much of which consists of extracts from her diary of continental travel; EVB is the subject of 25 pages, many of which are filled with letters and anecdotes to and of her by other, more famous people. By contrast, the dedicatee of the book, Elizabeth Thompson, is compressed into 4 pages, and Henrietta Ward – at this time the most established woman artist in the country still active – only 5. The way Clayton structured her material was to devote, in the first volume, chapters to individuals or groups of individuals and, in the second volume, to discuss artists in terms of genre. Thus, there is a chapter on Figure Painters, on Landscape Painters, on Humorous Designers, Decorative Artists, etc. Some artists are mentioned in more than one chapter, such as Adelaide Claxton (Figure Painters and Humorous

Designers). Within the genres dealt with by Volume II, the distribution is as follows: Figure Painters, 34; Landscape Painters, 18; Portrait, Miniature and Enamel Painters, 8; Painters of Flowers, Fruit and Still-Life, 18; Animal Painters, 6; Humorous Designers, 4; Decorative Artists, 2; Amateurs, 14. The size of this last category reflects, not so much the preponderance of non-professionals in the field of women's work, but rather the author's fascination with the wealthy and aristocratic, a snobbery which frequently distorts her accounts. Her exclusion of sculpture is also a limitation, of course. As a work of critical analysis and historical value, Clayton's work suffered from the same defects as had Ellet's nearly twenty years earlier: no illustration, little analysis of works, and a marked unevenness in the nature of the information given, characterised by a greater interest in the subject's biography than in her productions. The *Art Journal*'s reviewer summed it up, by saying: 'Without any attempt at art-criticism, Miss Clayton tells the stories, long or brief as they may happen to be, of our Art sisters very pleasantly and very creditably both to them and to herself.'

George Moore's essay 'Sex in Art' appeared in his book *Modern Painting* published in 1893. It is typical of the *fin-de-siècle* in its reversion to a prescriptive and paternalistic denunciation of the progress women had made during the previous 40 years in relation to the art world, though it is remarkable in its audacious espousal of this anti-woman position. It runs to about 3500 words, and is quite unillustrated (as is the book as a whole). At its simplest, it is an assertion of 'man for the sword and for the needle she' – a demand that men should be men and women be women, so to speak. He claims that the only and essential quality for the female artist to display is femininity (which he later more or less defines), and it is by this sole criterion that he judges the success or failure of the artists he mentions. These include writers and painters, though not sculptors, actresses or dancers: 'Sex is as important an element in a work of art as it is in Life; all art that lives is full of sex', he writes: 'There is sex in *Pride and Prejudice*; *Jane Eyre* and *Aurora Leigh* are full of sex; *Romola, Daniel Deronda*, and *Adam Bede* are sexless, and therefore lifeless.'

On this criterion, he condemns also George Sand and Rosa Bonheur, and praises Elisabeth Vigée-Lebrun and Berthe Morisot. Thus it may be hazarded that when Moore says that 'all art that lives is full of sex', he means what is prescribed as masculine and feminine passion. He goes on to equate 'sex' with what in post-Freudian terms could be called libido: 'I mean by sex that concentrated essence of life which the great artist jealously reserves for his [sic] art, and through which it pulsates.' What, then, he is requiring from female artists is the complement to what is in our own day commonly called 'balls'. This he claims to find only in the work of Morisot, and then due in large part to her acknowledgement of the greatness of Edouard Manet, Moore's chosen hero.[5] Her work is 'Truly, the art of Manet *transporté en eventail*'. This compliment refers to Moore's initial judgement on women in art: 'Women have created nothing, they have carried the art of men across their fans charmingly, with exquisite taste, delicacy, and subtlety of feeling, and they have hideously and most mournfully parodied the art of men.'

Such generalisations continue unabashed: 'Woman's nature is more facile and fluent than man's. Women do things more easily than men, but they do not penetrate below the surface, and if they attempt to do so the attempt is but a clumsy masquerade in unbecoming costume.' 'In her art woman is always in evening dress: there are flowers in her hair, and her fan waves to and fro, and she wishes to sigh in the ear of him who sits beside her. Her mental nudeness is parallel with her low bodice, it is that and nothing more.' 'Whatever women have done in painting has been done in France.' His prejudice for French art and his studied rejection of British painting and sculpture underpins, but does not overcome, his obsession with stereotypes of gender. He scorns George Sand and Rosa Bonheur, which latter he does not even deign to discuss, simply saying in a conventional coupling of her and Elizabeth Thompson Butler 'the failure of Lady Butler was even greater than Rosa Bonheur's'. As one would expect, he cannot even recognise passion that is not heterosexual as existing at all, because it might spoil his case.

Other artists he mentions by name include Louisa, Lady Waterford ('a fluent and facile talent, strangely unoriginal, but always sustained by taste'); Elizabeth Armstrong (Forbes) whom he puts 'easily at the head of English lady artists'; Annie Swynnerton whom he finds fatally impersonal ('Impersonality in art really means mediocrity'); a group of contemporaries whom he lumps together as 'ladies who marry painters, and who, after a few years of married life, exhibit work identical in execution with that of their illustrious husbands – Mrs E.M. Ward, Madame Fantin-Latour, Mrs Swan, Mrs Alma-Tadema'; and Angelika Kauffmann (1741–1807), whose success in Georgian Britain he put down to having had the good luck to be born at the right time: 'Though her work is individually feeble, it is stamped with the charm of the tradition out of which it grew and was fashioned.'

Moore's comment on Kauffmann shows not only his a-historical means of analysis, but also his prescriptive and contradictory approach to women's – and creativity's – aims, roots and ideas: for he goes on to say that Kauffmann 'was content to remain a woman in her art. She imitated Sir Joshua Reynolds to the best of her ability' yet he also vigorously discounts women artists in his own day who, he says, do nothing original. Indeed women's alleged lack of originality is his central and recurrent theme. In being thus preoccupied, he does not, however, discuss education, opportunity or prejudicial treatment; he talks only of those romantic intangibles, talent, genius and charm. In this, and in his opposition to women determining what they might do in art, in his covert concern to protect the (male) domain of great art (by which he means painting, though he fails to acknowledge this) and his insistence that women be ruled by men and by male definitions of their gender, George Moore gives us a clear idea of how vigorous the opposition to women in art still was at the end of the century.

Notes

1.   Ellet's career in literature was, indeed, rather that of an anthologist than anything else: her other publications included *The Women of the American Revolution* (Boston, 1848, 1850), *Pioneer Women of the West* (Boston, 1852), *Summer Rambles in the West* (Boston, 1853), *The Practical Housekeeper: a cyclopaedia of domestic economy* (Boston, 1857), and *The Queens of American Society* (Boston, 1867).
2.   Reported in the *Art Student*, 1 August 1864, pp.136–7; the Society had been formed, in January 1863, by South Kensington and Academy Schools students (see letter from F. Scarlet Potter, *Art Student*, 1 April 1864, p.57).
3.   J. Cordy Jeaffreson, 'Female Artists and Art Schools in England', *Art Pictorial and Industrial,* vol.1, no.2, August 1870, pp. 25–30, 50–52, 70–73; it is probable that the writer had the acquaintance of some female artists of his own time, since he appears in the family photograph album of the painter John Brett, and would therefore have known the painter's sister Rosa (Rosarius), and Louisa Starr (Canziani), who also appears in the album as a friend of the family. I am grateful to descendants of the Brett painters for showing this material to me. See *A Book of Recollections* (1894), for more about the writer himself.
4.   Clayton's other publications, *Notable Women* and *Celebrated Women* (1859/60 and 1875) featured no artists at all, but much more convention-

ally interesting women, such as wives, daughters, Christians and philan-
thropists. She also wrote *Female Warriors* in 1879 for Tinsley.

5.   Moore's claim to fame was as the English standard-bearer for the
Impressionists and their associate Edouard Manet. *Confessions of a
Young Man* (1888) had recounted Moore's time spent in Paris amongst
these artists, giving pride of place to Manet.

Select Bibliography

Ellen C. Clayton, *English Female Artists*, 1876.

Walter Shaw Sparrow, *Women Painters of the World*, 1905.

Jeremy Maas, *The Victorian Art World in Photographs*, 1984.

Pamela Gerrish Nunn, *Canvassing*, 1986.

Elizabeth Butler, *An Autobiography*, 1922.

Estella Canziani, *Round about Three Palace Green*, 1939.

William Frith, *My Autobiography*, 1887/8.

Jeremy Maas, *Gambart, Prince of the Victorian Art World*, 1975.

M.H. Spielmann and G. Layard, *The Life and Work of Kate Greenaway*, 1905.

Cornelia Carr, *Harriet Hosmer*, 1913.

Louise Jopling, *Twenty Years of my Life*, 1925.

Clara Thomas, *Love and Work Enough: the life of Anna Jameson*, 1967.

Anna Lea Merritt, *Love Locked Out* (ed. Galina Gorokhoff), 1986.

Cook and Wedderburn, *The Collected Works of John Ruskin*, 1903/12.

The Solomon Family of Painters, Geffrye Museum London, 1986.

Elfrida Manning, *Bronze and Steel*, 1930.

Henrietta Ward, *Reminiscences*, 1911.

Henrietta Ward, *Memories of Ninety Years*, 1924.

Augustus Hare, *Two Noble Lives: memorials of Charlotte Countess Canning and Louisa Lady Waterford*, 1893.

Virginia Surtees, *Sublime and Instructive: letters from John Ruskin to Louisa Marchioness of Waterford, Anna Blunden and Ellen Heaton*, 1972.

Art Journal, Athenaeum, Englishwoman's Review, Illustrated London News, London Society, Magazine of Art, Portfolio, Royal Academy Illustrated

Index